East Asia and the Global Economy

JOHNS HOPKINS STUDIES IN GLOBALIZATION

Christopher Chase-Dunn, *Series Editor*

Consulting Editors: Volker Bornschier, Christine Gailey, Walter L. Goldfrank, Su-Hoon Lee, William R. Thompson, Immanuel Wallerstein, and David Wilkinson

East Asia and the Global Economy

Japan's Ascent, with Implications for China's Future

STEPHEN G. BUNKER

and

PAUL S. CICCANTELL

The Johns Hopkins University Press

Baltimore

The Johns Hopkins University Press
2715 North Charles Street
Baltimore, Maryland 21218-4363
www.press.jhu.edu

Library of Congress Cataloging-in-Publication Data
Bunker, Stephen G., 1944–
East Asia and the global economy : Japan's ascent, with implications
for China's future / Stephen G. Bunker and Paul S. Ciccantell.
p. cm. — (Johns Hopkins studies in globalization)
Includes bibliographical references and index.
ISBN-13: 978-0-8018-8593-8 (hardcover : alk. paper)
ISBN-10: 0-8018-8593-0 (hardcover : alk. paper)
1. Industries—Japan—History—20th century. 2. Japan—Economic
policy—1945– 3. Japan—Foreign economic relations.
4. Raw materials—Japan. 5. International economic relations—History.
6. Globalization. 7. Capitalism. 8. Natural resources.
I. Ciccantell, Paul S., 1965– II. Title.
HC462.9.B852 2007
330.952—dc22   2006035480

A catalog record for this book is available from the British Library.

CONTENTS

Even by the standards of academic publishing, this book has a long history. Stephen and I began working on this project in the spring of 1993. Based on his extensive field-work and teaching in the Brazilian Amazon and my own fieldwork in Brazil and Venezuela, it was clear that Japanese investment and the economic development of Japan had changed the capitalist world-economy, as well as the prospects for raw ma-terials–based development in Latin America and around the world. Our challenge was to explain the new patterns of joint ventures, the ever-larger mines, smelters, dams, and ships, and the complex mixture of positive and negative impacts that these huge projects were having in areas like the Amazon.

We initially planned a comparison of four of the world's leading raw materials industries—aluminum, copper, iron, and coal—using a number of raw materials–producing regions as case studies. As we developed our empirical analysis and theo-retical model, it became obvious that we had far too many types of material and social variation to explain in the multi-material and multi-region comparison. We therefore reorganized our research agenda in two ways. We focused our analysis of Japan's eco-nomic ascent, the topic of this book, on coal, iron, steel, and shipping, which we had identified as the linchpins and pattern-setters for Japan's ascent. We also separated our broader theoretical model and long-term comparative analysis of the five most im-portant and transformative cases of economic ascent and the restructuring of the cap-italist world-economy over the past five centuries into another book, *Globalization and the Race for Resources* (2005).

As we worked on these two books in tandem during Stephen's long battle with can-cer, reviewers of the earlier book and our publisher added a third major change to our agenda. We had planned to include in *Globalization and the Race for Resources* an ex-tensive analysis of how the Amazon had been incorporated into the capitalist world-economy based on its natural resource wealth, and how the incorporation of the Ama-zon on the basis of its particular and often unique material and social characteristics had in turn shaped the capitalist world-economy. In order to focus that book on our theoretical argument and the empirical analysis of the transformative impacts of the ascents of Portugal, Holland, Great Britain, the United States, and Japan, the case study of the Amazon was reduced to only a small part of that book. As a result, our long-term analysis of the Amazon will be the subject of a third book, the completion of which will be my next task.

Our research methods for all of these projects combined a variety of comparative, historical, and qualitative research techniques, including hundreds of interviews with government officials, industry executives, workers, and community residents; extended visits to mines, dams, smelters, and ports; building extensive industry and regional databases; secondary data analysis; and archival research. Our most important analytic technique consisted of long arguments over how to make sense of the rich empirical data we collected across industries, materials, and regions. These sometimes took place at Stephen's farm or Murphy's Log Cabin in Hollandale, Wisconsin, on the terrace at the University of Wisconsin–Madison's Memorial Union, or, particularly during Stephen's illness, over the phone, but the ultimate outcome was a much stronger analysis of our empirical data and a much clearer theoretical argument. Stephen's wife, Dena, tolerated many of our long discussions and phone calls, and we both owe her thanks for that.

I know that Stephen would have liked to thank his colleagues and the staff members of the UW-Madison Department of Sociology for their constant friendship. Their personal and professional support and kindness were truly extraordinary and exemplary of what collegiality is supposed to mean. Stephen's fieldwork was supported by the National Science Foundation, Brazil's Conselho Nacional de Pesquisa, the Howard Heinz Endowment, the University of Wisconsin–Madison Graduate School, the University of Wisconsin–Madison Global Studies Institute, the World Wildlife Fund, and the Sloan Foundation. R. Tyler Priest, then a graduate student in history at UW-Madison, conducted invaluable archival research for us at the National Archives.

I would like to thank a number of people and organizations who have facilitated the long period of research on which this book is based. My department heads at Western Michigan University, Thomas Van Valey and David Hartmann, and the WMU Department of Sociology have provided extensive support in recent years. My research assistants at WMU, Nathan Christensen, Michael Macaluso, Flora Myamba, and Jon Van Wieren, located many seemingly arcane books and articles that contributed to this book and I would like to thank them for their work. During the earlier phases of my research, my department head at Kansas State University, Michael Timberlake, and the KSU Small Research Grants Program provided support for my research in difficult fiscal circumstances. The Canadian government's Canadian Studies Faculty Research Program provided significant funding for several periods of research on the coal industry in western Canada. The Social Science Research Council funded my field research in Brazil and Venezuela. I would also like to thank the many people who shared their time and insights with me during my fieldwork. My wife, Laura, and my children, Katie and Jack, patiently accepted several extended absences while I conducted fieldwork.

Paul S. Ciccantell

East Asia and the Global Economy

CHAPTER ONE

Growth and Crisis in the Japanese Economy

Japan's Rapid Ascent and Its Restructuring of the World Economy

At the end of World War II, a defeated Japan faced tremendous difficulties. U.S. bombing destroyed much of Japan's industry and cities, and an occupying army controlled the country politically and economically. Japan lost its empire and the area's tremendous natural and human resources. Japan's population desperately needed jobs, food, and even coal for heating to survive the winter. In the late 1940s, Japan apparently lacked even the necessities for survival; few could imagine creating an industrial powerhouse in the midst of this crisis.

By the early 1970s, Japan had become one of the world's wealthiest nations, with the most technologically advanced steel, automobile, shipbuilding, and other industries, dominating world trade in a variety of products. The dramatic economic growth and development that occurred were based on the difficult and conflictual process of creating and adapting a new model of economic development—a model that integrated domestic heavy industrialization, state-sector-firm coordination and conflict, and the globalization of raw materials industries to supply the material building blocks for Japan's development. This model imposed huge costs and risks on states and firms in Japan's new raw materials peripheries in Australia, Brazil, Canada, and other nations. With critical support from the existing hegemon, the United States, the Japanese state and Japanese firms, led by the steel industry, drove an incredible material expansion of globalization, moving millions of tons of iron ore, coal, and other raw materials distances that would have seemed unimaginably uneconomic in the late 1940s. Within two decades, this Japan-driven globalization fundamentally reshaped the world economy, making a resource-poor island nation the world's leading exporter of a variety of industrial goods and setting the stage for the collapse of these industries in the United States, the world's leading economic and political power.

This same successful model, however, created the economic problems that confronted Japan at the end of the twentieth century. State-subsidized credit created to meet the huge demands of state-of-the-art steel mills, shipyards, and other heavy industry during the 1950s became cheap credit for real estate speculation. Protection against imports that helped infant industries grow into global powerhouses during the 1950s and 1960s became tools and crutches for globally uncompetitive industries in Japan that imposed high prices on consumers and restricted economic growth. The crisis of the 1990s and early 2000s resulted from the same model of economic development that brought such success in the 1950s, 1960s, and 1970s.

The story of boom and bust does not end with the crisis of the 1990s. The rapid growth of China over the past decade derives in large part from Japanese investment and increasingly from efforts to emulate Japan's model of raw materials–based industrialization and its system of low-cost raw materials supplies from the globalized iron ore and coal industries. The long-term sustainability of Chinese economic development likely rests on the success or failure of the investment and technological partnerships between Chinese and Japanese firms seeking to replicate the Japanese model in the steel mills, shipyards, and automobile plants in coastal industrial parks and further inland in China. Support from the United States aided Japan's economic development in critical ways; Japan may or may not do the same for China.

Japan's rapid rise from devastation and defeat in World War II to being a dominant force in world trade by the 1970s stimulated extensive analysis of domestic systems—managerial, cultural, and political—for the causes of its success. The dramatic changes in international systems—of exchange, production, and transport—that the Japanese economy fomented while achieving its huge success received less notice. Japanese strategies and actions in the world economy significantly accelerated and expanded processes of globalization and enhanced global inequalities. Japan's power in the international economy both depended on and supported extraordinarily effective innovations in its domestic economic, political, and financial systems. These two outcomes, rapid domestic development and global trade dominance, and the relative impoverishment of its extractive peripheries depended on and mutually reinforced each other.

Japan's economic success fundamentally rested on heavy industries and related transport systems. It depended on closely articulated coordination of the state with industry associations and firms via state-sector-firm collaboration in selected sectors—steel, shipbuilding, and finance—to integrate domestic productive efficiencies and economies of scale with extremely favorable investment, trade, and transport arrangements with international sources of the huge volumes of raw materials that the rapidly expanding Japanese economy needed.

These state-sector-firm strategies emerged and evolved through long processes of cooperation, negotiation, adjustment, and conflict between diverse domestic interests and agencies (including several agencies of the Japanese state, industry associations, firms with often divergent interests, and political leaders) and a variety of international actors (including the Allied Occupation Forces, the U.S. State Department, the World Bank, transnational and local mining firms, and political leaders in Australia, Brazil, Canada, and other nations that supplied raw materials to Japan). The importance of the integration of innovations in domestic industries and institutions with international organizations and institutions leads us to analyze these crucial sectors as generative—that is, as generating new, more powerful, and closely linked interdependence, cooperation, and conflict between firms, sectors, financial interests, and the state to dominate an increasingly global economy.

To trace how the Japanese strategies drove globalization and global inequality, we use and expand on Giovanni Arrighi's (1994) explanations of how successive cycles of accumulation enlarged and intensified the world-system. Arrighi takes the revealed preference of capitalists for ever more rapid turnover times on investment, approaching an ideal state of absolute liquidity, to indicate a deeper goal of using money to make more money without passing it through the production of commodities. By focusing his arguments on highly abstract monetary relations as the goal and ultimate end of all systemic cycles of accumulation, Arrighi constructed a powerful model of the stages from maturity to decadence of different hegemons, with the contradictions of hegemonic overaccumulation being partially resolved by investment in other rising economies.

Part of this model's power lies in Arrighi's use of the strategy of incorporated comparisons to account for what we call the cumulatively sequential increase in size, scope, volume, and density of productive, financial, political, and commercial relations across ever broader spaces. In achieving a coherent model of how these cumulatively sequential increases simultaneously create the conditions of subsequent hegemonic ascent and structure the relations between mature or declining hegemon and new centers of accumulation (Amsterdam to Britain, Britain to the United States, the United States to Japan and China), Arrighi overcomes the stasis imposed by Wallerstein's dependence on tripartite categories whose relations remain fundamentally unchanged. Arrighi's analysis, however, says little about how Japanese firms and the Japanese state drove the globalization of key industries, such as coal, iron ore, steel, and shipbuilding, over the past five decades. He thus neglects the negative consequences for Australia, Brazil, Canada, and other nations that Japanese strategies restructured into key parts of Japan's raw materials periphery. In this book, we incorporate an analysis of the very material processes that Arrighi sees the capitalist stratum as bent on avoiding into an expanded model of cumulatively sequential increase and of the potential problems created by the strategies of the Japanese state and Japanese firms to develop so rapidly during the second half of the twentieth century.

We argue that raw materials and transport industries drove Japan's economic ascent after World War II. The state, economic sectors, and firms collaborated, often after protracted conflicts that established the terms of what we describe as a dynamic tension, to secure low-cost raw materials that Japanese firms turned into cars, ships, consumer electronics, and a plethora of other industrial products. A small island nation that lacked adequate domestic supplies of virtually all the raw materials essential to industrial production became a world leader in the production of steel, copper, and aluminum. Its domination of world trade in a wide variety of products required millions of tons per year of these materials. Japanese firms and the Japanese state turned an apparent material and economic disadvantage, the need to import large volumes of raw materials, into a competitive advantage over the United States, Europe, and the rest of the world economy. The strategies of Japanese firms and the Japanese state to resolve the problems of procuring bulk cheaply and reliably from multiple distant locales drove the technical and organizational innovations that underlay Japan's rapid industrial development. These innovations in competitive markets fundamentally and materially globalized the world economy.

As occurred in earlier cases of dramatic economic ascent, the model of development created in Japan to resolve this fundamental problem embodied a dynamic tension between material process, technology, processes of global economic and political competition, and collaboration between states, firms, and organizations in multiple nations. In Japan, a variety of social groups sought to shape this development model and capture the benefits that resulted. These groups included the steel, shipbuilding and other firms in the generative sectors; several state agencies (including the Ministry of International Trade and Industry, the Ministry of Finance, and the Japan Development Bank, among others); managers and labor unions in the generative sectors; firms, managers and workers in less-favored and less-successful sectors; the Liberal Democratic Party; private banks; and powerful business organizations like the Keidanren. Because this dynamic tension involved balancing the interests of various groups, it was very difficult to maintain and easy to disrupt. Concessions needed to maintain this balance of the dynamic tension between these groups created the problems of overvalued land, heavy corporate debt loads made possible by subsidized lending, protected and inefficient industrial sectors, and the increasing ability of Japanese firms to weaken national economic growth by relocating production outside Japan to increase firm competitiveness.

These strategies and the technical and organizational innovations they spurred drove a major share of the tremendous increase over the past fifty years in the volume of raw materials traded internationally and the distances these raw materials travel. In 1960 seaborne petroleum, coal, iron ore, and bauxite trade totaled 2,093 billion ton-miles (a measure that combines both the volume of trade and the distance each ton moves from the point of extraction to the point of industrial processing). Twenty years later, in 1980, these four raw materials accounted for 11,015 billion ton-miles of seaborne trade, an increase of 426 percent. Coal, historically one of the most localized industries in the world, experienced the most dramatic growth, with seaborne trade increasing from 145 billion ton-miles in 1960 to 1,849 billion ton-miles in 1990. At the same time, coal prices fell in real (inflation-adjusted) terms from US$86.65 in 1959 (in 1992 dollars) to US$43.63 in 1998 for coal imported into Japan. Similar dramatic changes took place in iron ore.

Surprisingly, the existing hegemon, the United States, had little to do with either the expansion of trade or the drop in prices. Instead, both resulted from Japanese firms and the Japanese state collaborating to achieve huge economies of scale and tight integration in the transportation and processing of raw materials. What started in the 1950s as a strategy to resolve the fundamental obstacles to economic ascent in the face of U.S. hegemony drove both of these changes and led to absolute trade dominance by the 1970s. Japanese firms and the Japanese state drove this latest phase of the progressive globalization of the capitalist world-economy in support of national economic ascent. This phase of globalization results from the cumulatively sequential nature of the increasing material, geographic, technological, organizational, and economic scale of the major cycles of economic ascent and hegemonic transition.

Japanese firms and the Japanese state constructed a series of iterative strategies based on the steel industry as a generative sector that drove Japan's economic ascent in the world-historical context of U.S. hegemony. Together these strategies created a tightly linked set of technological and organizational innovations to overcome the natural and social obstacles to Japanese development. They dramatically increased Japan's international economic competitiveness by lowering production costs in all sectors of the economy. They turned Japan into the world's largest exporter of manufactured products, restructured a range of global industries, and recreated the world-system hierarchy in support of Japanese development. In particular, their organizational and financial innovations in the use of long-term contracts and joint ventures in raw materials industries fostered global excess capacity and lowered rents to resource-extracting firms and states. This reallocated the costs of providing the material building blocks of Japanese development to the states and firms of its new raw materials periphery, with costs to Japan's coal and iron ore peripheries totaling tens of billions of dollars over the past fifty years. This gave Japanese firms a national competitive advantage that supported capital accumulation and economic ascent and simultaneously underdeveloped Japan's periphery.

The Central Questions of This Book

We address five central questions about the causes and consequences of Japan's role in the world economy over the past five decades:

1. What drove Japan's rapid economic ascent?

2. How did Japan globalize the world economy in support of its rapid economic growth?

3. What are the consequences of the new forms of global inequality created by this globalization?

4. Why did Japan's spectacular economic growth come to a dramatic end in the 1990s?

5. How is China utilizing and transforming the Japan-created global raw materials industries to support China's rapid development?

We develop a theoretical and methodological model, new historical materialism, that builds its sociological analysis on the foundation of material process.

In any rising economy, strategies for economic ascent must respond to and take advantage of contemporary technological, geopolitical, environmental, and market conditions in the rest of the world and of the nation's position and location within that particular global economy. They must also coordinate the physical characteristics and location in space and in topography of the various raw material resources actually or potentially available with the physical characteristics and location in space and topography of the national territory. Solutions to the raw materials problem require the coordination of multiple physical and social processes across geopolitical and physical space with domestic relations between firms, sectors, the state, labor, and new technologies. Rising economies resolve these problems at the same time as or even before they increase industrial competitiveness. These solutions stimulate complex processes of learning and of institutional change that fundamentally mold the organization of the national economy at the same time that they change international markets and the rules binding participants in them.

The challenges and the opportunities presented by the basic raw materials industries and by the transport systems on which they depend foster what we call *generative sectors*. Generative sectors create the backward and forward linkages that underlie the concept of a leading sector. They also stimulate a broad range of technical skills and learning along with formal institutions designed and funded to promote them, including vast and diversified instrumental knowledge held by interdependent specialists about the rest of the world. Generative sectors foment the creation of financial institutions adapted to the requirements of large sunk costs in a variety of social and political contexts. In the sociopolitical realm, generative sectors create patterns of specific formal and informal relations between firms, sectors, and states, and the form of legal distinctions between public and private and between different levels of public jurisdiction. Generative sectors will be more numerous, more easily observed, and more efficacious in those national economies that are growing so rapidly that they must achieve massive increases in throughput and transformation of raw materials. The concept is relational, however, within a world-systems perspective, and thus implies that generative sectors in a rising economy will also shape the economies that export raw materials or trade in other kinds of goods.

Contrary to claims that globalization supersedes the national state, the Japanese state, in coordination and often in conflict with firms and industry sectors, developed and applied these strategies. Maritime Industrial Development Areas (MIDAs), built on land reclaimed by the Japanese state, became the linchpin of these strategies of scale and integration. MIDAs incorporated port facilities to import raw materials and to export industrial products and the steel mills and their major customers, including shipyards and automobile plants. The MIDAs' deepwater ports allowed the use of larger and larger ships (often built with subsidies from the Japanese government in the adjacent shipyards owned by the same industrial group) to import raw materials at low costs to brand-new steel mills that were vastly larger than mills in the United States or Europe. These Japanese mills, also built with state subsidies, incorporated state-of-the-art technology that produced the world's largest, lowest-cost, most integrated, and most competitive steel industry. The technologies that increased economies of scale in processing and transport were tightly interdependent. Larger steel mills depended on larger ships to supply low-cost raw materials over longer distances and on shipbuilding and other large industries for consuming steel, while technologies for building larger ships and higher-quality industrial products depended on the increasing availability of progressively lower-cost and higher quality steel.

An increasingly complex set of social institutions developed by Japanese firms and the Japanese state in order to promote rapid economic growth created these dramatic physical and technological changes. A series of conflicts and coordinated actions to overcome the physical and economic obstacles to acquiring millions of tons of coal and iron ore each year to supply the Japanese steel industry shaped the development of the Ministry of International Trade and Industry. MITI became a locus for coordinated actions between firms within and between industrial sectors, and between firms, sectors, and the state, with the long-term goal of resolving Japan's growing demand for raw materials imports and careful management of scarce capital. The Japanese banking system, supported by a range of state subsidies and constrained by rules emerging from contentious battles between state agencies with different mandates, shipbuilding firms, manufacturing firms, the banks themselves, and a variety of other firms, carefully allocated scarce investment capital during the 1950s and 1960s to support key sectors, including steel, shipping and shipbuilding. *Keiretsu* corporate groupings and the Keidanren business organization promoted cooperation between competing firms to reduce potentially devastating internal economic and political competition.

These scale-increasing technologies in processing and transport drove a fundamental restructuring of the built environment simultaneously in Japan and in the areas that became raw materials peripheries supporting Japanese economic ascent. The efforts to achieve economies of scale to increase economic competitiveness in Japan created increasing diseconomies of space because of domestic raw materials depletion and the geopolitical unavailability of the nearest potential supplies in China. Japanese steel firms and the Japanese state created a model of coordinated strategies to develop progressively larger, lower-cost ships to transport raw materials and to reduce raw materials acquisition costs and increase security of supply. These strategies encouraged investments by a growing number of exporting regions' states and firms in the mines and infrastructure needed to supply the rapidly growing demand in Japan.

These raw materials supply arrangements shifted an increasing share of the costs of the system onto Japan's suppliers by fomenting competition between suppliers, reducing raw materials rents, and creating excess capacity by bringing new suppliers onstream. These strategies also reserved for Japanese importing firms any benefits of increasing economies of scale in transport by requiring that the Japanese firms handle ocean transport. These strategies imposed huge costs on and provided only limited returns to exporting states and firms. At the level of the world economy, the cumulative impact of the benefits to Japan, the growing costs to Japan's raw materials suppliers, and the rapidly declining economic competitiveness of Japan's competitors that could not match these developments restructured and exacerbated global inequalities.

After the steel, shipbuilding, and other linked industries built in the MIDAs were well established and leading the global economy, the constellation of firm strategies, bank lending policies, and state subsidies so critical to rapid growth became potential liabilities. The bursting of the property value bubble, heavy corporate debt loads, excessive bank lending, declining state ability to subsidize industry, growing opposition to extensive political corruption, and recognition of the environmental problems in port areas combined to create years of economic stagnation and revealed the weaknesses of the post–World War II model of development. These problems, paralleling in many ways the recurrent banking and consumption crises in the United States between the 1890s and 1930s as its model of development matured, derived from the social solutions to the profound material challenge of acquiring and processing the raw materials that underlay Japan's rapid growth. Government-subsidized low-interest loans that could have funded a new, state-of-the-art steel mill in a MIDA could just as easily be used to bid up the price of an office building in central Tokyo. However, the two investments had vastly different implications for long-term national economic growth. We argue that the roots of Japan's rapid economic growth, its recent problems, and its globalization and restructuring of the world economy are all to be found in a range of social, political, economic, and spatiomaterial processes that underlaid each major systemic cycle of capital accumulation in the world economy over the past five hundred years.

Existing Models of Japan's Rise, Global Expansion, and Decline

Explanations for Japan's rise to challenge U.S. economic supremacy include management techniques, cultural characteristics such as the Japanese work ethic and preference for consensus, and extensive state-firm cooperation, among many others. A similarly wide range of answers has also been offered to explain a second, equally surprising, and phenomenal change in Japan's economy, how and why its successful model came to a sudden halt. In addition to our first and fourth questions on what drove Japan's remarkable rise and fall, two largely neglected questions emerged from our efforts to address these issues. How did Japan globalize the world economy in support of its rapid economic growth? What are the consequences of the resulting new forms of global inequality? These two questions receive relatively little attention both in the literature on Japan's economic growth and from analysts of political economy and globalization, most of whom focus on the role of the United States

Japan's rapid rise and dramatic transformation of world industrial and trade patterns and of space and the global environment (as well as its crisis) can best be understood by analyzing the raw materials and transport industries that provided the material foundations for Japan's competitive advantages in a variety of industries. These Japanese industries drove a profoundly material process of globalization led by Japanese firms and the Japanese state in support of domestic development.

Answers to the first question about how Japan rose to global trade dominance initially focused in the 1970s and 1980s on one or a few characteristics of Japanese industry, such as management techniques, just-in-time delivery, and an emphasis on quality. In the past decade, analysts emphasized previously neglected dimensions of Japan's political economy and analyzed these characteristics as part of a larger system. A broad consensus emerged in the literature about the main components of the Japanese economic system since World War II, although analysts vary in their emphasis on the importance of different elements, and a few even seek to refute the importance of some elements altogether.

Management techniques often quite different from those used in the United States and Western Europe first drew attention. They included just-in-time delivery, permanent employment for some workers at large firms, the use of temporary and part-time workers and subcontractors to offset the burden of permanent employment, a lack of shareholder accountability for management because of cross-shareholding and a reliance on bank lending rather than capital markets for funding, and a combined emphasis on production for the domestic market and for export by large firms to take advantage of economies of scale (Abegglen and Stalk 1985; Calder 1993; Johnson 1982:229; McMillan 1985; Okimoto 1989; Ouchi 1981; Pascale and Athos 1984; Pempel 1998; Thurow 1992).

Japanese firms developed a relatively peaceful system of labor relations, including company unions and lifetime employment for some workers. This system prevented disruption of production and distributed the benefits of development broadly and in a largely egalitarian manner that legitimated the overall political and economic system (Bernier 2000; Nakamura 1981:18; Nishizawa 2002; Odaka 1999; Okimoto 1989; Pempel 1998; Thurow 1992).

Keiretsu groups composed of affiliated firms in a variety of industries and centered on a group bank dominated many areas of the Japanese economy. These keiretsu groups typically employ a full-set strategy of investing in many branches of industry because of MITI's and other agencies' risk reduction. These keiretsu include cross-shareholding of other group members' stock, sharing of information and personnel, financial support by banks to group member firms, and other forms of cooperation and risk sharing by group members (Aoki and Dinc 2000; Calder 1993; de Bruin and de Bruin 2002; Hoshi 1994; Johnson 1982; Katz 1998; Nakatani 1984; Okazaki and Okuno-Fujiwara 1999; Okimoto 1989; Sawabe 2002; Sheard 1994; Teranishi 1999). A few analysts determined to prove that "Japan is just like the West" and had no meaningful keiretsu or main bank system question this characteristic (e.g., Miwa and Ramseyer 2002; Ramseyer 2000), but their thought experiments and limited empirical evidence selected to support their argument are methodologically and empirically unsound (Hamada 2000) and unconvincing.

Trading companies, banned by the Allied Occupation Forces after World War II, recreated themselves and expanded by the 1960s. The trading companies coordinated interfirm cooperation and gathered information to increase Japan's global competitiveness, particularly in raw materials imports and the multifaceted deals often needed to create or expand trade relations with many nations (Calder 1993:146; Kojima and Ozawa 1984; Kunio 1982; Tsurumi 1980; Yoshino and Lifson 1986; Young 1979). These trading companies helped create and facilitate Japan's model of raw materials access.

The Japanese state developed a significant degree of planning capability and the ability to implement development strategies in some areas by using its power over limited capital resources from the late 1940s through the early 1960s, its control over credit allocation and foreign exchange, and its regulatory powers regarding firms and international trade. Key government agencies included MITI and its predecessor and successor agencies that controlled foreign exchange from 1949 through 1964 (Calder 1993; Johnson 1982:79–80; Lincoln 1984; Nakamura 1981; Okazaki 1997); the Ministry of Finance (MOF) (Sawabe 2002; Ueda 1999); the Fair Trade Commission that was created to enforce antitrust regulations under the Supreme Commander of the Allied Powers (SCAP) (Johnson 1982; Okimoto 1989; Tilton 1996:30–31); and the Bank of Japan (Johnson 1982; Nakamura 1981:139–44). Johnson (1982:236–37) outlines seven steps in MITI's typical program for supporting the development of a new industry: formulating a policy statement that justifies supporting the industry; allocating foreign currency and funding from the Japan Development Bank; providing licenses to import foreign technology; designating the industry as strategic to grant accelerated depreciation allowances; providing free or cheap improved land for industry facilities; providing tax breaks; and creating an administrative guidance cartel incorporating the firms and trade association in the industry to control competition and coordinate investment.

This state capacity and power formed part of a system of state-firm relations, including administrative guidance and *amakudari* movements of state agency personnel into leadership positions in firms, that sought to achieve consensus between the government and the private sector (Bernier 2000; Johnson 1982; Samuels 1987; Usui and Colignon 1995; Yakushiji 1984). State power maintained a system of severe constraints on imports and on foreign investment in Japan to protect Japanese firms and Japan's economic security (Katz 1998; S. Pekkanen 2000; Pempel 1998). This system of state-firm relations created the "Japan Inc." stereotype of the 1970s and 1980s (Nakamura 1981:83; Prestowitz 1988), but several analysts challenged and reformulated this stereotype (including Calder 1993; Okimoto 1989; and S. Pekkanen 2003). These analysts highlight the limited powers of the state and the independent role of the private sector, including the role of the Industrial Bank of Japan, a private bank, in providing credit to new industries, a role often attributed to MITI and government banks (Calder 1993:158).

These analysts also highlight the roles of private-sector innovation, investment, and initiative, often in the face of government neglect or outright opposition, as critical components of Japan's rapid economic growth in many sectors, including electronics. They emphasize the role of the private Industrial Bank of Japan as a lender and strategic analyst for firms neglected by government agencies or that sought to bypass government plans. Their research also reveals the roles of the private banks at the center of keiretsu groups and their nonbank subsidiaries, such as life insurance companies, that provided investment funds largely outside government control or influence (Calder 1993; Okimoto 1989; Morita 1986). Even in sectors in which the government played a key role, such as steel, private-sector initiative and direct conflict with state agency efforts to control their actions shaped Japan's development trajectory (Calder 1993;Yonekura 1994; see chapter 3 on the steel industry). The private sector and local governments even combined to create an international commercial information-gathering service in 1951 to market Osaka's products in other countries, and MITI took over and expanded this operation in 1954 to form the Japan External Trade Organization (JETRO), a key element of MITI's international operations (Johnson 1982:230–31).

The analysis of previously neglected industrial sectors and characteristics of Japan's political economy built an understanding of the often conflictual and uncooperative relations between the state and firms. These conflicts included the tremendous rivalry between government agencies and the limits placed on planning and coordination by these rivalries (Johnson 1982, who was an early exception to the failure to recognize the interagency rivalry; Calder 1993; Okimoto 1989; Tilton 1996). A complex system of government financial institutions that allocated government funds for a wide range of economic and political purposes exacerbated these difficulties of coordinated state action (Calder 1993:58), as did the increasing intervention of Liberal Democratic Party (LDP) politicians in agency decisions about tax breaks, subsidies, and other assistance to various sectors (Johnson 1982:247–48; Katz 1998).

Industry associations, another previously neglected factor, managed domestic competition, facilitated flows of information between firms as well as between firms and the state, and mediated between firms and the state (Calder 1993; Katz 1998; Okimoto 1989; Tilton 1996; Yonekura 1999;Johnson 1982, who was again an important exception).

The hegemony of the LDP for most of the period following World War II and its strategies for retaining power by incorporating a variety of social groups shaped Japan's political economy of rapid growth. Large contributors, including construction companies and banks that benefited from the maintenance of this system, supported this hegemony. LDP hegemony also rested on the excessive electoral power of agricultural and rural interests because of the structure of the parliamentary election system (Calder 1993; Katz 1998; Okimoto 1989; Pempel 1998; Tilton 1996). LDP hegemony faced significant challenges, most notably during the battle over renewing the Japan-U.S. security treaty in 1960, but the LDP eventually created a new form of national identity and unity based on the broader distribution of the gains from economic growth during the 1960s that preserved its hegemony for a long period (B. Gao 2001).

The relative weakness of consumer and citizens' power over corporations, except in times of crisis (e.g., the pollution crises in late 1960s and early 1970s) also shaped Japan's political economy (Katz 1998; Nakamura 1981:100–102), although one recent analysis highlights the long-standing role of some types of civil society groups (R. Pekkanen 2004). This relative weakness supported high prices in domestic markets, formal and informal limitations on imports, and the operation of cartels that limited competition, protected inefficient firms, and supported high prices in the domestic sphere that benefited firms, state agencies and the LDP and its supporters at the expense of consumers (Katz 1998; Okimoto 1989; Tilton 1996).

U.S. support for Japanese development in the 1940s and 1950s as part of its Cold War efforts in Asia helped drive rapid economic growth (Arrighi 1994). Analyses of Japan's domestic development acknowledge but often minimize the importance of the period of Allied Occupation and the role of SCAP headed by General MacArthur in the postwar reconstruction of Japan (Calder 1993; Johnson 1982; Nakamura 1983, 1994, 1998; Okazaki and Okuno-Fujiwara 1999; among many others). This counterbalances interpretations that the Occupation "changed everything" about Japan via *zaibatsu* dissolution, writing the new Japanese constitution, and reconstructing Japan as a Cold War ally in Asia (Ball 1949; Bisson 1949, 1954; Borden 1984; Hadley 1970; Pauley 1945; U.S. State Department 1949), but it leads to a startling neglect of the role of the United States in Japan's economic ascent, especially in the external arena.

Many researchers analyze Japan's economic miracle in a comparative framework to show the exceptional or unexceptional nature of Japan's political economy and developmental trajectory, either by comparing Japan to other "late developers" or to the other core nations since World War II (see particularly Katz 1998 and Pempel 1998 as examples of these contrasting tendencies). Only Arrighi (1994) places Japan's rise in a longer-term historical comparison with the other most rapid, dramatic, and important cases of economic ascent: Holland, Great Britain, and the United States. We build on Arrighi's pioneering analysis by identifying the key mechanisms in the generative sectors that link the internal and external dimensions of Japan's ascent and that drove its ascent.

None of the analyses of Japan's economic ascent discussed thus far recognize that Japan fundamentally transformed the world economy in support of its postwar economic development. Movements of vast quantities of raw materials and, more recently, of manufactured goods did not happen and were technically and economically impossible until Japan globalized the world economy. The generative sectors in steel, shipbuilding, and shipping simultaneously drove Japan's rapid development, created a new raw materials periphery to supply Japanese industries at low cost, and globalized a series of raw materials and manufacturing industries. In short, Japan's development changed the world.

This Japan-driven globalization and restructuring of the capitalist world-economy is what led us to systematically compare the economic ascent of Japan to earlier cases of transformative economic ascent in economies that eventually became hegemonic: Portugal, Holland, Great Britain, and the United States. This long-term comparative analysis, presented in Bunker and Ciccantell (2005a), revealed a consistent pattern of the creation of generative sectors in raw materials and transport that were maintained in a dynamic tension that drove economic ascent in each nation for several decades. Over the past five centuries of these systemically cumulative cycles, each nation's ascent restructured and further globalized the capitalist world-economy. Our comparative analysis also revealed that, despite periods of rapid economic growth in many other nations since the 1500s, no other nation's economic ascent had the kind of transformative and globalizing impacts on the world-system that the ascents of Portugal, Holland, Great Britain, the United States, and Japan have had.

This multipronged comparative strategy led us to develop the analysis of Japan's economic ascent presented in this book, even though Japan has not and may never rise to the position of global hegemon, as these earlier ascendants did. Moreover, it led us to incorporate into the analysis of Japan's ascent and stagnation an examination of China's rapid economic ascent since 1980. China's ascent, by far the most important change in the capitalist world-economy in recent decades, is closely linked to and dependent on both the United States and Japan. Japanese firms, markets, institutions, banks, technologies, and development model are playing much the same role that earlier ascendants have done for later ascendants, supporting and guiding ascent via investments in and relations with more rapidly growing economies, even as economic and geopolitical rivalries grow. Understanding China's economic ascent in relation to and comparison with Japan leads us to formulate the fifth research question guiding this book: how is China utilizing and transforming the Japan-created global raw materials industries to support China's rapid development?

Several works advanced our understanding of Japan's economic growth by linking many aspects of Japan's success in the past fifty years to the social institutions created during the Meiji Era and in the first half of the twentieth century, particularly during the period from 1930 to 1945. This corrects interpretations that depicted the post–World War II era as a dramatic break with Japan's past. Historically, Japan served as an extractive periphery for hundreds of years for China and, to a smaller extent, for Europe, including the Dutch, in copper, sulfur, precious metals, silk, and rice. This history made the successful industrialization and the initially successful but ultimately failed imperialism of the period from the Meiji Era through World War II an extremely remarkable accomplishment.

During the Meiji Era, the Japanese founded the original zaibatsu groups and developed the ongoing concern on the part of successive Japanese governments about the danger of zaibatsu-created monopolies and the need to promote oligopolies comprising competing firms in many industries to control the zaibatsu (Mosk 2001:67). The oligopolies led by the keiretsu groups remain an important issue for the state and the economy today (Katz 1998). A pattern of collaboration between the national state, regional, and local governments and private firms also emerged during the Meiji Era. This collaboration was often focused around infrastructural needs in port areas such as Osaka, the development of electric power, and railroad construction (Calder 1993:25; Mosk 2001:83, 137). The state often provided financing for private firms and for the building of factories later sold to private firms (Calder 1993:25). Large firms created the system of private banks during this period (Calder 1993:26), and the Japanese state created the original government bureaucracies during the Meiji Era (Johnson 1982:37–38).

The Maritime Industrial Development Area program after World War II built on the model developed during the Meiji Era to use port development as a means of economic development and as a way to gain the support of local warlords for the national government by combining national, prefectural, and city government subsidies. Interestingly, the Meiji program relied on Dutch engineers and technology during its early years, due to the contacts between Japan and Holland established during the period of Dutch hegemony and maintained during Japan's isolation prior to the Meiji Era. This borrowed technology often failed due to the much more severe climatic and tidal conditions in Japan than in Holland, and some of these development efforts failed. The Ministry of Transport and Japanese engineers learned from these early experiences and developed expertise and technologies better suited to Japanese conditions (Inamura 1993; Japan Port and Harbour Association n.d.; Kita and Moriwaki 1989; Kudo 1985; Masuda 1981; Miyaji 1990; Rimmer 1984; Takamura 1990; Yuzo 1990).

Changes during the first three decades of the twentieth century also helped lay the foundation for Japan's growth after World War II (Johnson 1982; Nakamura 1983, 1994, 1998). Key changes during this era included the electrification and mechanization of industry (Mosk 2001:119–26), the development of private banks (Teranishi 2000), the creation of heavy industry by the state and private firms (Johnson 1982:86–87), and the first state industrial policy efforts (Johnson 1982:98–101).

From the 1930s through 1945, a variety of key elements of Japan's post–World War II political economy developed (Dower 1999; Johnson 1982; Nakamura 1981, 1983, 1994, 1998). These included a growing role of the state in the planning and management of the economy via direct control and through administrative guidance of private firms (often based on the model of Nazi Germany), increased concentration in the banking sector, an emphasis on employment stability and labor peace, the creation of a syndicate loan system that served as the model for the main bank system (Johnson 1982:108–10; Okazaki and Okuno-Fujiwara 1999:2–3), and the central role of industry associations in forming cartels (Johnson 1982:162–63; Nakamura 1981:13; Tilton 1996:29). The shift from light to heavy industrialization and the concentration of manufacturing in the hands of large firms accelerated during the war (Johnson 1982:157–62), with small firms increasingly tightly linked to large firms as subcontractors (Nakamura 1981:15). Despite efforts of the Japanese military to take complete control of Japan's economy, strong resistance by private firms forced the military and other government agencies to compromise and leave a significant degree of control in private hands, even though this hindered war efforts. Japanese firms maintained an unbroken legacy of a significant degree of freedom from government control (Dower 1999; Johnson 1982:133–56).

The Allied Occupation created or consolidated several key elements of Japan's postwar political economy from 1945 through 1952 (Ball 1949; Bisson 1949, 1954; Borden 1984; Dower 1999; Hadley 1970; Johnson 1982; Nafziger 1995; Nakamura 1981; Pauley 1945; So and Chiu 1995; Vogel 2002; U.S. State Department 1949). Many of the members and leaders of Japan's state agencies, including MITI, served during the war and escaped SCAP's efforts to purge the wartime leadership. SCAP considered these experienced bureaucrats, many of whom spent the war directing Japan's industrialization drive in Manchuria, as indispensable to the rebuilding of Japan's economy (Dower 1999; Johnson 1982:41–46). The purge of zaibatsu leadership and seizure of the wealth of the founding families left MITI and other government agencies with an unprecedented degree of control over the Japanese economy in the early postwar period (Johnson 1982:173–74; Nakamura 1981:23–26).

No analysis of MITI (including Johnson 1982) pays much attention to its role internationally in gathering information about raw materials suppliers and industries and in facilitating the formation, operation, and negotiations of the Japanese steel mills' raw materials–purchasing cartel. All discussions of the role of steel and MITI simply assume that iron ore and metallurgical coal will appear at the new coastal steel mills, without examining how MITI and the Japanese steel firms constructed global iron ore and coal industries to supply their mills at progressively lower cost. This Japanese purchasing cartel presented a united front as the world's single largest buyer of metallurgical coal and iron ore in negotiations with uncoordinated individual exporting firms. Many analysts neglect the international role of MITI, facilitated in the 1950s and early 1960s by its control over foreign exchange earnings and enhanced by its efforts to acquire and analyze information and to develop a highly skilled and widely experienced staff. Analyses typically focus only on MITI's domestic role, the failures of some of its efforts to plan development and control firms' actions, and its battles with other government agencies, most notably the MOF (Calder 1993; Johnson 1982; Okimoto 1989). We highlight this international role of MITI and the inseparability of its international efforts from the development of the steel, shipbuilding, shipping, and other industries in Japan.

The creation of the Priority Production System in 1947 to solve Japan's economic crisis of energy and food shortages, inflation, high unemployment, extreme poverty, economic stagnation, and social unrest utilized the government agencies and private firms developed in earlier eras. In combination with critical support from the U.S. government, the Japanese state resolved this crisis, despite often significant conflicts between SCAP and the Japanese bureaucracy (Dower 1999; Johnson 1982:179–93; Nakamura 1981:21–22, 56; Vogel 2002), and laid the foundation for Japan's dramatic economic ascent.

U.S. support to establish a new Japanese model of raw materials access that did not require the costs of and the resistance to empire sharply differentiated the era following World War II from the period between 1930 and 1945. The earlier eras created key elements of Japan's postwar domestic political economy, but in the external arena, the Japanese state learned from earlier periods that imperialism had failed and that the United States and the resistance of neighboring nations foreclosed this strategy.

An entirely new model of external relations, especially in terms of raw materials access, had to be created if the heavy industrialization strategy that emerged out of the cooperation between and conflicts among SCAP, Japanese government agencies, the steel industry association and the three members of the steel oligopoly, and other steel firms like Kawasaki was to succeed. This model, pioneered in the late 1940s by SCAP, the U.S. State Department, and the Ministry of Commerce and Industry, or

MCI (MITI's predecessor), and supported by the World Bank and some political leaders in Australia seeking to promote Australian development, resolved Japan's postwar coal crisis. This new model gradually developed and expanded from the 1950s onward into a system of raw materials access based on long-term contracts and limited Japanese joint-venture investments. This model, in combination with Japanese domestic investment and innovation in steel and shipbuilding, progressively reduced the cost of Japan's raw materials imports and guaranteed supply security, making Japan's economy the world's most competitive in a range of industries and driving Japan's dramatic economic ascent.

The firms, state agencies, banks, and other social institutions that created and sustained the generative sectors in steel and shipbuilding in the era after World War II emerged from a conflict-filled process of bargaining and accommodation domestically between the firms and state agencies that survived World War II, between Japan and the United States in the context of the Cold War, and between Japan and several other nations, most notably Australia, Brazil, and Canada, that became Japan's key suppliers of raw materials.

This Japanese political economic system drove Japan, through several business cycles between the mid-1950s and 1973, on a trajectory of sustained, rapid growth led by generative sectors in steel, shipbuilding, and automobiles. The disruption of cheap energy supplies in 1973–74 by the first oil shock, in combination with Nixon's ending of the gold standard of fixed exchange rates and the increasing trade conflicts with the United States and other buyers of Japanese manufactured goods, severely disrupted this system. Japanese firms, industry sectors, and the state reacted comparatively quickly (relative to the United States and Western Europe) to this new global context and shifted rapidly away from petroleum use in industry and electricity generation to coal and nuclear power. This industrial transformation, which eventually included the virtual elimination of some energy-intensive industries in Japan, such as aluminum smelting, was not smooth or fully planned and controlled by the state (Calder 1993; Samuels 1987).

The Japanese political economic system adjusted relatively quickly and suffered only relatively mild disruption from the second oil price shock of 1979–80, supported particularly by an automobile industry that led the world in fuel efficiency by using progressively lighter and stronger steels and incorporating growing quantities of other, lighter materials. Economic growth continued through the 1980s, with steel and automobiles maintaining their leading roles and now joined by other sectors, such as electronics and computers; however, the shipbuilding industry entered an ongoing period of decline in the 1970s.

The 1990s, after the collapse of the bubble economy in 1990, proved to be a decade of crisis. This crisis ended the world-leading competitiveness of steel and many other industries in Japan, leaving them mired in a long-term stagnation and decline. This led many firms to shift investment abroad (Katz 1998; Pempel 1998).

Many of these analysts address our fourth research question: why did such a successful model come to such a sudden halt? Some focus on the political causes of Japan's decline (e.g., widespread political corruption, the loss of LDP hegemony, the growing power of various civil society groups, and the ascendance of the interests of noncompetitive, protectionist sectors). Some analysts focus on the economic causes of Japan's decline (e.g., speculative investment, the rise of new, low-cost competitors, the increasing value of the yen, inadequate domestic consumption, and the role of liberalization in the financial sector). Other analysts blame the Japanese state for decline (e.g., too much state intervention in the economy, recognition of the environmental problems, increased politicization of the regulatory process, and atrophied embeddedness that reduced competitiveness). We return to the relative roles of these factors in contributing to economic stagnation in the concluding chapter of this volume.

The linked second and third questions—how did Japan globalize the world economy in support of its rapid economic growth and what are the consequences of the resulting new forms of global inequality?—receive much less attention in the literature. The foreclosure of the imperial model of raw materials access by defeat in World War II (Barnhart 1987; Borden 1984; Marshall 1995; McDougall 1993) made a new model necessary after the war. The most important analyses of these questions focus on the so-called ABC raw materials access strategy of depending mainly on Australia, Brazil, and Canada for raw materials since World War II (Akao 1983; Anderson 1987; Graham, Thorpe, and Hogan 1999; Katada 2002a, 2002b; Koerner 1993; McMahon and Harris 1983; Ozawa 1979, 1986; Panda 1982; Swan, Thorpe, and Hogan 1999; Vernon 1983). Many analysts recognize the concern of the Japanese government to assure raw materials supplies (e.g., Johnson 1982; Okimoto 1989). Even in the most insightful of these analyses, however, the raw materials problem receives scant attention: "a further aspect of the international environment beneficial to Japan was the availability of cheap and stable supplies of the raw materials and energy needed for heavy and chemical industrialization" (Nakamura 1981:63).

These second and third questions also receive relatively little attention from analysts of political economy and globalization, most of whom focus on the role of the United States in driving globalization (for alternative perspectives on this debate, see Amin 1996; Arrighi 1998; Biersteker 1998; Boxill 1994; Ciccantell 2000; Garrett 1998; Harvey 1995; Kiely 1998; Shaw 1997; Sklair 1998; and Yaghmaian 1998) and pay insufficient attention to the role of Japan. The strategic efforts of the Japanese steel firms and MITI, initially supported by the U.S. government, *created* cheap and stable raw materials supplies by globalizing formerly localized raw materials industries, most notably coal and iron ore.

The attempts to address our first four questions in the existing literature provide a starting point for developing an outline of the key factors analyzed in our work. The Japanese development model of the postwar era embodied what we term a dynamic tension between the material processes underlying economic ascent, processes of global economic and political competition, and a constellation of social groups seeking to shape this development model and capture the benefits that resulted. Domestically, these social groups identified in the literature include firms and industry associations in the generative sectors; labor in the generative sectors; managers and other professionals in the generative sectors; government agencies charged with national development, led by MITI; other government agencies, including the Ministry of Finance, the Ministry of Transport, and the Bank of Japan; banks and other financial institutions; firms and industry associations in other, often less-favored and less-competitive sectors; labor; managers and professionals in these less-favored, less-competitive sectors; and particular spatial and sectoral interests, represented by political leaders and various levels of government whose support was critical for legitimacy.

At the global level, key factors identified in the literature include economic and political alliances and rivalries with the existing hegemon and other rivals that shape national development strategies and competitiveness, embodied in the efforts of the Allied Occupation Forces and the U.S. State Department to secure access to coal from Australia to resolve the coal crisis of the late 1940s and the modeling of Japanese corporate accounting law on U.S. standards (Chiba 2001); political competition, including warfare and efforts to set the rules of the global economy, that similarly shape the success or failure of any strategy of national economic ascent; market forces and relative competitiveness that shape the nature and relative success of any nation's development strategy, particularly evident in the crisis in Japan because of efforts to ignore global competitiveness that led to growing state subsidies, growing burdens on other social groups (Katz 1998), and ultimately halted the pattern of state-sector-firm relations and the economic ascent of the nation; and, finally, the relationship between the ascendant economy and its extractive peripheries that supply the ascendant economy and critically support global competitiveness.

If any component of this constellation of social forces becomes too powerful and overwhelms the interests of others, this dynamic tension collapses and economic ascent will end. These patterns are both long-lasting (even staying in place long after ascent is halted) and very difficult to maintain in dynamic tension. This helps explain why dramatic ascent and the resulting restructuring of the world economy occur so infrequently, despite the efforts of many states and firms to accomplish this transformation in support of their own interests over the past five centuries. The creation and maintenance of these patterns of dynamic tension result from the efforts of states and firms to resolve the fundamental material challenge for rapidly ascendant economies: acquiring, transporting, processing, and utilizing the rapidly growing amounts of raw materials essential for economic growth. The loss of dynamic tension as political payoffs, financial and land speculation by fractions of capital focused on making money without investing in the productive process, misdirection of state subsidies to uncompetitive industries, and competition from the existing hegemon and other rising economies, including China, in the context of the global economy that Japan's ascent helped create exposed the limitations of Japan's postwar development model and the opportunities the increased economies of scale in steel, shipbuilding, shipping, and other industries created for other rising nations.

Answering these four questions requires a longer-term and comparative perspective to identify not just the unique characteristics of Japan's economic ascent but, more importantly, the commonalities between Japan's postwar rise and earlier cases of successful economic ascent that restructured the capitalist world-economy. Understanding Japan's economic ascent led us to conduct a long-term series of historical comparisons of several cases of economic ascent (Bunker and Ciccantell 2005). These comparisons helped to reveal how Japan achieved such intensive domestic development and far-reaching external restructuring to create its raw materials peripheries. We found a clear pattern of rapidly ascending economies that simultaneously developed their domestic industrial economies, restructured and progressively globalized raw materials and transport industries, and restructured increasingly distant regions into raw materials peripheries supplying increasingly diverse sets of raw materials at progressively lower costs. Japan's rapid rise and dramatic transformation of world industrial and trade patterns and of space and the global environment (as well as its long crisis) can best be understood by analyzing the raw materials and transport industries that provided the material foundations for Japan's competitive advantages.

Extending this comparative analysis to the so-called new economy of the "Information Age" of the late twentieth and early twenty-first centuries (Aoyama and Castells 2002; Castells 2000a, 2000b, 2000c; Harvey 1990) revealed another critical case for analysis: the economic ascent of China. Although some analysts talk about "post-materialism" (Herman et al. 1989) and networked societies (Castells 2000a; Wellman 1999), raw materials now pour into China on a scale far larger than that achieved by Japan as the Chinese state and Chinese firms seek to replicate the Japanese model of economic development. Long-distance global flows of raw materials are larger than ever before, with a huge and rapidly growing share headed to China rather than the existing core powers. The capitalist world-economy has not "de-material-ized"; instead, the materials are simply traveling from mining areas developed to serve the Japanese market in large ships developed by Japanese shipbuilding firms to new coastal industrial areas in China built following the model of Japan's coastal MIDAs (often in cooperation with the same Japanese steel firms), where these raw materials are transformed into the industrial products that flood the U.S. and global markets. This profound material restructuring of the capitalist world-economy, based largely on China's relationships with Japan and the United States, led to our fifth research question: how is China utilizing and transforming the Japan-created global raw materials industries to support China's rapid development?

Outline of the Book

In the next chapter, we explain our methodology to analyze these processes in the case of Japan and of earlier ascendant economies that rose to dominate global trade and restructure the world economy in support of their national economic ascent. We describe our approach to the challenges of conducting comparative analysis over very long periods in the context of the evolution of the capitalist world-economy as the result of the strategies of ascendant economies to confront the power of and system created by the existing hegemon in pursuit of their own national development.

We then present our theoretical model, new historical materialism. We highlight our concept of generative sectors that drive economic ascent and provide the templates for the construction of broader patterns of state-sector-firm relations, financial systems to concentrate and allocate funds to generative sectors, patterns of international relations to ensure low-cost, secure access to raw materials, and other elements of the broader process of national development and of restructuring the world economy and global environment to support economic ascent. In cases of successful economic ascent, these generative sectors resolve an important contradiction between economies of scale in raw materials extraction and processing and of diseconomies of space created by the need to transport increasing quantities of an increasingly diverse set of raw materials over increasing distances to supply the expanding industrial sector in the ascendant economy. We outline key findings from our comparative case studies of successful economic ascent in Portugal, Holland, Great Britain, and the United States in order to provide the context of and framework for understanding Japan's economic ascent after World War II.

In chapter 3, we first describe the position of Japan materially and sociopolitically after World War II, highlighting Japan's depleted domestic raw materials supplies, its poverty, the opposition of Japan's neighbors to reestablishing trade relations with

Japan, and the development of the existing hegemon's need to support the redevelopment of Japan as part of U.S. Cold War strategies in Asia. We then analyze how Japanese firms and the Japanese state, supported by U.S. and World Bank financial assistance, created a new model of domestic development based in the steel, shipbuilding, and shipping industries. MITI developed its capacity and role in Japan's development via both cooperation and conflict with the Japanese steel firms and their needs domestically and internationally, supporting the development of increasingly large-scale and tightly integrated blast furnaces and steel mills. We describe the MIDA program begun in the 1950s that coordinated firm and state investment in new greenfield ports and steel plants utilizing the latest technological advances developed in Japan and imported from other nations to reduce costs and increase Japanese economic competitiveness in steel, shipbuilding, and all other sectors that used steel and the steel-based transport infrastructure. We also analyze the development of the Japanese shipbuilding industry that provided the increasingly large ships needed to bring rapidly growing quantities of coal, iron ore, and other raw materials from distant raw materials peripheries to Japan via technological innovations and close state-firm coordination.

In chapter 4, we extend and deepen our examination of coal procurement in our analysis of how and why the steel industry catalyzed a generative sector crucial to Japan's rapid development in the second half of the twentieth century. The locus of our narrative remains the MIDAs, where organization and technology designed to import vast bulk from multiple distant sources cheaply and steadily intersects with the organization, technology, and construction of space and environment designed to transform the imported bulk into high-quality steel at the lowest possible production and distribution costs. In the previous chapter on steel, we primarily looked inland from the MIDAs. In this and in the following chapter, we primarily look overseas from the MIDAs to the sources of coal and iron. As with steel, we locate the Japanese solutions to coal procurement within these technological and scale imperatives of competition at the world-historical moment of Japan's ascent.

We first analyze the key material characteristics of metallurgical coal and then outline the stages of the development of Japanese raw materials acquisition strategies for coal over the past five decades, because this historical evolution in Australia, western Canada, and in other nations provided the model for these strategies in other raw materials industries. MITI and the Japanese steel firms became increasingly skilled at transferring the burdens of financing the growing costs of building mines, railroads, and ports to states and firms in Australia, Canada, and other raw materials peripheries, as well as at fomenting increasing competition between coal suppliers in order to drive down Japan's coal acquisition costs. We then analyze the consequences for

Japan's coal-exporting periphery of this new model of periphery formation, including bearing the costs and risks of supplying raw materials to Japan and receiving reduced prices and rents because of increasing competition, and the impacts of the rapid ascent of China in recent years on these raw materials peripheries. The conclusion highlights the role of coal in supporting the generative sectors in Japan.

In chapter 5, we show that the Japanese steel mills and the Japanese state gradually replicated and adapted the strategies and trade relationships developed to resolve the challenge of coal supplies in the iron ore industry. The Japanese steel firms and the Japanese state promoted exploration of new areas, pushed new transport technologies and infrastructure, and devised new contractual and rent forms that significantly reduced their equity participation and capital risk. As in the coal industry, their emerging strategy created intense competition between suppliers within a market characterized by excess capacity. This strategy essentially evaded the ability of large mining oligopolies to restrict supply in order to support ore prices. The Japanese steel firms and MITI devised strategies and instruments to restructure the world industry and its transport characteristics so that they revolved around and favored Japanese steel mills and MIDAs.

After outlining the key material characteristics of iron ore, we focus particular attention on Australia and Brazil, the two largest suppliers of iron ore to Japan and the key partners in the development of Japan's iron ore acquisition strategies, as well as the bearers of the burdens of the immense costs of opening remote raw materials frontiers in Western Australia and the Amazon to supply iron ore at low cost to Japan. We also examine the impacts of China's recent economic ascent on these peripheries and the strategies of the Japanese steel mills to respond to Chinese ascent.

In chapter 6, we focus on the process of transporting raw materials to Japan and the role of the Japanese shipping industry in creating economies of scale in shipping that contribute significantly to lowering Japanese raw materials costs for the steel plants and their customers in the MIDAs. We analyze the growing scale of ships and ports as the outcome of the strategies of Japanese firms and the Japanese state to create global raw materials and transport industries that dramatically reduced raw materials transport costs during the second half of the twentieth century. We then outline the consequences of these strategies for Japan's coal- and iron ore–exporting peripheries. Finally, we examine how China's ascent affected the shipbuilding and transport industries.

In the last chapter, we summarize how Japanese firms and the Japanese state constructed a development model based on the steel industry as a generative sector that drove Japan's economic ascent in the world-historical context of U.S. hegemony. These strategies created a tightly linked set of technological and organizational innovations to overcome the natural and social obstacles to Japanese development, dramatically increased Japan's international economic competitiveness by lowering production costs in all sectors of the economy, turned Japan into the world's largest exporter of manufactured products, restructured a range of global industries, and recreated the world-system hierarchy in support of Japanese development. Organizational innovations in the use of long-term contracts and joint ventures in raw materials industries, designed to foster global excess capacity and lower rents to resource-extracting firms and states, reallocated the costs of providing the material building blocks of Japanese development to the states and firms of its new raw materials periphery. This competitive advantage drove Japanese capital accumulation and economic ascent, and simultaneously underdeveloped Japan's periphery.

These Japanese innovations became key elements of globalization as U.S. and European transnational corporations and states sought to compete with Japan. Joint ventures, long-term contracts, and other forms of interfirm cooperation replaced vertically integrated foreign direct investment, the earlier U.S. model of capital accumulation and international economic linkage, as the model for global industries. This new model of capital accumulation redistributed the costs and benefits of development between core and peripheral regions of the capitalist world-economy in a wide range of global industries. We then highlight comparisons between Japanese economic ascent and earlier cases of successful economic ascent, outlining the lessons for understanding national development and the transformation of global industries and environments that can be drawn from the cases of Japan, the United States, Great Britain, and Holland. We then discuss the emerging parameters of the evolution of the world economy in the twenty-first century, focusing particular attention on the economic ascent of China that is replicating in many ways the Japanese model of development in a much larger territory and population.

CHAPTER TWO

Economic Ascent and Hegemony in the Capitalist World-Economy

Relations of production are profoundly social, but they occur within, are constrained by, and catalyze material processes. Material processes manifest a higher degree of regularity and generality than occurs in social processes, so explanation of the physical can be more precise (Bunge 1997). National development as a field emanating from purposive action of states, firms, and sectors comprises multiple intersections and interactions between social and material processes. We explore the methodological and empirical contribution that physical regularities may impart to analysis of the social phenomena of national development within a dynamically expanding world economy. We focus on Japanese development after World War II, both domestically and in its relations with other national economies, and in comparison with other cases of rapid, systemically transformative economic ascent as the empirical base for building a model flexible enough to be applied to other countries, contemporaneously and at different historical moments in the development of the world-system.

New Historical Materialism and Generative Sectors

Our analysis of national economic development and economic ascent focuses on the emergence of hegemonic potential, rather than on its maturity and decline. The beginnings of economic ascent require successful coordination of domestic technological advances, particularly in heavy industry and transport, with the external solution of access to cheap and steady sources of the raw materials used for heavy industry. The raw materials used in greatest volume present the greatest challenge and best opportunity for economies of scale. These economies of scale, however, drive a contradictory increase in transport cost, as the closest reserves of raw materials are depleted more rapidly as the scale of their industrial transformation increases.

The tension of this contradiction between the economies of scale and the cost of space foments technological innovation in transport (e.g., vessels, loaders, ports, rails); in chemical and mechanical means of reducing component inputs per unit of output (e.g., coal and iron in steel); and in improvements in control of heat, pressure, and the mix of chemicals that make each unit of material inputs stronger and thus enable smaller, lighter amounts to perform the same work. All of these technological fixes drive each other, and all of them tend to generate increases of scale, thus exacerbating over the long term the very contradiction between scale and space that they are designed to solve.

The national economies that most successfully initiated technological and organizational solutions—internal and external—of this contradiction simultaneously generated their own rise to economic dominance, restructured the mechanisms and dynamics of systemic and hierarchic accumulation, and expanded and intensified the commercial arena of raw materials trade and transport. We call these sectors generative (see also Bunker and Ciccantell 2003a, 2003b, 2005; Ciccantell and Bunker 1999, 2002, 2004): "sectors that create backward and forward linkages and stimulate a much broader range of technical skills and learning, along with formal institutions designed and funded to promote them; vast and diversified instrumental knowledge held by interdependent specialists about the rest of the world; financial institutions adapted to the requirements of large sunk costs in a variety of social and political contexts; specific formal and informal relations between firms, sectors and states; and the form of legal distinctions between public and private and between different levels of public jurisdiction" (Ciccantell and Bunker 1999:116).

We build on leading-sector theory (Modelski and Thompson 1996) and on Chandler's (1977) notion of template to posit that generative sectors emerge around the most complex challenge facing states, firms, and sectors in rapidly rising economies. A generative sector, however, is not necessarily the sector with the highest rate of profit. A generative sector stimulates innovation and development across other sectors, as Rostow (1960) argued in his model of leading sectors. Cooperation, and therefore trust, between firms, sectors, and the state are essential to overcoming the costly contradiction between economies of scale and diseconomies of space. Moreover, cooperation and trust become more essential at each successive stage in the evolution of the capitalist world-economy because the complexities and scales of the social and natural material processes increase over time (Chase-Dunn 1989).

Generative sectors are conceptualized much more broadly than as simply leading economic sectors. Generative sectors serve simultaneously as key centers of capital accumulation, bases for a series of linked industries, sources of technological and organizational innovations that spread to other sectors, and models for firms and for state-sector-firm relations in other sectors. These generative sectors in raw materials and transport industries drove economic ascent throughout the history of the capitalist world-economy in core economies and simultaneously underdeveloped peripheral regions both within and external to the national boundaries of these rising core economies.

The linkages from these generative sectors spread throughout the ascendant economy, supplying direct inputs for other industries at lower cost, providing infrastructure available for use by other industries and consumers, serving as profit centers, generating capital for investment in existing and new industries, providing markets for other industries, stimulating the development of capital markets that are then available to other industry sectors, and shaping the general pattern of relations between firms and the state. The myriad direct and indirect linkages from the generative sector lower raw materials costs, increase labor productivity, and improve international competitiveness in many sectors of the ascendant economy via this range of direct and indirect linkages.

This exacerbated tension between the contradictions of scale and space is sequentially cumulative, so each systemic cycle of accumulation confronted more complex tasks, requiring greater and more efficacious state participation, promotion, and protection, together with more and greater coordination of firms and sharing of both the costs and the benefits of technological innovation within and across sectors (even if they remain competitive for market share). These internal dynamics must also achieve reduction in the costs of the raw materials and of the transport infrastructure in the external exporting zones. The cumulatively sequential increases in scale of raw materials transformation and in the size and capacity of transport vessels and infrastructure correspond to and make economically viable the expansion of the practical commercial space in each systemic cycle of accumulation.

The technological and social organizational developments generated in response to the contradiction between scale and space for the most voluminously used raw materials provide the critical impulses that create, expand, and restructure the world-system as a series of punctuated cumulative sequences. Commerce in the most voluminously traded raw materials—from wood and grain to iron ore and coal—proceeded from river-based to lake- and railroad-based to ocean-based transport through the Dutch, British, and American systemic cycles of accumulation and Japan's successful restructuring of these trades into truly global sourcing. Each step of this expansion allows and employs huge increases of scale in transport technologies. The introduction of new scales of transport and of industrial transformation, by broadening the sources of raw materials from river basin to continental and then to global networks, systematically reduced ground rents (see Coronil 1997; Marx 1967; Ricardo 1983) available to the resource-rich economies that export these raw materials.

The interaction between scale, scope, technological innovation, and denser political and material relations between firms, sectors, and the state increase the productivity, the profitability, and the financial and political power in the national economies that initiate, regulate, and structure each systemic cycle of accumulation. Simultaneously, the same set of skills and interactions lowers the rents to and increases the infrastructural investments of raw materials–exporting economies. Thus, each hegemonic cycle simultaneously increased the commercially integrated space, the movement of raw materials in this space, and global inequalities between raw materials exporters and raw materials importers (see Bunker and Ciccantell 2005; Ciccantell and Bunker 1999).

Our concept of generative sector extends and refines Rostow's (1960) notion of leading sector. Generative sectors drive technological, financial, organizational, and political relations, stimulating cooperation across and efforts to reduce conflict between firms, sectors, and states in strategies and actions both domestic and international. Technological advances that occur within the generative sectors follow both forward and backward linkages (cf. Hirschman 1958), most importantly by providing templates (cf. Chandler 1977) for direct application to other sectors that directly or indirectly constitute clusters or linked nodes in chains of production (Marx 1967; Schumpeter 1934). The spread of innovation through such clusters constitutes a consistent theme in economic history. For example, Landes (1969) follows Marx in identifying the complex mutual stimuli that coal mining fomented between advances in the technologies of generating heat and pressure from steam and of transforming heat into mechanical energy in order to lower water tables in the deepening mine shafts; advances in metallurgy required to contain pressures in the boilers; advances in metalworking required to sustain vacuums and pressures in moving pistons and their cylinders; standardization of components used in these boilers, pumps, and machines; and advances in the fuel efficiency of all of these processes. The chemical advances in technology, particularly in metallurgy, and the control over the pressures generated required collaboration between firms as well as surveillance and support by the state. All of these technological advances fed into other sectors, including rail and ship transport needed to move the raw materials whose consumption each technical advance cheapened and thereby accelerated.

Historically, those sectors with the densest forward and backward linkages to other sectors utilize the most voluminously used raw materials, especially when we include the chemical transformations and improvements of these raw materials and the ways in which they are transported. Historically as empirical process and chemically or logically as material process, technical advances in the fuel efficiency and in the strength of these materials and in their transport consistently created cumulative sequences toward ever greater scale. Heat and pressure both become more economical in larger containers, and higher heats and pressures create chemical transformations and mechanical energy more efficiently (Landes 1969). We have shown similar processes at work in maritime transport and bulk-breaking or handling (Bunker and Ciccantell 1995a, 1995b, 2005).

We propose that matter and space, as naturally given aspects of physical reality, manifest themselves socially and economically in built or manipulated environments as cost, scale, and distance. In these and related manifestations, matter and space pose regular, specifiable conditions of production and exchange. The conditions, once specified, may reveal their explanatory status and the intensity of their links both to the local and temporal particularities of instances and to temporally evolving global systems in which they participate and which they partially form. We propose that comparison based in highly specified physically and spatially grounded material analysis resolves some of the problems of comparisons of cases or instances that participate in complex systems of highly dense interaction, especially when the system itself evolves over time, driven by and driving changes in its component parts (on comparative study of long-term change, see, e.g., Abbott 1997; Evans 1995; Lieberson 1992, 1997; McMichael 1984, 1990, 1992; Paige 1999; Ragin 1987; Robinson 1996, 1998, 2004; Sassen 1995; Tilly 1995a, 1995b; Wallerstein 1974, 1980; Woo 1991).

The social processes of production depend fundamentally on matter. Production-enhancing technologies entwine comprehensively with the historically accumulating social knowledge of and capacity to manipulate ever more precise differentiations between the chemical and physical properties and attributes of different material forms, in their pure instances, in their transformation into energy, and in their reaction to and incorporation of each other under different conditions and combinations, including particularly temperature and pressure. Space defines and organizes the world economy as a system because of the ways that matter is distributed in and across space.

Different kinds of matter are located in different places. As technology advances, material forms used for particular production processes or for particular products become progressively more specific. The locations of specific kinds of materials correspondingly become more rare, so that the total distance—that is, the space—between the locus of production and the locus of extraction increases. Thus, space and matter are integrally entwined in both production and extraction. Expanded production consumes more matter across broader spaces, and thus the expanding interaction of scale and distance of matter and space drives the expansion and the intensification of the world-system.

Space is simultaneously a means of production, a condition of production, a barrier to or cost of production, and an obstacle to circulation of commodities. Space impinges on extraction even more directly than on production, as the space in which the resource extraction occurs is naturally, or geologically and hydrologically, determined. The attributes of this space include not simply location on a two-dimensional plane, but the topographic characteristics of the site and of the entire space between the site of extraction and the site of transformation, and the amount of space across and within which a given amount of the resource occurs. In minerals, space is reduced to a percentage of pure ore and a measure of overburden—that is, to the amount of other matter in whatever space must be excavated to extract a given amount of the mineral in question. The composition—hardness, friability, moisture, and such—of the surrounding matter combines with this space to determine cost of extraction and processing, as well as the environmental impacts of the extraction. Thus, the relevant space of matter (or the space that matters) in extraction includes depth and extent of one form of matter within other forms of matter (i.e., the ground), as well as the naturally determined distances between the sites of natural occurrence and of social transformation.

To reduce the cost of space, expanded production generates large and complex technological innovations in material and energetic forms that permit increased economies of scale in transport vehicles, loaders, and infrastructure. Marx (1967), Mandel (1975), Innis (1956), Landes (1969), Chandler (1965, 1977), and Harvey (1982) explained in different ways the multiple and complex links between expanded production, technological advance in material use and in energy capture and containment, and new means of transport. Marx (1967), Innis (1956), and Harvey (1982) all noted the high cost of the building of the environment required for rail and shipping, and the role of the state and of high finance in overcoming the inadequacies of individual capitals or of private ownership of land. Although the role of raw materials procurement and transport and the technical or physically determined economies of scale in heavy industry are consistently undertheorized by all of these authors, the cases or instances in which they discovered and then presented these relationships of capital and innovation consistently involve the movement of matter across space and the questions of property in both matter and space.

This confluence of space and matter in the formation, expansion, and intensification of the world-system demands a specific focus on the strategies to procure and transport raw materials as these have structured cumulatively sequential systemic cycles of accumulation. The resolution of the contradictions between scale of transformation and cost of space created generative sectors in all of the economies that became serious candidates for hegemonic status. The material processes and physical attributes of the raw materials and their extraction and transport can be specified in precise, regular, and commensurable, and thus in comparable, terms theoretically independent of any of the social processes that constitute a relational analysis of the capitalist world-economy or comparison of its component parts. We can explain their links to the generative sectors that drive the expansion and reorganization of the world-system. Their explanatory status can thus be quite high.

In our new historical materialist approach, we examine the ways that society and nature interact through social creation and use of technologies that can perform their intended functions only if they conform to naturally determined material processes. We also examine the consequences of the laws of thermodynamics on the ways these technologies enable humans to extract, transform, consume, and discard naturally produced matter and energy. In order to do this, we have to organize our data, and our analysis, along three distinct spheres of understanding that appear to reflect three different kinds of reality. The first sphere entails *physical and mathematical laws* and rules that appear to apply universally. Most relevant to this study are gravity, the conservation of matter and energy, and the ratios between volume and surface. These are fundamental to the economies of scale, the diseconomies of space, and the reiterated scalar expansions as solutions to the tension between them. To the extent, though, that these laws and rules are universal, they remain totally abstract, and humans have only approached some understanding of them when and where they are manifest in the second sphere, *material processes,* such as the rate and timing of the growth and reproduction of, for example, turtles, caymans, rubber trees, the reiterated cycles of evaporation, condensation, rainfall, and downward flow of water, the effects of water and wind on particular geological formations, the interaction of oxygen and flame, or the transformation of gravity into various other forms of energy, including electricity. All such processes obey multiple abstract physical and mathematical rules and laws that configure differently to give them their varied material and empirically observable manifestations in a wide range of different material forms. In other words, because they are manifest in matter, the empirically observable patterns they produce vary according to the composition of this matter. For example, the gestation and life-span of a flea, a buffalo, and an elephant all obey the same physical laws and biological rules, but they vary because these laws and rules configure differently through the different material composition of each species.

Similar regularities and variations occur in geological formations, which result from varied configurations of universal laws through different material compositions. These range from climatic patterns to the chemical reactions between different elements to the reproductive cycles of plants and animals. These give rise to the different technological potentials of different metals and of different deposits of the same metals that are so important in understanding how different nations have developed new technologies that conformed to particular types of raw materials and how these same nations sought for those kinds of deposits that gave them the greatest technological advantage. The regularities observable within each such configuration, and in the interactions between them when they are conjoined or simultaneous, provide the potential for human discovery and for technological innovations. The intersection of geological process and technological discovery provides the third sphere in our analysis, in which we see the role of contingency, chance, interpretation, and communication that constitute *story,* or *history.* This is the sphere where the inevitability of law and process are joined with human choice, intention, and agency in the formation of society. It is also the sphere where the laws and rules configure as process creating very different geological, climatological, and biological events according to the accumulation of site-specific material formations that we humans know as topography, vegetation, mineral composition, hydrology, and such. This sphere shapes the development of technologies and the elaboration of national strategies for trade dominance that drive the evolution of the world-system. Moreover, these social stories or strategies succeed only if they occur within and adapt to the material forms naturally produced in geological stories configured in specific locations.

The outcomes of the stories in this sphere are determined by the laws and processes that regulate their component ingredients. In the social realm, this means that technological discoveries and the search for the materials they transform will succeed only if they conform to these laws and processes, and that they will succeed competitively only if they conform better than alternative technologies then in use. The actual discovery, or the insight that leads to it, does not occur, nor can it be explained, through these laws and processes. Similarly, the elaboration of the political organization, the financial system, or the productive organization that enabled particular countries to become trade dominant must obey physical laws and rules in order to succeed.

Obedience to physical law does not explain their success, however. Different human groups have different goals and interests. They thus have different intentions and are differentially successful in inventing technologies and strategies to achieve them. At the same time, they react to each others' technologies and strategies, thereby changing each others' relative chances of success. Nations that rose to dominate trade succeeded in part by anticipating or taking into account competitive or resistant behaviors of both their competitors and their different suppliers. The complexity of the world context to which these nations adjusted their strategies and actions, and the close-coupling and scope of coordination these required, increased as the scale and scope of the world economy expanded, and as the scale and cost of transport fell, bringing more and more potential players into the same competitive game.

Each of these stories, or strategies, depends on advancing human understanding of and ability to use physical laws and rules, but these cannot explain their formation, and can explain only part of their consequences. The highly variable, and necessarily contingent, elements of choice, skill, and information in all of the different human groups involved in particular outcomes drive their formation and shape their consequences. Successful trade strategies incorporate the responses of raw materials suppliers and of competitive domestic firms into national strategies. Successful ascendant economies interpret past stories, or history, in terms that encourage supplier nations to behave in ways that fit the interests of the ascendant nation. Successful interpretations become hegemonic and achieve the acquiescence, and even the complicity, of the subordinate supplier nation with trade policies that benefit the industrial core while prejudicing the economy and environment of the extractive periphery.

Other recent theoretical advances in analyzing long-term social change shape our analysis in important ways. Chase-Dunn and Hall (1997) highlight the importance of Bulk Goods Networks over the long run. Our focus is on these Bulk Goods Networks as sources of the most fundamental challenges to economic ascent, and, in those rare cases where these challenges are met by technological and social organizational innovations that give one rising economy large competitive advantages, these innovations drive the restructuring of the capitalist world-economy in support of this ascent.

Other analysts highlight different economic sectors at different points in history as playing critical roles in long-term change. Agriculture and agriculture-based industries throughout human history and even today certainly shaped key elements of long-term social change. Tomich (1994) and Mintz (1985) showed how the environmental, technological, social organizational, and consumption characteristics of sugar shaped colonial strategies and competition between core powers for hundreds of years. Moore (2003) demonstrated that efforts to find workable technologies and social systems of production for mining and agriculture in Latin America shaped Spanish and Portuguese colonial strategies and the long-term consequences of colonialism for these core powers and for Latin America. Eric Williams (1944), Walter Rodney (1982), and many others showed how the transatlantic slave trade to supply labor for colonial plantation agriculture and mining shaped long-term social and economic change in Africa, Europe, Latin America, and North America. O'Hearn (2001) analyzes the pastoral and agriculture-based textile industry as shaping the development trajectory of Great Britain, its colonies, and the larger world economy. Arrighi's (1994) model of long-term change often focuses on the critical role of mining, agriculture, transport, and industries based on processing raw materials in shaping long-term change.

Even theories that focus on recent decades and on higher-value-added industries such as electronics and fashion and the commodity chains that produce them (Gereffi and Korzeniewicz 1994; Smith 2005) acknowledge the important roles of raw materials and transport in shaping these commodity chains, even when their analytic emphasis lies elsewhere. Sklair (2000), Robinson (2004), and other analysts of globalization raise fundamental challenges to the state-centered models of political economy, requiring us to sharpen our analytic explanation about why these sectors still remain critically important in what is often assumed to be a post-material "new economy" and about why patterns of state-sector-firm cooperation and conflict remain central. More generally, our approach to commodity chains follows Hopkins and Wallerstein's (1986) approach, focusing on the political economy of imperialism and globalization and the consequences of this political economy for both core and peripheral economies (Bunker and Ciccantell 2005).

The theoretical model we present in this book, its companion volume, *Globalization and the Race for Resources* (Bunker and Ciccantell 2005), and our other research complements these theoretical and empirical studies by focusing more narrowly on the raw materials and transport sectors that we argue drove economic ascent and long-term change by resolving the fundamental challenges that raw materials and transport pose for economic ascent. This analytic focus simultaneously broadens our model far beyond a study of a subset of important sectors to show that these particular sectors lowered costs, increased competitiveness, led technological and social innovation, provided templates for business organization and strategy and for patterns of state-sector-firm cooperation and conflict, generated a dynamic tension that sustained economic ascent, and over the long run shaped the repeated restructuring of the capitalist world-economy in support of the economic ascent of the most successful nations over the past 600 years. These industries may be playing the same role in the most recent spectacular case of economic ascent, China.

Firm and State Strategies for Competitiveness, Profit, and National Development

Increasing overall economic competitiveness in the capitalist world-economy depends on reducing production costs across a variety of industries sufficiently to dominate domestic and international markets. Reduction in the cost of the most voluminously used raw materials creates savings across the entire economy, from the construction of plant and shared infrastructure through the production of goods and on to their distribution. This increasing competitiveness across many sectors drives economic ascent in the capitalist world-economy.

The costs of extracting, transporting, and processing high-volume raw materials utilized in many economic sectors such as oil, coal, and iron have historically been highly scale-sensitive. Scales of procurement, transport, and processing all dictate large amounts of inflexibly sunk capital (Barham, Bunker, and O'Hearn 1994). These can be profitable and competitive only if they operate at or near full capacity, and so are viable only if they articulate with broad and stable markets in which their output is competitively cheap. In other words, steady, high-volume throughput from mine to market of the most voluminously used raw materials undergirds economic ascent. High rates of throughput are possible only if processing, production, and distribution of the raw materials are cheap enough to achieve cost-competitive production. This cost competitiveness is the key element of the economic rivalry that underlies the evolution of the systemic cycles of capital accumulation identified by Arrighi (1994).

Rising economies historically developed or adopted and then implemented more completely and rapidly technologies and social organization that move the raw materials from extraction through production to market more efficiently and at lower cost than their competitors under the socioeconomic and technological conditions of a particular historical era. As scale of enterprise, volume of matter, and distance of procurement increase, the technical and organizational components become more interdependent and time, as the medium in which they must coordinate their multiple complex interactions, decreases. Social and material process both become more diverse and more complex, and their management becomes increasingly tightly coupled. The infrastructure used to extract, transport, and process the bulkiest raw materials (machinery, trains and railroads, ships and ports) also consumes a large share of them, enhancing the tight coupling of this cycle (Bunker and Ciccantell 2005; Ciccantell and Bunker 1999).

The capital requirements of domestic plant and infrastructure, and the protection requirements of capital invested internationally in the spatially diverse and diffuse sources of raw materials and in the extensive transport systems used to move them back to the industrial center, typically exceeded the capabilities of individual firms or sectors. In order to increase economic competitiveness by lowering relative costs, coordinated actions by states, sectors, and firms in ascendant economies reduced competition in obtaining raw materials. In the domestic market, state-owned and privately owned financial institutions provided low-cost financing and helped control domestic competition that could reduce prices and returns on investments. State agencies developed that gathered information on a global scale and negotiated agreements between firms and the state, all of which combined to resolve the high costs of the contradiction between increasing economies of scale and increasing geographical scale.

Three broad strategies evolved historically to reduce raw materials costs. First, ascendant economies can conquer resource-rich peripheries, followed by wars or diplomatic actions that impede access by the established economies. Second, ascendant economies can incorporate new technologies that effectively change established relations between economy and environment. These include new forms or expanded scale of mining, processing, and transport. Third, ascendant economies can induce host countries to assume a significant share of the cost of reorganizing world markets, introducing new technologies, and developing new transport routes.

These three major strategies evolved to allow ascendant economies to continue their advance. The first strategy predates the emergence of the capitalist world-economy. Direct imperial conquest of resource-rich peripheries and the defense of these formal and/or de facto annexations by force and/or diplomatic actions helped many states seeking to ascend in the capitalist world-economy in the context of rivalry with existing hegemons and other potential ascendants. Britain's construction of its empire in North America, India, and later in Africa (Bayly 1989; Innis 1956; Williamson 1965, 1967), U.S. conquest of half of Mexico's territory and the incorporation of these resource-rich regions into the United States in the mid-1800s (Ciccantell 2001), Belgium's conquest of the copper-rich Congo region of Africa (Pakenham 1991), and Japan's conquest of Manchuria and much of Southeast Asia during World War II (Borden 1984; Bunker and Ciccantell 1995a, 1995b; Marshall 1995) all resulted from this strategy. Beginning during the colonial rush to Africa in the late 1800s and to the Middle East after World War I and especially following the extensive process of decolonization after World War II, this strategy became increasingly difficult and expensive to carry out and maintain. Led first by U.S. transnational corporations (Keohane 1984; Krasner 1978), particularly in the aluminum industry (Barnet and Muller 1974; Ciccantell 2000; Hymer 1979; Jenkins 1987) and then in new ways by Japanese firms and the Japanese state after World War II (Ciccantell and Bunker 2002), other strategies replaced colonialism for ensuring raw materials access.

The second strategy emerged over the past five centuries to resolve the challenge of securing raw materials access to support economic ascent. The adoption of James Watt's vastly improved steam engine to remove water from coal mines in Great Britain during the last twenty years of the eighteenth century made vast reserves of deeply buried and previously unextractable coal suddenly available on a large scale at low cost to power Britain's Industrial Revolution (Mathias 1969:134–35; Rosenberg and Birdzell 1986:150–51). Similarly, the rapid expansion of a domestic transportation infrastructure in the United States in the mid-nineteenth century based on the newly developed technology of railroads linked widely dispersed raw materials– and agriculture-producing peripheries to markets and industrial centers in the East (Chandler 1965; Douglas 1992; Stover 1961). This creation of a low-cost transport network drove the rapid industrialization that was key to U.S. ascendance in the capitalist world-economy.

Under the third strategy, ascendant core powers induce and sometimes force raw materials–producing nations to pay a significant share of the costs of reorganizing world markets, introducing new technologies, and developing new transport routes. Imperial core powers taxed their colonies to support armies to control indigenous populations and used corvée labor to construct infrastructure in earlier eras. In nonimperial situations, ascendant core powers induced raw materials–extracting peripheries to finance the construction of railroads, often justified in terms of local economic development but mainly benefiting foreign investors and raw materials consumers. Numerous examples of the employment of this strategy by Britain occurred in Latin America during the nineteenth century (Coatsworth 1981; Duncan 1932; C. Lewis 1983). Similarly, British and North American rubber buyers and consumers induced members of the economic elite in the Brazilian Amazon to finance the expansion of the wild rubber industry in the region to supply the core's industrial plants in the late nineteenth century (Barham and Coomes 1994a, 1994b; Bunker 1985). This strategy dramatically reduced both the costs to and risks assumed by the ascendant core economy's firms and state in the raw materials–extracting region.

Economies of scale in processing raw materials reduce costs, but they can occur only with standardization of process and therefore of inputs. Assuring constancy of supply from the same source standardizes inputs. However, as distances to sources become greater, this may involve special problems of establishing and maintaining property and contractual rights, as well as transport rights and costs, across national boundaries and on the seas. Preparing and blending ores from different locations to particular specifications standardizes inputs, but the costs of these procedures increase with the variability of the ores received, so this second option also depends on some constancy of supply from different sources.

Contriving to lower the rents and prices paid for their extraction also reduces raw materials costs. Direct imperial conquest of suppliers, close holding of technical information, knowledge about the internal politics and economies of resource-rich nations, stimulating competition between multiple suppliers, transferring the costs of providing infrastructure to exporting firms and states, and creating buying cartels all allow ascendant economies to negotiate rent and price bargains (Amin 1976; Anderson 1987; Ciccantell 2000; Graham, Thorpe, and Hogan 1999; Girvan 1976; Jalee 1968; Koerner 1993; Swan, Thorpe, and Hogan 1999).

Lowering the cost of transport via larger, more efficient vehicles, vessels, terminals, and ports also reduces raw materials costs. The technical and organizational innovations create a major demand for the raw materials themselves and can be implemented only via complex negotiations and agreements with foreign states and firms. Ports and terminals are needed at both ends of a voyage, so cheapening transport of raw materials historically entails cross-national coordination and guarantees of construction, ownership, and management of these costly facilities. The large costs sunk in enabling infrastructure and vessels to handle very large volumes create pressure to reduce loading and unloading time, and thus create incentives to develop technologies and management to accelerate turnaround (Drewry 1976; Frankel et al. 1985; Goss 1967; Goss and Mann 1977; Jansson and Shneerson 1982; Kendall 1972; Robinson 1978; Stopford 1988). In this instance as well, solutions involve the coordination of the technical and the political, and of the domestic and the external.

Finally, lowering the cost of raw materials depends on security of supply. Smelting and refining, the generic terms for simplifying the physical and chemical complexity of mineral ores into useful forms, and bulk transport are scale-sensitive and capital-intensive. They entail large investments of capital sunk in technologies specific to the particular mineral, and often to the particular ores (Barham, Bunker, and O'Hearn 1994). The greater the capital intensity, the greater are the costs of operating at less than full capacity. The more specific the technology to the process, the less flexible it is in shifting to other inputs or other products. Interruptions of supply threaten mineral processors with heavy losses. Resulting increases in raw materials costs reverberate through the entire economy. Security of supply becomes a pressing concern for individual firms, for entire sectors, and for the national state. The solutions developed required coordinated actions domestically and internationally and between firms, sectors, and the state.

The huge scale and lumpiness of sunk capital in the raw materials and transport sectors, and the relatively long economic life of the infrastructures developed, mean that, once established, these solutions tend to endure over the medium term. Their immediate costs diminish, but they no longer generate the technical and organizational innovations they did at the beginning. Once established, the motivation for close-coupled collaboration also tends to diminish. Firms are far less likely to accede to collective decisions and to direct state intervention or restriction when they no longer depend on state support, subsidies, or regulation to achieve solutions to problems beyond the individual firm's capacity. Nonetheless, even if close coupled collaboration declines, the spillover of the original technical and organizational solutions, both into other sectors and into the institutional relations between firms, sectors, and the state, ensures that their social and economic impacts endure.

Four Earlier Cases of Rapid Economic Ascent and Restructuring the Capitalist World-Economy

Four earlier cases of economic ascent, Portugal, Holland, Great Britain, and the United States, provide instructive examples of the role of generative sectors in creating and restructuring inequality between national economies, driving ascent to dominance within the capitalist world-economy, and driving the material intensification and spatial expansion of production and trade in the capitalist world-economy (see Bunker and Ciccantell 2003a, 2003b, 2005 for extended discussions of these cases).

Protection fees from Genoa and Venice eventually generated sustained financial and institutional support from the crown that built on Portugal's seafaring traditions and felicitous location to foment the technologies and navigational skills needed to couple the sheltered natural environment and prosperous consumer markets of the Mediterranean with the far broader trade opportunities of the Atlantic. Inventing the three-masted ship, adopting and then perfecting the Chinese compass, and figuring out how to mount iron cannon on ship deck enabled the Portuguese to open and then dominate new maritime trade routes to Africa and to East and South Asia.

The routes through the Atlantic replaced the overland trade routes that Genoa and Venice, in the eastern Mediterranean, dominated until the Ottoman Empire rose to challenge them. Portugal's innovations in maritime transport vastly expanded the material volumes of this trade; even small sailboats carried cargo more cheaply than horses and camels. Portuguese ships soon turned westward across the Atlantic, incorporating new space and new materials (American sugar, tobacco, turtle oil, and spices as well as silver and gold) into the Mediterranean-based world trade in Asian spices, silks, and drugs.

Genoa's and Venice's demands for naval protection and for carriage in the Mediterranean of bulkier, cheaper trade goods provided the initial motivation and then patronage and protection for Portugal's seafaring commercial development. Portugal's geographic location where the Mediterranean meets the Atlantic enhanced the commercial and political opportunities of this patronage. Adventurous entrepreneurs and a supportive, trade-oriented crown familiar with Chinese maritime technological accomplishments provided the local energy and capital for innovations in navigation and exploration. Eventually, the interaction between the natural and social features of Portugal's location within the contemporary world-system gave it dominance of the most recently devised transport technologies, control over the richest trade routes, and privileged access to highly prized commodities (tobacco and sugar) that rewarded crossing the greater transatlantic distances to their sources. Portugal advanced marine technology enormously, but rudimentary ship technology limited Portuguese long-distance trade to luxury goods.

Portuguese and Spanish maritime expansion, and the gold, silver, tobacco, and sugar it introduced into European commerce, generated demand for more and higher-quality materials for shipbuilding, port construction, grain, and fish than the Mediterranean could supply. Amsterdam's location on low-lying flat lands down the Rhine, the Elbe, and the Weser from some of the densest and oldest oak forests and richest agricultural lands in Europe allowed cheap access to and transport of high-quality timber and wheat. Privileged access to high-quality wood, abundant grain, and cheap bulk transport sustained early development of Holland as provider of high-volume, low-value raw materials to Spain and Portugal.

Agents of Amsterdam firms induced large landowners to organize serfs and peasants for cultivating, harvesting, and shipping wheat and for felling, sledding to river edge, and binding together vast numbers of oak logs into huge rafts that carried small temporary villages of peasants and mountains of grain down the Rhine, Elbe, and Weser and then along canals to the wind-driven sawmills in the Zaan. The high quality and abundance of the oak, the savings of rafting logs downriver over the expense of loading logs in seaworthy boats for ocean crossing, and the labor economies of wind-driven sawmills and plentiful cheap grain and fish gave Amsterdam enormous advantages in raw materials and labor costs in building boats and in the construction of canals, bridges, docks, and warehouses.

These savings supported major innovations in boat design that allowed for greater cargo capacity and lower manning requirements. The efficiencies and low cost of the herring *buss* contributed to Amsterdam's dominance of the incipient market for fish in Europe. The subsequent development of the easy-to-load, labor-saving *fluyt*, arguably an adaptation of boats designed for canal transport, provided such economies of shipping that Amsterdam soon dominated world carriage, realizing huge profits while offering the lowest rates. The competitive advantage of the Dutch carrying trade and sale of boats increased effective demand for Dutch-built ships and for the raw materials to make them. The resulting throughput was so great that shipyards could stock enough standardized parts for multiple boats to have raw materials on hand for customized production for specific clients. Dutch timber agents could buy in such bulk that some Norwegian woods were reputed to be cheaper in Holland than in Norway. This ability to buy cheaply and then to stockpile parts was particularly important for those parts of a boat that demanded particular types, shapes, and sizes of wood, such as keels and hulls (Unger 1978; see also Albion 1926).

Cheap raw materials, innovative technology, and new forms of labor organization combined to allow Amsterdam builders to design more efficient boats and to build and sell them so cheaply that Amsterdam had the largest carrying capacity in the world and also sold the most ships to competitor nations. The high throughput of materials in the busy shipyards allowed economies of scale in procurement of inputs and standardization of boat construction. Amsterdam was located near the Zaan, a large sheltered bay with river and canal connections to fertile inland hinterlands, on the coast that bounded the shortest maritime distance from the North Sea and the Baltic to the Mediterranean. This provided an enormous advantage for Amsterdam, first as a subordinate unit within the Hapsburg Empire, then as politically indepen-dent but economically subordinate republic, and finally as an economically dominant financial and product market. Its competition for trade with Spain and Portugal, then Europe's wealthiest nations, provoked both periodic attacks and prohibitions on Dutch shipping, but neither could do without the benefits that Dutch trade offered.

Privileged raw materials access and consequent competitive advantages in boat building and in transport created opportunities and rewards for new forms of state power and economic intervention that supported innovations in commerce and fi-nance. Innovations in shipping construction, management, and finance allowed the Dutch to transport profitably relatively low-value-to-volume goods (timber, fish, grain, potash) between the resource-rich Baltic and North Seas and the socially de-veloped Mediterranean. Dutch innovations thus expanded the space and broadened the material base of world trade. Dutch innovations lowered transport costs enough to extend plantation agriculture into South American and Caribbean interiors and to provide these plantations with African slaves. These events started the transformation of sugar from a luxury to a staple commodity for mass consumption. The Dutch took full advantage of this transformation, both by expanded sugar cargoes overseas and by increased sugar refineries at home.

All of these achievements originated in the confluence of topography and geogra-phy with Dutch social and political organization. As the timber trade and the ship-ping industry grew, the state invested directly in infrastructure such as dams and docks and in machinery such as cranes that were beyond the capital capacities of in-dividual boatyards and which could be shared between multiple boatyards. In addi-tion to state innovations in tax collection, as well as in fiscal incentives and subsidies for long-distance trade, state regulation and support enabled a proliferation of new forms of civil finance, from letters of credit for long-distance trade and commerce to joint stock in small lots invested in boats (Barbour 1950; Boxer 1965; de Vries and van der Woude 1997; Israel 1989, 1995; Unger 1978;).

The Dutch extended their advantage provided by the short voyage from the mouth of the Baltic, sheltered from the North Sea winds and currents by the Frisian Islands, into extensive close links, managed by resident Dutch agents, with landowners further inside the Baltic. The Oder, flowing through Poland, replaced the Weser and the Elbe as the forests in those drainages became depleted. Dutch merchants established close commercial relations along the Vistula, which provided increasing volumes of timber, and intensified the older connections to the Weser and the Elbe, where grain now replaced the earlier volumes of wood. Amsterdam's establishment of the world's first public bank in 1609 guaranteed the credits and loans that Dutch merchants used to organize the extraction, cultivation, harvest, processing, and export of timber, pitch, flax, potash, sulfur, leather, quicksilver, iron, copper, and even sails, boats, and guns from Sweden, Norway, Poland, and Russia (Barbour 1950).

The state licensed and encouraged guilds' development of specialized skills and collectively owned tools, thus assisting in the creation of a labor force that inspired envy and attempts at emulation in other nations (Barbour 1950; Unger 1978). Amsterdam's spatiomaterial advantages in access to raw materials and to wind power and in geographic proximity to potentially rich trade routes facilitated and catalyzed collective and state investments in productive and transport-related infrastructure, in the development of and investment in new technologies, in new financial instruments and institutions, and in new functions, powers, and capacities of the state and its relations to capital.

High rates of throughput, economies of scale, labor-saving technologies, an increasingly skilled and specialized work force, and shared interests between multiple firms, the state, financial institutions, small investors, and downstream consumers converged to create synergies or feedback loops that reinforced and extended economic growth and social development. The state grew in power, capacity, and legitimacy (and won increasing acceptance of its right to tax) by providing an expanding infrastructure for boatyards, harbors, locks, dams, bridges, and warehouses that enabled cheap, efficient transport and trade. The state also chartered and regulated financial systems and a rudimentary stock exchange so well and transparently that Dutch banks could charge the lowest interest rates in Europe. Cheaper, more efficient boats coupled with cheap credit allowed Amsterdam to extend, deepen, and cheapen its access to other sources of timber and stores.

The highly competitive shipbuilding and shipping industries created the means for Amsterdam to dominate first the bulk trades of Northern Europe and then the luxury trades with the Mediterranean and the Orient. Amsterdam became, simultaneously, the entrepôt of Europe, the financial center of the world economy, the first modern state, the inventor of risk sharing and the sharing of capital via insurance, and the dominant city in the wealthiest nation in Europe. The transport innovations that initiated local economic and social expansion also transformed and expanded the world economy. Grotius's arguments that *mare liberum* was prescribed by natural law, an eloquent defense of principles of security and freedom for international maritime commerce, established precedents that are still invoked in support of free trade and globalization.

The Dutch bulk trades provided the initial impetus for the innovations in transport, finance, and foreign relations that enabled them to dominate world trade. Under Spanish and Portuguese patronage and protection, and aided by the influx of capital brought by Protestant and Sephardic refugees from those countries' religious persecutions, Dutch city-states and then the Dutch republic extended the technological and commercial innovations in the bulk trades to include trade in and then manufacture of higher-value-to-volume and thus more profitable goods. The bulk trades, limited to the relatively small space between the North Sea, the inner Baltic, and the Mediterranean, supported the longer-distance trade in high-value-to-volume spices, drugs, textiles, and wines that the bulk shipping technologies made possible. They also brought in a growing variety of raw materials, from sugar to potash to copper, which served as inputs to expanding, export-oriented, Dutch manufacture.

Struggles to overcome Dutch trade dominance expanded the capitalist world-economy further. Unable to compete with Dutch access to raw materials in the Baltic and North Sea, Britain extended its raw materials procurement to the Atlantic, annexing fishing grounds and forests first in Ireland and soon in North America. Britain's location and size deprived it of Amsterdam's ability to import timber cheaply. Rather than competing with technological innovations in cheap construction and design for enlarged cargo capacity and smaller crews, the British designed costly, highly maneuverable warships with large crews and little cargo space.

Unable to match Amsterdam's spatiomaterial efficiencies of raw materials access and transport, the British state used military prowess backed by increasingly sophisticated metallurgy to capture and keep Dutch boats in prolonged and repeated wars through the seventeenth century. The British also captured and administered broad areas of timber in the Americas, first for the import of lumber and then for the construction of boats. Innovative British colonial and military strategies for the procurement of bulky raw materials and their transport across broad spaces ultimately created the bases for the Industrial Revolution, but not before they had stimulated revolt and political separation by New England colonists anxious to reap for themselves the spatial and material advantages that their environment provided.

The New England colonies converted abundant timber accessible by short rivers across diverse ecological zones into the most effective carrying fleet in the world. They were well positioned to exploit the demand for carriage and for supplies in the

Caribbean, whose sugar was the most dynamically expanding commodity in world trade and the most dependent on external supplies of fuel and food. The North Americans soon surpassed the British in cargo capacity and carriage. British attempts to contain this competition contributed importantly to eventual rebellion.

U.S. independence directly reduced British carrying capacity. The growing volume and economic importance of cotton imports from the United States eventually forced Britain to relax the Navigation Acts. American ships could carry these cargoes more cheaply than could the British. British industrialists could make more profits in textiles than in shipping. Owners of textile factories pressured the state to open to foreign-controlled shipping in order to lower their raw materials costs.

The British did not regain a carrying or a raw materials advantage until new technologies allowed them to combine domestic sources of coal with steam-powered machines to transform cheaper and more versatile smelting and manufacture of metals into machines that enhanced mining, transport, and production capabilities. Iron and coal steadily displaced wood as the most voluminously used raw materials. Britain enjoyed social, technological, and spatial advantages in access to these materials. Steam-driven steel hulls were freed of the size and weight restrictions that even the largest and best timbers imposed, while trains and rails were freed of the topographical and hydrological shackles that previously bound bulk transport to rivers and canals.

The trinity of iron, coal, and steam fomented and was steadily enlarged and strengthened by scientific discovery and practical innovations. These enabled improvements in the control of the chemical and physical interactions of different raw materials and energy sources in metallurgy, in the conversion of thermal to mechanical energy in engines and motors, and in the control of material composition and of thermal energy in order to strengthen iron, and later steel. These improvements permitted the higher temperatures, greater weights, and more intense pressures that new technologies and their economies of scale demanded.

James Watt's steam engine began a shift away from wooden shipbuilding and toward the development of internal canal and railroad transport and iron industries as generative sectors. Watt's steam engine made vast reserves of deeply buried coal suddenly available on a large scale at low cost to power Britain's Industrial Revolution. Coal output doubled between 1816 and 1840, doubled again by 1859, and doubled again by 1880 (Mitchell 1980:382, 385). A massive canal-building effort to link internal coal fields to industrial and population centers became a major focus of capital accumulation in Britain (Mathias 1969:134–35; Rosenberg and Birdzell 1986:150–51), linking internal raw materials peripheries to rapidly growing industrial and urban centers.

Within a few decades, British firms adapted the steam engine for railroad transport, simultaneously freeing Britain from increasingly expensive, complex efforts to build canals to supplement natural watercourses and creating a growing synergy between railroad transport and the iron and later steel industries. British ironmasters developed a series of innovations in iron and steel production that made British iron and steel the most efficient and highest quality in the world and created many new uses in infrastructure, transport, and industry for steel (Albion 1926; Harris 1988; Hobsbawm 1968; Isard 1948). Pig iron production increased from 0.6 million tons in 1825 to 4.9 million tons in 1865, railroad lines increased from only 43 kilometers in 1825 to 18,439 kilometers in 1865, and railroads moved more than 114 million tons of cargo by 1865 (Mitchell 1980:413, 610, 618), all of which surpassed the *combined* totals of Great Britain's continental rivals, France and Germany, over the same period.

The subtle interplay between the internal dynamic of capital and the interactions between space, matter, and technological innovation accelerated and became more complex and more consequential as iron and steel and coal replaced wood as the most voluminously used raw material. Most of the new iron and steel technologies, particularly the use of coal in blast furnaces and the development of the Bessemer process to make uniform high-grade steel at costs that allowed mass production and consumption, emerged from British experience in military metallurgy. British industrialization and its dominance of world trade and world shipping all flourished as a consequence. However, the United States, with access to a more appropriate spatio-material configuration, adopted these technologies and soon surpassed British industry.

In the mid-nineteenth century, British firms also adapted the steam engine to oceangoing water transport on a reliable, large scale, rejuvenating Britain's shipbuilding and shipping industries on the basis of steamships that linked the distant parts of the British Empire. Shipbuilding became a massive consumer of raw materials often transported on steamships themselves (Mathias 1969; Rosenberg and Birdzell 1986). Steamship registrations in Great Britain rose from 1 in 1814 to 2,718 in 1865, totaling 823,000 deadweight tons; France and Germany together had only 469 steamships totaling 142,000 deadweight tons in 1865 (Mitchell 1980:643, 646), with iron and steel providing the vast majority of inputs for these ships' construction in the British shipyards that dominated the world shipbuilding industry.

British financiers and the British state adopted many Dutch banking innovations and adapted them to the new political relations of the capitalist world-economy and to the expanded spatial scale on which it operated. The invention of bonds, a means by which the state could effectively sell shares in a public enterprise and then buy back that share, strengthened, broadened, and tightened financial cooperation between capital and the state, while making possible state support of fixed investments in shared infrastructure beyond the means or interest of individual firms.

Canals and ports were steadily expanded to accommodate the vastly increased carriage of coal and iron. Britain's greatest, most costly, and most consequential infrastructural increase in the spatial scale of the world economy came with the Suez Canal, which instantly and effectively shortened and cheapened the link between Britain's Atlantic and its Indian Ocean sources of raw materials and markets for industrial output. The opening of the Suez Canal and the improvements in ship and motor size and fuel efficiency combined to enable Britain's dominance of trade between Europe and the rest of the world. These technological innovations and infrastructural investments spilled over into other industrial applications that constituted the second industrial, or machine-based, revolution. The development and proliferation of machines to make machines vastly increased Britain's imports of raw materials and thus the transport networks required to support them (Hobsbawm 1968).

Eventually, the Suez Canal played a major role in extending and deepening the economic significance of the technologies whose first development it had originally stimulated. The canal provided direct commercial and military access to the newly discovered oil fields of the Middle East. Access to these oil fields, and control over the dependent monarchies that the British colonial office put in power, facilitated cheap and secure access to a raw material that powered cheaper, faster ships and trains with far less cargo space sacrificed to fuel than was possible with coal and steam. The internal-combustion engine ratcheted up the technological means of expanding the reproduction of capital by enabling faster production machines, creating a machine appropriate for mass consumption and personal use, and cheapening and accelerating transport of raw materials (see Hugill 1994).

Just as access to abundant, high-quality oak along relatively flat rivers with sites of steady wind power supported the technical, social, political, and financial synergies that drove Amsterdam's ascent to economic dominance, British coal originated and supported many similar synergies, but in a spatially vaster, materially more diverse and intense, and financially and institutionally more complex economy. Myriad innovations that cheapened and expanded the procurement of iron and coal enabled additions to and refinements of the multiple means and forms in which they could be combined to produce steam and convert steam heat to mechanical forces, or to drive chemical and physical conversions. Improved, cheaper iron and steel enabled the invention and adoption of new production machines and of new consumer goods. Together, the new machines and higher-quality, cheaper metals enabled profit-enhancing technological and social organizational innovations to follow and extend each other along more complex and diverse trajectories and with far greater and faster increases in scale and in cost of construction than had been possible in the wood-based economy that Amsterdam expanded in rising to trade dominance. The new technical initiatives and their increased scale both depended on and fed the new and expanded instruments and institutions of finance developed to satisfy and to profit from the growing demand for investment capital.

Like the Dutch, the British developed technological, organization, financial, and political innovations that transformed their geographic proximity to large sources of the most voluminously used, lowest-value-to-volume raw materials into dominance of industrial, then transport, and finally financial markets. Like the Dutch, the British extrapolated their technological, commercial, and financial advantages in heavy industry to expand their access to higher-value-to-volume industrial inputs across far broader spaces. The transition from wind-driven wooden hulls to coal-powered steam engines driving steel hulls greatly increased the maximum distances economically viable for the transport of the highest-bulk, lowest-value raw materials as well as for the less voluminously used and higher-priced specialty inputs. Where the Dutch extended the advantages of river transport of vast quantities of oak to longer-distance trade in higher-value-to-volume goods, the British extended their advantage in river and canal transport of coal and Baltic sources of iron to much more distant sources for the higher-value-to-volume goods that new technologies demanded and made possible: copper, guano, and nitrates from Chile and Peru; tin and rubber from Malaysia, Bolivia, and Brazil; grain from around the world; and eventually refrigerated meat from Argentina and New Zealand.

In these cases, the higher-value-to-volume raw materials appear to lead the spatial extension of integrated commerce. Closer examination over a longer period of analysis, though, demonstrates that the demand for these more valuable materials, and the ability to transport them at economically competitive rates, were both driven by technological innovations that economies of scale and enhanced throughput of the most voluminously used raw materials required and simultaneously enabled in each economy. Historically, empirically, and logically, the higher-value, lower-volume trades that provide such profits to the trade-dominant nation are possible only because of prior dominance of lower-value, higher-volume bulk trades and the infrastructural, technological, financial, and organizational innovations that they engender.

Over time, British technology and British finance returned the advantage to the United States, not because capital was overaccumulated in Britain, but because the huge and sustained demand in Britain for American raw materials encouraged technological, organizational, infrastructural, and financial innovations and investments in the expanding American economy. Massive industrialization in nineteenth-century Europe created demand for food (cheap grains, meats, and sugar) to reduce the cost of factory labor, and for cheap raw materials (cotton, timber, iron, and copper) for manufacture. The diversion and concentration of agricultural labor from subsistence crops to sugar and cotton cultivation and processing, and the fuel required for the mechanized processing and transport of these commodities, created peripheral demand as well for foodstuffs and fuel.

The opportunities offered by sparsely settled, or depopulated, and fertile lands to produce or extract food, wood, and minerals for dynamic international and national markets stimulated the westward expansion of populations, transport infrastructure (canals, roads, railways, and harbors), and capital (accumulated in logging, fishing, shipbuilding, and shipping) from the narrow, rocky, northern coastal fringe between the Atlantic and the Appalachians to the broad, flat, fertile plains between the Appalachians and the Rockies. Railroad building across vast, fertile continental expanses that the United States could incorporate politically and economically with little or no resistance from existing populations was supported by the cheap, strong steel enabled by the introduction of the Bessemer process and trade-and-wage-oriented immigrants from an already industrializing Europe or a resource-poor New England looking for better returns to their labor. The same steel was rapidly incorporated into a series of locally invented agricultural, industrial, and transport machines and structures that enabled the sparse American population to use more resources and land and thus to produce more per person-hour. American production and productivity both soared as the young nation incorporated more of its continental interior, exploited its vast resources, and learned how to transform its raw materials into locally useful tools and locally consumable food that enabled it to export more raw materials and more finished goods. Expanding production and export in the continental interior, in turn, pushed demand for more steel-built machines, railroads, and ships.

The steel industry grew on mass production of steel for rails and at the same time provided a market for iron and coal that supported the integrated development of extensive rail lines and shipping systems. Two great river systems, the Mississippi and the St. Lawrence, combined with the Great Lakes and augmented by state-financed canals and smaller navigable rivers, supported the synergies between the accelerated consumption of iron and coal, the development of a rail network, and the growth of increasingly mechanized commercial agriculture (Agnew 1987; Fishlow 1965; Meinig 1986, 1993, 1998; Parker 1991; Temin 1964; Vance 1990). The United States thus incorporated into the national economy its major sources of the most voluminously used raw materials at the same time that its transport systems expanded the spaces of both the national and the world economies. The territorial expansion as well as the transformations in state-capital relations gave rise to the United States' particular mode of spatiomaterial intensification and expansion.

Because its raw materials periphery was a vast, practically unclaimed, violently depopulated, highly cultivable, and easily transitable plain, topographically and hydrologically amenable to railroad and steamboat (at the time the most recently developed and most efficient technologies of bulk transport), the United States could incorporate this space and its material resources economically, demographically, and politically. The arriving Northern European populations adapted existing and developed new social and political organizational forms, culture, and ideologies compatible with and favorable to the resource base and the mode of production and exchange that attracted them to migrate into this space (Parker 1991). The resulting internalization of its own extractive periphery that the United States' solution of the contradiction between scale and space created engendered homologous cultural and political systems in both extractive and productive regional economies. With its mythologization of trappers, loggers, miners, and cowboys, this culture symbolically and practically tended to be more egalitarian than its European origins. Labor and agricultural political movements steadily achieved a broader articulation of expanded production with a broad-based and growing popular market and a labor force specifically formed around the emerging mode of production rather than displaced from earlier modes of production.

The benefits of expanded production were thus more broadly diffused and political resistance was less than in extractive peripheries incorporated during the ascent of other trade-dominant nations. These exceptional nineteenth-century circumstances created the material and ideological bases for the extraordinary insularity and immunity from (and blithe disregard of) the environmental destruction, resource depletion, political and financial chaos, and brutal and destructive wars that its continuing economies of scale and voracious appetite for mineral raw materials and for huge, unfettered speculative profits in finance and real estate in deregulated markets engendered later in the twentieth-century raw materials peripheries it had to create as it overshot its own natural resources.

Britain pioneered many of the nineteenth-century technologies and the financial institutions required to implement them, but the far broader unclaimed and relatively unsettled territories of the United States, the varieties of ores and coals available there, and the topographies and hydrologies that defined the locations of these material resources shaped the geographical space in which technical, financial, material, social, and political dynamics intersected, vastly increasing the synergies in their economies of scale. U.S. firms adapted imported technologies of smelting to fit the booming demand for steel, used the stronger, cheaper metals they produced to improve and strengthen steam engines and steel-hulled boats, and then invented and improved steam shovels and unloaders. First local states and then the federal state invested in canals, locks, and dams to facilitate transport from huge iron and coal deposits around the Great Lakes. Firms and state negotiated new, and often tentative, forms of collaboration to combine matter and space with capital and technology and to form the world's leading producer of steel and the world's leading layer of steel rails.

The adaptation of European technologies to the broader spaces and more abundant mineral and vegetable resources of North America illuminates the interdependencies between space, matter, technology, and capital. The synergies between natural resources, fertile soils, stronger machines, and a rapidly growing, trade-oriented immigrant population moving into a large, relatively unpopulated and weakly defended space around the Great Lakes generated the U.S.-led material intensification and spatial expansion of the nineteenth century. This episode in globalization underscores the subtle interplay between the internal dialectic of capital, its external dialectic with space and matter, technological innovation, and social organization.

This interplay accelerated and became more complex and more consequential during the second half of the nineteenth century. Most of the new iron and steel technologies, particularly the use of coal in blast furnaces and the development of the Bessemer process to make uniform high-grade steel at costs that allowed mass production and consumption, emerged from British experience in developing military metallurgy. British industrialization, and its dominance of world trade and world shipping, all flourished as a consequence, but these technologies were adopted by economies with access to more appropriate spatiomaterial configurations. First Germany surpassed British steel production, and then the United States surpassed both Britain and Germany, surging to production of 70 percent of the world's steel within three decades of the introduction of Bessemer converters and the huge increases in scale of production and scale of transport that Bessemer techniques allowed.

This remarkable advance in U.S. steel production emerged from reiterated cycles of scale-enhancing technological innovations. These innovations drove huge investments to rebuild the environment to fit the new scale in a spatiomaterial and social context that enabled and rewarded the reiterated improvements and expansions of prevailing technologies, scales of capital, and state-sector-firm organization and relations. The Bessemer process allowed mass production of steel just as the technologies of metallurgy and transport were developing sufficiently and the organization of capital and of the state had expanded enough to support huge investments, first in railroads, ships, canals, and locks, and then in newly developed machines that mechanized mining. These investments in new technologies and infrastructures made the huge iron ore reserves around the north coasts of the Great Lakes and the rich deposits of coal further south available to steel mills along the south coasts of the Great Lakes. The expanding demand for raw materials stimulated scale increases in both transport and infrastructure.

Commerce on the Great Lakes had already been hugely enhanced by the proximity of dense forests of high-quality timber. The spread of grain agriculture and the demand for coal drove a vibrant shipbuilding industry. Highly decentralized charcoal-fueled iron plantations supported early U.S. industrialization, but by the mid-nineteenth century both metal and trees were becoming scarcer around the established plants. The discovery of copper and iron in huge, high-grade deposits in the Upper Peninsula of Michigan in the 1840s supplied the first expansion of iron production. The coincidence of increased demand with the opening of new transport routes and with the discovery of new and richer deposits fed back into the further investment in mining, locks, and canals. Expanded cargoes generated need for larger, heavier vessels; these required further investments to expand the locks.

The completion of the Sault Ste. Marie locks in 1855 opened up the vastly larger Mesabi Range iron ore deposits in Minnesota. The U.S. state expanded the locks several times over the subsequent decades. Boat sizes increased, stimulating innovations in boat motors to develop greater machine power. Shipbuilders increasingly built hulls of metal to support the extra size and weight of cargoes and the extra thrust of more powerful motors. Mines increasingly mechanized mining and loading. Integration with rail systems proceeded, both physically as infrastructure but also as corporate strategy, as combines, trusts, and corporations of unprecedented size combined the capital of multiple firms with new forms of finance and equity ownership to meet the investment requirements and take advantage of the opportunities for control and profit that the new economies of scale offered in mining, transporting, processing, and selling iron and coal.

Detailed examination of this particular phase in the long-term spatiomaterial expansion of the world economy provides a useful template for comparative analysis. Great Lakes mining and transport fed each other in very much the same way that logs and boats did in Holland, but at a vastly larger scale of material and space and capital with larger corporate and financial units, and a more active state. Like Holland before it, the United States was first incorporated into the capitalist world-economy as a raw materials and transport supplier to the world-trade dominant nation, Portugal in Holland's case, Britain in the case of the United States. British capital invested in North American extractive and infrastructural projects and British markets for North American fish, whale oil, logs, crops, ships, shipping, and minerals catalyzed much of the initial economic and demographic growth of New England, and then augmented the New England population, capital, and markets that incorporated the Midwest's supply of timber, wheat, meat, copper, coal, and iron into the world markets that drove the expanding U.S. economy.

The close entwining between the U.S. rise to world trade dominance and its roots in extraction and transport of bulky raw materials for the preceding hegemon parallels, at a huge increase in scale and space, Holland's early political and economic subordination to imperial Spain and Portugal as supplier and transporter of high-volume, low-value goods such as timber, fish, grain, flax, pitch, tar, and other ship stores. Portugal earlier served similar functions at an even smaller material and spatial scale to then dominant Venice and Genoa. In each case, the protective aegis of the dominant nation freed the provider of raw materials and bulk shipping from the need to support a military force against piracy, so all available capital and labor could be devoted to economic activity. Italian, then Portuguese, and finally British commerce, technology, capital, and entrepreneurial and technical skill flowed to the geographically and politically most convenient source of the raw materials most in demand for their own markets, both domestic and foreign. In each case, economic and political skills and institutions, developed when the subordinate economy was still relegated to bulk trade and shipping of low-value but industrially or commercially critical goods, later enhanced the now-independent nation's continued access to raw materials and proximity to major trade routes that led to its economic expansion and eventual trade dominance.

As in the Dutch and British cases, the United States' ease of access to the sources of the most voluminously used raw materials, now iron and coal, and the adoption of new technologies to transport and process them, engendered high levels of throughput and economies of scale that enhanced technological innovations in iron- and coal-dependent industries. These new technologies and the markets their existence helped create, in turn, engendered technical discoveries of uses for and enhanced demand for other raw materials, most notably manganese, aluminum, cobalt, and titanium, that, in different combinations with iron and with other metals, provide strength, lightness, and resistance to impact, corrosion, or heat. All of these had military applications in the new transport technologies based on jet engines and their capacity for high speeds at the cost of huge metal stress and heat. Like the Dutch and the British before them, the North Americans lengthened their commercial networks furthest around these higher-value-to-volume goods, supported by a base in the most voluminously used, lowest-value-to-volume raw materials.

Like the Dutch and the British as well, the Americans invented new regimes of international relations to assure their access to industrially and militarily critical raw materials, especially when World War II threatened their access to tin, manganese, and rubber, and then with even greater assiduity when the Cold War endangered access to the far greater panoply of specialty metals that the intervening years of technological advance had made essential to U.S. industrial growth and military security (see Eckes 1979; Marshall 1995). High-quality manganese, cobalt, and titanium are available only in a few places in the world, and U.S. diplomatic relations were sometimes distorted by their existence in politically awkward and potentially hostile locations like Soviet Georgia, the Congo, and South Africa. Domestic politics were also affected, as the southern and western U.S. states that had low-grade manganese and aluminum deposits invoked isolationist rhetoric again the East Coast business and political interests that favored free trade and no tariffs to import these industrially critical raw materials.

The Great Lakes mining and transport complex set the competitive standards that the spectacular spatiomaterial innovations of the Japanese shipping and steel industries had to surpass to achieve trade dominance in the 1960s and 1970s. The U.S. case provides a useful baseline for comparison of security, both military and political, between international and domestic supply lines. The United States' incorporation into its own sovereign territory of resource-rich, fertile, easily transitable lands created essential self-sufficiency in most raw materials during the nineteenth century. This reduced U.S. needs to protect investments in foreign extractive and transport systems at the beginning of its rise to trade dominance. The industries, transport infrastructure, and overall pattern of state-firm relations established by these generative sectors remained in place and slowly obsolesced (Ciccantell 2001), but they continue to shape the U.S. political economy, as the ongoing conflict over the future of the steel industry demonstrates.

In each of these cases of economic ascent, generative sectors in raw materials and transport industries drove these nations' development and their restructurings of the world economy. The pattern of tightened coupling of state-sector-firm relations, necessitated by the increasing complexity of raw materials access created by each of these ascendant economies, contributed to the cumulatively sequential evolution of the capitalist world-economy, raising the bar for each subsequent potential ascendant. Once each rapidly ascendant economy matures, however, the incentives for close cooperation and coordinated actions decline, and the raw materials supply systems constructed during ascent begin to obsolesce in the context of the strategies of potential new ascendant economies.

CHAPTER THREE

The MIDAs-Steel-Ships Nexus

In this chapter, we first describe the position of Japan materially and sociopoliti-cally after World War II. We highlight Japan's depleted domestic raw materials sup-plies, its poverty, the opposition of Japan's neighbors to reestablishing trade relations with Japan, and the development of the existing hegemon's need to support the re-development of Japan as a linchpin of U.S. Cold War strategies in Asia. We then ana-lyze how Japanese firms and the Japanese state, supported by U.S. and World Bank fi-nancial and technical assistance, fought and cooperated to create a new model of domestic development based in the steel, shipbuilding, and shipping industries. The Ministry of International Trade and Industry (MITI), established in 1952, developed its capacity and role in Japan's development in relation to the Japanese steel firms and their needs domestically and internationally, supporting the development of increas-ingly large-scale and tightly integrated blast furnaces and steel mills. The Maritime Industrial Development Area (MIDA) program, also begun in the 1950s, coordinated firm and state investment in new greenfield ports and steel plants utilizing the latest technological advances developed in Japan and imported from other nations to re-duce costs and increase Japanese economic competitiveness in steel, shipbuilding, and all other sectors that used steel and the steel-based transport infrastructure. The same system of financial and technical innovations drove the rapid expansion of scale in-creases of the Japanese shipbuilding industry that provided increasingly large ships needed to import rapidly growing quantities of coal, iron ore, and other raw materi-als from distant raw materials peripheries.

We analyze the tight linkage of the steel and shipbuilding industries by building and integrating state, sector, firm, and financial organizations across domestic and ex-ternal spheres. The analysis integrates material and spatial processes with technolog-ical, financial, and political processes to explain what drove Japan's rapid economic ascent. By outlining how the generative sectors in steel, shipbuilding, and shipping propelled this era of rapid growth from the 1950s through the early 1970s and how the steel industry maintained this role through the renewed period of growth in the 1980s, until its stagnation in the early 1990s, this chapter also sets the stage for questions raised in subsequent chapters.

The Japanese Economy in the Aftermath of World War II

Efforts to deepen industrialization in Japan took place during the first third of the twentieth century, most notably through expanding the steel, copper, and shipbuilding industries and through the creation of a domestic aluminum industry. All of these efforts involved the development of close state-sector-firm coordination in which the state played a central role. The first modern ironworks in Japan utilized locally mined iron ore and charcoal (Fujimori 1980:100). The Japanese steel industry began with the Yawata steel mill in Fukuoka prefecture in the northern Kyushu coal-producing region. The mill was built on the Japan Sea to allow imports of iron ore from China. The Japanese government built the mill and the Ministry of Agriculture and Commerce (the predecessor to the MCI and MITI) operated it as a development strategy for both economic and military purposes. This created a very close relationship between Yawata and its successor firms (New Japan Steel and then Nippon Steel) and MITI, the eventual successor to the MAC. Privately owned Kobe Steel and Nippon Kokan entered the steel industry in 1911–12, and Sumitomo entered in 1937 (Fujimori 1980:100–101; Johnson 1982:86–87; Murata 1980:26; Yamamoto and Murakami 1980: 139–41).

During the 1930s and 1940s, the Japanese state sought to take over the private steel firms as part of the military-driven government, but the private firms successfully resisted this effort. As a result, the Japanese state worked through the Iron and Steel Control Association, the predecessor to the postwar steel industry association, in its efforts to control the industry and to promote the expansion of steel production, including in its colony in Manchuria. This pattern of state-sector-firm relations formed the basis for the postwar system in the steel industry (Yonekura 1999:185–98) and helped move Japan into a competitive position with the world's leading powers in both steel and the tightly linked shipbuilding industry (see table 3.1).

The industrialization drive from the late 1800s through the end of World War II depleted Japan's limited coal, iron ore, and copper reserves. To overcome this obstacle to continued industrialization, the Japanese state and Japanese firms sought to gain access to raw materials via direct imperial conquest of neighboring resource-rich areas of China, East Asia, and Southeast Asia (So and Chiu 1995). The *zaibatsu*, large industrial groups that each included a variety of firms, including mining, shipping, and textiles, served as key actors in this raw materials access strategy until the military gained ascendancy over foreign policy in the occupation of Manchuria.

TABLE 3.1
World Powers in Steel and Shipbuilding

	1900	1913	1919	1929	1936
Steel (in millions of tons)					
Britain	4.9	7.7	9.7	7.7	7.8
Germany	6.4	18.9	15.0	16.2	19.2
United States	10.2	31.3	45.2	57.3	47.7
France	1.6	4.7	1.8	9.7	6.7
Japan	0	0.2	0.8	2.3	5.0
Shipbuilding (in thousands of tons)					
Britain	1,442	1,932	1,620	1,523	1,030
Germany	205	465	135	249	479
United States	191	228	3,580	101	163
France	117	176	33	82	47
Japan	5	65	612	164	441

SOURCE: Murata 1980:19.

This raw materials access strategy brought Japan into direct military conflict with the United States, Great Britain, the Soviet Union, and China. As historian Jonathan Marshall (1995:x) argued "the United States' war with Japan from 1941 to 1945 was primarily a battle for control of Southeast Asia's immense mineral and vegetable wealth." The defeat of Japan in World War II and the dismemberment of Japan's empire brought about severe economic and political crises in Japan. Japan's defeat in World War II foreclosed this ascendance and development strategy, because the U.S. government recognized that "Japan has her tentacles firmly embedded in the richest sources of many of the world's raw materials—materials which became necessary to the normal economies of the rest of the world. . . . As long as these vital materials are denied to the rest of the world, as long as access to them and to the trade routes of the east are hers to dominate and exploit for selfish and aggressive purposes, neither we nor our allies can hope for any return of peace, normal trade, or a decent standard of living for mankind" (Acting Secretary of State Joseph Grew, cited in Marshall 1995:185).

During World War II, Japanese raw materials industries sharply increased output, but at the cost of further deterioration of already aging small-scale plants located near iron ore and coal deposits in Japan. By the end of the war, this depleted Japanese coal, iron ore, and copper deposits, and the steel plants deteriorated (Ackerman 1953; Hein 1990; Yonekura 1994).

From the end of the war in 1945 until late 1947, the U.S.-led occupation of Japan headed by the Supreme Commander for the Allied Powers (SCAP), General Douglas MacArthur, had a number of mandates, including purging Japan's wartime leaders from positions of military, economic, and political power and breaking up the giant zaibatsu industrial holding companies (Borden 1984:62–67; Pauley 1945; U.S. State Department 1949). U.S. policy toward its defeated enemy focused on the creation of a democratic, self-sufficient society in Japan that would not be able to threaten its neighbors militarily again. SCAP sought to prevent rearmament by restricting steel output, in part through planned dismantling of Japanese plants for shipment to China and other Asian nations as war reparations.

These U.S. efforts to restructure Japanese economic and political life largely failed because the Japanese government bureaucracy remained virtually intact. Japanese economic and political elites defeated, delayed, and subverted many of these efforts because SCAP worked through the structure of the Japanese government bureaucracy (Maki 1947). As Chitoshi Yanaga (1968:28) argued, "the most important functions of the bureaucracy involve the protection and promotion of business and industry, in whose behalf it formulates long-term economic plans, makes forecasts, sets goals, and establishes priorities." The three closely linked bases of the Japanese political system— organized business, the party government, and the administrative bureaucracy (Yanaga 1968:28)—acted in coordination first to neutralize SCAP and later to guarantee long-term access to increasing supplies of raw materials to Japanese industry.

Also in the early postwar period, raw materials and industrial production in Japan collapsed, despite the attempts of the leaders of the old steel industry to revive their old plants (see Yonekura 1994). The supply of coal was critical:

> Coal output, the primary source of energy for Japan, ran at 3–4 m[illion] tons a month at the war's end. Immediately after the war, production dropped to barely 1 m[illion] tons a month. The reason was, as one Japanese author mildly puts it: "With Japan's defeat, the Koreans and Chinese who had been subject to forced labour in the coal mines were refusing to continue, and coalmining was in a state of virtual collapse. . . . Restoring coal output to its end-of-war level required investment in new equipment, which, in turn, required steel. Unfortunately steel production also slumped. Without adequate coal supplies, the railways could not run and the steelworks could not operate. Without steel, coal output could not be expanded. When the prohibition on trade was lifted, Japan had nothing to export to earn foreign currency with which to buy additional energy supplies from abroad." (Reading 1992:51)

In response to this crisis, in 1947 the Priority Production System focused on resolving this domestic crisis for the short term: "all available coal supplies, not required for running the railways, were allocated to the steel industry, together with all emergency fuel imports. All additional steel output was allocated to the coal industry to enhance coal production. This process was continued until coal production was increased to the point at which a surplus became available to supply other sectors" (Reading 1992:54). In fact, as Chalmers Johnson (1982:179) argued, "the priority production system is significant because it and its institutions were clearly based on prewar and wartime precedents and because, except for the fiscal innovations made in 1949 and 1950 to control inflation, it was the prototype of the high-growth system that MITI and other ministries were to forge during the 1950's." In other words, the Japanese state, supported by the United States, reconstructed the pattern of state-sector-firm cooperation and coordination that marked Japan's rapid rise between the mid-nineteenth and mid-twentieth centuries in order to resolve this raw materials–based economic crisis. This reconstructed system then drove Japan's dramatic rise to challenge U.S. hegemony in the late twentieth century.

Beginning in late 1947, a dramatic "Reverse Course" of U.S. policy toward Japan undid many of the efforts of the initial Occupation period to restructure the Japanese economy, such as breaking up the powerful zaibatsu and reducing the power of prewar elites and the state bureaucracy. This resulted from the perceived geopolitical threat to U.S. hegemony in the region presented by communist regimes in the Soviet Union and, after 1949, in China. Additionally, U.S. business interests with ties to zaibatsu prior to the war saw Japan as a prime location for foreign investment and sales and therefore opposed the initial postwar plans (Ball 1949; Bisson 1949:95–99, 1954: 41–43; Borden 1984:62–76, 83–88; Hadley 1970:144–46). As Arrighi (1994) demonstrates, financial capital interests in existing hegemons historically invested in a potentially ascendant economy because of the great opportunities for profit during the phase of rapid growth and technological innovation. U.S. banks financed Japan's economic ascent, just as Dutch financiers funded Holland's military rivals and British investors financed U.S. railroads.

The growing "dollar gap" global trade imbalance threatened the construction of a U.S.-led postwar global economy and U.S. economic growth via exports. For Japan, cut off geopolitically from previous raw materials supply sources in China, this meant raw materials had to be imported from dollar area sources, significantly exacerbating this global problem. For the U.S. government, financing this dollar gap through foreign aid became a heavier and heavier burden, creating a tremendous incentive both economically and politically to find new sources of raw materials for Japan that did not have to be paid for with scarce dollars (Borden 1984:5–8).

In the U.S. government, geopolitics quickly became paramount: the aim was now to rebuild Japan to provide a bulwark against communism in Asia, even if that meant reconstructing Japan's raw materials supply network in Japan's World War II colonies in Southeast Asia (Borden 1984:196–97), and promote the growth of the steel industry (Tiffany 1988:80–81). Economic and geopolitical concerns in the existing hegemon, coupled with resistance to restructuring by Japanese political and economic elites and their U.S. business allies, created the initial conditions for Japan's resumption of an ascendant course in the world economy.

This restored to political and economic power the elite leadership that planned and carried out Japan's imperial strategy in the 1930s and 1940s (Ball 1949; Bisson 1949:95–99, 1954:41–43; Borden 1984:71–76; Hadley 1970:144–46). Industrialization and the maintenance of the existing economic and political order once again became the central foci of Japanese government and Japanese firms' strategies. However, imperial conquest had been foreclosed as a raw materials access strategy by Japan's defeat and the restrictions on Japan's military imposed by the SCAP-written constitution.

As a result, coordinated efforts of the SCAP and the Japanese economic and political elites and government bureaucracy in the late 1940s formulated new raw materials access strategies in order to build up Japan as a bulwark against communism in Asia. As McDougall (1993:673) argues, this rebuilding would require "access to markets and raw materials, either in the United States itself or in East Asia"; the United States would have to take the lead in creating a peacefully constructed Co-Prosperity Sphere for Japan.

To accomplish this, SCAP and the Japanese leadership in the late 1940s and early 1950s carried out extensive efforts to assess Japan's domestic raw materials resources and their potential to meet the needs of the rapidly growing but severely impoverished Japanese population. Out of the forty minerals considered of major importance to industrial production at that time, Japan had domestic resources of only eleven adequate to its needs for the foreseeable future, including coal for electricity generation. Substantial reserves of copper and three other minerals existed, although at a relatively high price. Eight minerals were in deficient supply domestically, including iron, manganese, and tin, while seventeen minerals were strongly deficient or completely lacking in terms of domestic resources, including aluminum (Ackerman 1953:303).

Japan lacked high-quality coking coal for steel production, forcing reliance on imports. Steelmakers typically mixed low-quality Japanese coal with higher-quality imports. Northern China supplied coking coal to the Japanese steel industry prior to 1945, but the geopolitical foreclosure of this supply option meant that the United States became Japan's dominant coking coal supplier after 1945, even though this required scarce dollars (Ackerman 1953:182).

The need for imported raw materials led first to a "Little Marshall Plan for Japan," a US$165 million grant from April 1948 through July 1949 requested by the U.S. Army as part of the Economic Recovery for Occupied Areas aid program. This aid provided funds to purchase industrial raw materials (Borden 1984:75). The U.S. and Japanese governments also established other aid and loan programs to finance raw materials purchases, most notably the Export-Import (ExIm) Bank of Japan, whose regional mandate of trade promotion later expanded to include the promotion of overseas raw materials production to support heavy industrialization in Japan (Ozawa 1986:600).

SCAP and other U.S. government agencies began to promote and manage Japanese foreign trade and negotiated trade agreements between Japan and other governments, including the British Empire (Borden 1984:75–76). This U.S. effort to rebuild Japan emphasized establishing Japan as the center of the Asian noncommunist economy: "to facilitate Japanese trade recovery, Acheson directed American officials in Asia in July 1949 to cooperate with SCAP. They were to encourage increased food and raw materials production for all industrial nations, but especially for Japan. . . . By dealing with weak Southeast Asian nations individually the United States could dominate the discussions and channel development efforts toward primary production" (Borden 1984:119–20). This U.S. effort encountered strong resistance in the nations of Asia that the United States sought to transform peacefully into Japan's raw materials periphery. One U.S. official, Thomas Blaisdell, responded to this resistance in spring 1950:

> We don't take the position that a country has to industrialize. One of the points that the United States Government has been trying to put across in discussions on economic development in the UN is the point that you can have economic development along agricultural lines, along lines involving production of primary commodities. Of course the difficulty is that a lot of people conceive of economic development as involving industrialization, in many cases more than mere production of textiles or first stage processing of primary products. (cited in Borden 1984:134)

The Korean War created a large-scale demand for Japanese industrial products to supply U.S. forces in Korea. This combination of conditions opened the door for the rapid development of the Japanese steel industry.

The Creation of a New Development Model in Steel and MIDAs

Despite the initial U.S. reconstruction goals of denying Japan a large-scale steel capacity because of steel's role in military supplies, the economic and geopolitical conditions of the late 1940s and early 1950s combined to make the development of a domestic steel industry an essential need for national development and for U.S. geopolitical strategy. Japanese firms and the Japanese state recognized the essentiality of steel and the benefits of economies of scale for the steel, automobile, machinery, shipbuilding, and other industries, as well as the mutual benefits of developing the Japanese steel, shipbuilding, and shipping industries to reinforce and reduce costs for all three industries simultaneously (Okazaki 1997:78–81). This laid the groundwork for creating these generative sectors that drove Japanese economic development and reshaped the world economy in the following decades.

However, without domestic metallurgical coal and iron ore and given the prohibitively high cost of transporting these raw materials thousands of miles with existing transport technologies, an internationally competitive steel industry seemed to be an impossible dream, particularly to the newly created MITI, formed on the basis of the previous Ministry of Commerce and Industry. Efforts to plan the development of the steel industry in the early 1950s identified raw materials costs as the key obstacle to international competitiveness in the steel and steel-consuming industries. The high cost of coal was the greatest challenge, with coal accounting for 50 percent of steel production costs because domestic coal cost US$14–15 per ton, in comparison with U.S. steel producers' coal costs of US$7 per ton. High coal costs created high steel prices that left Japanese shipbuilding, machinery, automobile, and other industries uncompetitive (Nakamura 1981:33, 43; Okazaki 1997:83–87).

MITI's establishment law of 1952 assigned it regulatory duties for the steel industry as part of its responsibilities for the mining and minerals processing industries. MITI in the early 1950s actively opposed the targeting of the steel industry by the government because of concerns over the industry's ability to be internationally competitive. The economic boom that began in 1955 led to a reevaluation of the potential of the steel industry as a leading economic sector. MITI became involved as a coordinating agent for the steel sector in a number of areas, including a partially successful system of administrative guidance and control over capacity expansion in an effort to keep steel plants operating at full capacity without severe price competition during the late 1950s and 1960s (O'Brien 1992; Yonekura 1994:212–37).

The increasing scale of plants and capital requirements and the resulting severe domestic competition during the 1950s provoked government intervention, Yonekura (1994) argues, in the form of two rationalization programs coordinated by MITI (Tiffany 1988:126). This conflictual pattern of state-sector-firm relationships shaped the investment of US$2.1 billion in the steel industry between 1951 and 1960 (Tiffany 1988:126). This investment, supplied in part by the U.S. government, included US$176 million between 1957 and 1960 to aid the steel industry, with US$97 million from the U.S. ExIm Bank. The World Bank also supplied US$73 million to the industry during this period. This U.S. and World Bank assistance provided part of the necessary financing and the justification for lending by other international banks to the steel industry (Tiffany 1988:169; USBM/USGS 1958b:584–85). The U.S. government also provided technical information and the scrap metal needed to supply the steel industry's rapid growth during the 1950s and early 1960s (Tiffany 1988:169–70). This support from the existing hegemon as part of its Cold War geopolitical strategies provided critical resources for the phenomenal growth of the Japanese steel industry and the Japanese economy during the 1950s and 1960s, driven by generative sectors in steel and shipbuilding.

MITI confronted the vested interests of the old steel companies and their still highly influential leaders. On the other hand, the industry depended on MITI and the ExIm Bank for access to raw materials, foreign exchange to purchase imported raw materials, negotiations with the U.S. government, and capital for investment. MITI parlayed this leverage into regulatory powers over the entire industry, which it used to promote new technologies of unprecedented scale and efficiency. MITI sought to limit capacity to projected minimum demand, with imports making up shortfalls during booms. MITI argued that the costly new plants would be competitive only at full or nearly full capacity utilization. To achieve this, MITI had to quell the expansionist ambitions of individual firms. MITI succeeded only partially (O'Brien 1992), but it learned a great deal, achieved enormous prestige and legitimacy, and became essential to the industry as a whole as it simultaneously promoted the most advanced technology in the world, coordinated access to cheap raw materials, and held the line on excess capacity. This form of tightly coupled state-sector-firm coordination became a key strategy for resolving the challenges of increasing scale and global sourcing for the steel industry.

The resulting state interest in the creation of a domestic steel industry coordinated by MITI created the opportunity for the entrepreneurial efforts of Kawasaki Steel in the context of increased domestic competition following the breakup and privatization of Japan Steel under SCAP's authority. The MCI and then MITI sought to work with the three members of the steel oligopoly and the steel trade association to expand capacity gradually (Calder 1993; Johnson 1982). However, the growing demand for steel and the entrepreneurial independence of other firms seeking to free themselves from dependence on the three-firm oligopoly led to an important break with the existing structure of the industry (Calder 1993; Yonekura 1994). Kawasaki Steel led the way by making huge investments in building a modern, coastal steelworks to dramatically lower the cost of producing steel in Japan. Kawasaki overcame resistance and outright opposition from some government agencies, using a very high debt-equity ratio of 75 to 25 and a loan from the World Bank (Calder 1993), and, by relying on high amounts of debt, solving the problem of the limited capital available in Japan. These innovations provoked responses from other large steel firms, constructing their own modern steelworks in order to compete with Kawasaki (Yonekura 1994:190–200, 207–11).

Some analysts claim that these battles between individual firms and MITI over MITI's efforts to coordinate investment and production (Abe 1999; Kipping 1997;

Yonekura 1994) prove that MITI played only a minor role in Japan's economic development and that Johnson's (1982) analysis of MITI is false (Calder 1993; Ramseyer 2000). However, we argue that these conflicts result from the dynamic tension between firms with divergent interests, the agencies and political actors of the Japanese state, and other social groups that underlay Japan's sustained economic ascent. The often coordinated but sometimes conflictual goals, strategies, and actions of these actors drove the social and technical creativity, innovation, and compromise that made Japan's steel industry and other generative sectors global leaders.

After the resolution of the conflict with Kawasaki, MITI and other agencies of the Japanese government focused their resources on promoting economic development through heavy industrialization, most notably the steel industry. In addition to financing and export promotion, the Japanese government also helped other steel mills replicate Kawasaki's coastal greenfield expansion by

> establish(ing) huge industrial parks. The first was on land reclaimed from Tokyo Bay. Kawasaki Steel . . . built the most modern integrated steel facility in the world. Located close to a new, modern harbour, a continuous production line was established covering all stages of production from raw materials to finished products on the same site and using the most modern technology in the world. With labour still relatively cheap, Kawasaki Steel became the cheapest in the world. Here the results of dividing up the old zaibatsu came into play. Neither Yawata Steel nor Fuji Steel was prepared to allow a newcomer, Kawasaki Steel, to steal a march on them. Both launched similar developments, creating a large and modern Japanese steel industry in the world-beating class. (Reading 1992:70–71)

Inland transportation of raw materials in industrial-processing and consuming countries is in important ways susceptible to human manipulation. Preexisting industrial and consuming centers located inland from ports, often near former sites of domestic raw materials extraction, may force firms and/or states to invest heavily in railroad, water, and/or road transport facilities to link processing and consuming sites. When the depletion of domestic resources forces a shift to dependence on imported raw materials, the cost of moving these raw materials to existing inland processing plants often becomes prohibitive. Japan's first iron and steel works had been located near domestic coal and iron resources. Between World War I and World War II, new Japanese steel mills were built near the existing industrial and market centers of Tokyo and Osaka (Yamamoto and Murakami 1980:145). However, the Yawata steel mill began a pattern of coastal location to utilize imported Chinese resources (Yamamoto and Murakami 1980:145), a pattern built upon by Kawasaki and the other steel firms in the 1950s.

Relocation of raw materials industries through the construction of new raw materials–processing plants in port areas offers tremendous savings for raw materials–importing nations and firms. Yawata and Kawasaki became the pattern for all major new Japanese steel mills, with most steel firms building plants to serve the eastern and western markets from nearby steel mills on the coast (Yamamoto and Murakami 1980:145–48).

Governments in Japan and Western Europe offered significant incentives to promote the relocation of processing plants that are dependent on raw materials imports to port areas through MIDA programs beginning in the 1950s. The iron and steel industry, oil refineries, petrochemical complexes, aluminum smelters, and power plants almost entirely relocated to MIDAs. Large ships using firm- or government-financed ports can unload directly into stocking yards at plants in the port area, eliminating inland transport costs in the importing area (Hanappe and Savy 1981:13; Takel 1981; Vigarie 1981:24–25).

The Japanese MIDA program coordinated firm and national, regional, and local government investment (Murata 1980:178–82; Yamamoto and Murakami 1980:146–48) in new greenfield ports and steel plants. This complex coordination enabled the expanding steel industry to utilize the latest technological advances developed in Japan and imported from other nations to reduce costs and increase Japanese economic competitiveness in steel and shipbuilding. These advantages supported all other sectors that used steel and the steel-based transport infrastructure. In many Japanese ports, facilities for importing coal and iron ore and the steel plants that used these raw materials became the core components of the industrial area (see, e.g., Osaka Port and Harbor Bureau 1987, 1999; Yuzo 1990).

The MIDA ports served as growth poles that generated a variety of linked industries in the port and the region. This economic development model justified a combination of national, prefectural, and city government subsidies for MIDAs. The MIDA program built on the model developed during the Meiji Era to use port development as a means of economic development and of gaining the support of local warlords for the national government (Inamura 1993; Japan Port and Harbour Association n.d.; Kita and Moriwaki 1989; Kudo 1985; Masuda 1981; Miyaji 1990; Rimmer 1984; Takamura 1990; Yuzo 1990).

Japanese MIDAs were typically built on reclaimed land because of the lack of available land along the Japanese coast. Between 1954 and 1970, 33,200 hectares were reclaimed, with another 42,700 hectares reclaimed between 1971 and 1975 for MIDA development. Land reclamation methods included excavating deep channels leading to the new port, hydraulically moving sand and mud from river deltas, moving mountains into the sea, and disposing of urban garbage in the reclaimed area (Hotta 2002).

A combination of national, prefectural, and local government subsidies provided funds to local government port authorities for this construction, and the port authorities then sold the land to private firms to repay the cost of reclamation.

Reclaimed areas used for MIDAs include Port Island (4.3 square kilometers) and Rokko Island (5.8 square kilometers) in the port of Kobe, several piers and islands in Yokohama Bay, and, in Tokyo Bay, Kawasaki, Tokyo, Chiba (36 square kilometers), Kisarazu, and Yokosuka (Karmon 1980:285–97). The Kawasaki Steel mill in Chiba that opened in 1952 led a rapid movement of heavy industry into reclaimed land in Chiba prefecture on Tokyo Bay, including Nippon Steel, Nippon Kokan, and Sumitomo Metals, among others, in this area very close to the largest Japanese market of the Tokyo region. A similar pattern led by the steel industry on government-reclaimed land totaling 2,300 hectares also followed on Osaka Bay at Sakai-Senhoku and on another 1,000 hectares west of Kobe in the Harima district (Fujimori 1980:86). The MIDA model also created new steel and other heavy industrial locations around the Seto Inland Sea in a much less developed region. These MIDAs utilized land previously used by the military and by the salt industry, as well as newly reclaimed land, most notably in the Mizushima district in Okayama prefecture, in the neighboring Fukuyama district in Hiroshima prefecture (Fujimori 1980:96), and in Niigata in central Honshu. The old steel-producing region of northern Kyushu (where steel mills had been located in the first half of the twentieth century to take advantage of local coal) declined as a result of the development of steel capacity in these other MIDAs. However, the Japanese state subsidized the construction of a MIDA that included a large new steel mill at Oita City in Kyushu (Fujimori 1980:102).

This pattern of state-sector-firm relations in supporting the development of the world's most competitive steel industry restructured the industry geographically in terms of relocation to the MIDAs and built the world's newest steel industry. Of the twenty-one steel mills operating in Japan in 1975, two opened in the early 1900s, one in the 1920s, two in the 1930s, three in the 1940s, one in the 1950s, nine in the 1960s, and three in the 1970s, and even the older mills received technological updates during the 1960s. These relatively new and extremely large steel mills (the mills opened between 1961 and 1972 ranged from 2.3 million to 12.3 million tons of crude steel production in 1975) (Kawata 1971; Warren 2001:247; Yamamoto and Murakami 1980:142–43) were far larger and more competitive both technologically and in terms of raw materials costs than their major competitors in the United States and Europe.

By 1982 twelve iron and/or coal ports in Japanese MIDAs could unload ships with a capacity exceeding 100,000 deadweight tons (dwt), and all of the major Japanese steel firms had their own dedicated large-scale ports (CSR 1982:37–38; Penfold 1984:29). By 1990 a total of nineteen Japanese ports could unload vessels of 100,000 dwt or larger, with ten able to unload ships exceeding 200,000 dwt and the largest, Oita, capable of unloading ships up to 310,000 dwt (Lloyd's 1990:314–60).

This new steel industry in the MIDAs eliminated the need for internal transshipment in Japan of raw materials imports. As one analysis of the period of high economic growth between 1955 and 1970 argued,

> Japan is not only short of raw materials. For geographical reasons the amount of land suitable for industry is also limited. There is, however, one factor that makes the land available very advantageous for heavy industry. This is the abundance of harbours and coastal areas suitable for industry. As marine transport has improved and its cost fell, industries on the coast were able to obtain raw materials and export finished products much more cheaply than those inland. Thus Japan's long coastline was a great advantage. (Kosai and Ogina 1984:60–61)

The volume of raw materials in transmaritime trade quadrupled since 1960, in large part as the result of Japan's economic growth, and the available economies of scale increased proportionately. Capturing economies of scale in transport requires the construction of massive port systems, capable not only of accommodating large boats but also of loading them and unloading them quickly enough to prevent incurring the huge costs of tying up the capital-intensive ships too long in harbor. The costs of building such ports enhanced a feature of all constructed transport systems: to the extent that exporting and importing systems must be physically compatible to take advantage of cost-saving technologies, importers can tie exporters to their markets by fomenting mutually compatible port systems at both ends of the voyage. These investments in large-scale ports physically and economically tie raw materials exporters to only a very small number of potential customers, almost all of them located in Japan and Western Europe (Sullivan 1981) because the high capital investment in large-scale ports and mines can be repaid only by a high rate of capacity utilization.

A high rate of capacity utilization depends on the use of large-scale ships in these large-scale ports. Japan's much more rapid construction of such systems at home and compatible construction by its raw materials peripheries clearly indicate Japan's increasing power in the capitalist world-economy. Japan's topography favors such port systems, but the state and heavy industrial firms collaborated in building the domestic and the international environment in such a way as to maximize these advantages. Specifically, this pattern of state-sector-firm relations and the development of the greenfield steel industry in the MIDAs were tightly integrated with a series of technological innovations in pig iron and steel production that created economies of scale for the Japanese steel firms that further enhanced their global competitiveness.

Technological Innovations, Economies of Scale, and International Competitiveness

The combination of state, sector, firm, and financial collaboration in MIDAs and their ports made it possible and profitable to develop a series of technical developments and economies of scale in metallurgical processing and fabrication. Similar state-sector-firm financial collaboration overcame capital barriers to expanded scale as well.

To improve the first stage of processing iron ore and metallurgical coal, the production of pig iron in the blast furnace, Japanese steel firms beginning in the 1950s undertook a long series of efforts to increase the scale of blast furnaces. Japanese technological innovations increased blast furnace capacity from 1,500 tons per day in 1950 to 4,000 tons per day by the late 1960s (Kawata 1971; Manners 1971:27, 34) and to 22,000 tons per day by the early 1990s (McGraw-Hill 1992:425–26). The Japanese adopted, perfected, and diffused a second significant improvement in blast furnace operation, the improvement in the quality of the burden (the charge of raw materials into the furnace) through the sizing, agglomeration, and beneficiation of iron ore (Manners 1971:160). Limiting the variation in the size of iron ore, sinter, and pellet feed increases the efficiency of the furnace, reducing the volume of coal required and increasing the productivity of the furnace and lowering production costs (Manners 1971:36–37). Japan's global sourcing of iron and coal facilitated blending and provided significant raw materials cost savings.

A similar process of blending varieties of metallurgical coal also reduced the costs of blast furnace operations. The premium prices commanded by metallurgical coals because of their useful properties for metallurgical use stimulated extensive efforts by steel firms to develop Pulverized Coal Injection (PCI). PCI partially replaces metallurgical coal with a wider variety of grades of coal that are injected into the steel-direct reduction furnaces, rather than being processed into coke before being added to a blast furnace. PCI uses lower-cost coal and reduces the need for coking batteries, the most environmentally destructive aspect of steel making (McGraw-Hill 1992). Although Armco Steel in the United States first developed PCI in the early 1960s, low U.S. natural gas prices created a disincentive for the adoption of PCI. Japan and Europe took the lead in PCI technology, with twenty-three of Japan's thirty blast furnaces using PCI by 1992 (McGraw-Hill 1992). Substituting less expensive steam coal reduced Japanese steel firms' production costs and let them escape this "tyranny of metallurgical coal."

Japanese steel firms also reduced the amount of coke needed to produce each ton of pig iron in the blast furnace. The average amount of metallurgical coal required to produce coke declined from 1.1 tons per ton of pig iron in 1950 to 0.83 tons per ton in 1965 (Manners 1971:35) and to 0.4 tons per ton in the early 1990s (McGraw-Hill 1992:425). This dramatically cut raw materials cost for a blast furnace, because only about 36 percent as much coal must be acquired and transported to the blast furnace. For the Japanese steel industry, faced with a lack of domestic metallurgical coal and the need to import this essential input thousands of miles, increasing efficiency of coal consumption contributed significantly to lowering production costs. Increasing the scale of blast furnaces also contributed to lowering energy costs, as did computer control of the process of blast furnace operation (McGraw-Hill 1992:425–26), another technology pioneered by the Japanese steel firms.

As Manners (1971:38) concludes, "all iron- and steel-producing countries benefited from the improvements of blast-furnace technology, but none perhaps quite so rapidly as Japan." This rapidity resulted in large measure from the role of MITI and other agencies in providing capital and raw materials access support, imposing critical regulations, and fostering cooperation between firms and the state in the face of intense domestic and global competitive pressures. By combining increasing scale of the blast furnace with careful control of blending multiple ores and controlling the size of feed, Japanese steel mills became the largest and most efficient in the world by the mid-1960s. These efficiencies and reduced transport costs underlay Japan's competitive advantage in steel production from the late 1950s through the 1980s.

Expanding the scale of the blast furnace that produces pig iron achieved large fuel economies in the first stage of processing steel. The scale of the second steel-making stage limited the potential for scale increase, and therefore fuel economy, as the blast furnace and the second stage had to be made compatible. Fuel economy depends on scale of processing, and the scale of processing advances through myriad technical discoveries that progressively cheapen steel making, but does it through scale increases that progressively accelerate the consumption of raw materials. This increases the cost of space across which raw materials must be transported and within which there is an ever smaller number of deposits large enough to support the consumption of ever larger integrated smelters.

The Japanese steel firms led the way in adopting a new technology, the basic oxygen furnace, that had significant advantages over the open hearth furnace that dominated U.S. steel production, and in adapting this technology to increase scale and efficiency. The basic oxygen furnace reduces the time required to produce one batch of steel to half an hour from the four to five hours per heat required in an open hearth furnace by injecting pure oxygen under high pressure (Ohashi 1992:542). Japanese steel firms adopted the basic oxygen furnace far more rapidly than any other nation's steel industry (Warren 2001:249–52; Whitman 1965:853–55). This innovation dramatically increased the scale of production, because a basic oxygen furnace in Japan could produce eight to ten times as much steel in a given length of time relative to a U.S. open hearth furnace.

The initially small scale of the basic oxygen furnace made matching the increasing scale of blast furnaces with basic oxygen furnaces a more difficult technological and organizational problem than for the open hearth furnace. Japanese innovations to increase the scale of the basic oxygen furnace resulted from the need to catch up with rapid increases in blast furnace size. The Japanese steel mills put the increasingly large blast furnaces, basic oxygen furnaces, and continuous casting together into large-scale production before any other steel producers did so.

The Japanese steel firms led a dramatic increase in economies of scale in steel production. In the early 1950s scale economies existed up to 1 million tons per year of capacity, whereas by 1965 economies of scale existed up to 5 million tons per year and potentially up to 10 million tons per year (Manners 1971:59).

From a raw materials perspective, the need for iron ore with a phosphorus content of less than 0.8 percent created a difficult challenge for adopting basic oxygen converter technology. In most parts of the world, iron ore typically has a higher proportion of phosphorus. The diffusion of the basic oxygen converter resulted in a premium price for low-phosphorus content ores (Manners 1971:49). Global sourcing reduces this problem by allowing Japanese steel firms to create supply relationships with mines producing iron ores of various qualities that the steel mills blended to satisfy this technical requirement.

Japanese steelworks installed basic oxygen converters by the late 1970s, utilizing top-blown oxygen injection. However, "the first bottom-blown converter was introduced to Japan from the United States in 1977. Extensive experience with both top-blown and bottom-blown converters led to the development of top-and-bottom-blown vessels, and most of the converters now in use are of the combined type" (Ohashi 1992:543), an excellent example of technology import and then further research and development to produce a qualitatively new and more efficient technology for steel production in Japan. Other Japanese technological innovations in steel production included pretreating pig iron with fluxes to remove sulfur and phosphorus before charging the basic oxygen converter, eliminating more of the impurities in the pig iron, focusing the converter stage on removing carbon and heating the molten steel, and making remaining adjustments in steel quality during a secondary refining step of vacuum degassing to remove carbon and dissolved gases and to add small amounts of alloying materials after the basic oxygen converter step.

Computer control of the basic oxygen converter step now achieves precise quality and temperature control. The technological and processual innovations shortened re-fining times and almost eliminated the need to reheat a batch of steel in order to change its chemical composition (Ohashi 1992:543–46). These improvements in turn mean that "the steelmaker has better control over the scheduling of the subsequent continuous casting process. Indeed, steelmakers now speak of continuous continuous casting. By this they mean the successive casting of many heats of steel, including ones with differing chemistries, in an unbroken slab" (Ohashi 1992:543). Continuous cast-ing further enhances the advantages of global sourcing from multiple deposits with multiple physical characteristics. This continuous rapid throughput puts a premium on ensuring steady supplies of huge volumes of diverse sets of both metallurgical coal and iron ore that can be blended to produce desired qualities in the pig iron and steel. Acquiring coal and iron ore from mines able to guarantee long-term supplies of very reliable known quality became an essential element of Japanese raw materials access strategies.

Rapid growth in the Japanese steel industry necessarily meant construction of greenfield projects, which did not suffer the innovation-retarding drag of capital vested in obsolete plants, depleted sources, and restrictive distribution networks. As a result, Manners (1971:116) argues, "there is a good deal of evidence . . . to suggest that, on average, Japanese steelmaking costs in 1965 were substantially below those of the United States iron and steel industry, and that Western European costs by and large lay somewhere between the two." Savings in raw materials and transport costs, com-bined with technological innovations and adoptions, in less than twenty years trans-formed the Japanese steel industry into the world's lowest-cost, fastest-growing steel industry.

As a consequence, by the late 1970s and early 1980s,

> for a wide variety of steel products, a Japanese manufacturer of steel products can buy Japanese steel at prices ranging from 15 to 30 percent lower, depending on the gauge, than his American counterpart can buy it in the United States. This handily gives the Japanese manufacturer a cost advantage of 5 to 8 percent less over his U.S. competitor for prod-ucts such as forklift trucks, construction equipment, automobiles, and ball bearings. (Abegglen and Stalk 1985:77–78)

This cost advantage for domestic steel consumers in Japan also translated into in-ternational competitiveness in steel exports. As a result, Japanese steel firms domi-nated world steel trade beginning in the early 1960s. Japanese steel exports rose from 8.8 percent of total world exports in 1960 to a peak of 40.8 percent in 1976; in volume terms, the increase was from 2.3 million tons to 36 million tons over the same period.

Japanese steel exports ranged from 19 million to 33 million tons per year over the past three decades, constituting 20–30 percent of total world steel exports during this period (data calculated from OECD 1985 and USBM/USGS various years b).

The tight coordination of all aspects of the steel industry that MITI and the Japanese steel firms pioneered and regulated produced major savings of transport costs for steel products. MIDAs simultaneously took advantage of deep ocean ports and of internal waterways, including Tokyo Bay and the inland sea. Barges ferry steel products across Tokyo Bay to other industrial plants (Manners 1971:71) that are not located in the immediate vicinity in the same MIDA. The tight articulation of the steel and shipbuilding industries also allowed for savings on the reexport of the finished steel.

Internationally, freight rates for steel product shipping increased between 1950 and 1965 for most steel exporters; however, "the major exception to this upward drift in rates was achieved by the Japanese, who, in pioneering the use of vessels solely for steel exports, were able to make dramatic reductions in their freight charges" (Manners 1971:72). Freight rates for steel products exported from the United States to Japan in the early 1960s ranged from $28 to $33 per ton, while Japanese exports to the United States faced freight rates of $15 to $21 per ton (Manners 1971:73). Just as was the case in international ocean shipping of iron ore and coal to Japan, the Japanese steel, shipbuilding, and shipping industries, in coordination with the Japanese state, worked to lower transport costs of finished steel products through technological innovation and vertical integration between steel firms and their internal shipping capacity in order to increase the competitive advantage of Japanese steel firms' exports to world markets. The same skills and powers to coordinate and negotiate across sectors extended this competitive advantage to international transport of raw materials.

The capital barriers to establishing this scale of smelting and the potential for crippling overcapacity in the still underdeveloped Japanese and Asian markets set the stage in the 1950s and 1960s for state-sector-firm cooperation, regulation, and resolution of disputes. On this stage, various agencies of the Japanese state, most notably MITI and the ExIm Bank, took the lead in the creation of the most tightly coupled relationship between capital and the state in history. MITI learned technical and political skills that made it essential to the steel, shipbuilding, and shipping industries. MITI's competence and power allowed it to combat and at least partially restrain the self-interests of particular steel companies in the interests of the sector and those of the national economy as a whole, thus playing a key role in maintaining the dynamic tension essential to continued Japanese economic ascent.

In short, as the U.S. government and Japanese development planners foresaw in the late 1940s, the steel industry became the linchpin of a number of linked industries that complemented one another in a "virtuous cycle" of economic development. The

TABLE 3.2
Japanese Steel Industry and GDP
(in millions of tons and billions of yen)

	Steel Production	Steel Exports	Coal Imports	Iron Ore Imports	GDP
1946	0.6	0	0	0	
1950	4.8	0.7	0.8	1.5	3,947
1960	22	2.3	8.3	15	15,500
1970	93	18	50	102	73,300
1980	111	30	68	134	240,000
1990	110		104	125	424,000
2000	106	29	142	132	513,534
2005	112				

SOURCES: Mitchell 1994; USBM/USGS various years a.

steel industry became a generative sector providing the raw materials foundation for reducing production costs for many sectors of the Japanese economy, transforming Japan into the world's second largest economy and the United States' most formidable economic competitor (see table 3.2).

The phenomenal growth of the steel industry during the 1950s and the 1960s and of steel-consuming industries drove Japan's rapid economic growth, but it also created rapidly growing demand for imported coal and iron ore to supply the industry. This raw materials challenge is our focus in chapters 4 and 5.

This virtuous cycle led by steel as a generative sector continued without interruption until 1973. The steel industry reacted to the oil price shock by virtually eliminating petroleum as a source of energy (petroleum became important for blast furnace use in the late 1960s because of the high cost and scarcity of metallurgical coal [Kawata 1971]), replacing it with larger quantities of coal. Combined with other technological and organizational innovations that increased efficiency and productivity, the Japanese steel industry survived the global economic and steel industry crisis of the 1970s still as a world leader in production and technology, and enjoyed another successful decade during the 1980s. However, the steel industry was not immune to the broader crisis that affected the Japanese economy beginning in 1990, and, as we discuss in chapter 7, the steel industry faces serious threats to its survival in Japan. Japanese steel firms undertook a variety of strategies to survive, including industry cartels, partnerships with U.S., European, Chinese, Brazilian, and other steel firms, exporting technology and expertise as participants in these partnerships around the world (Hanmyo 2002), and merging with each other, including the merger of NKK and Kawasaki to form JFE Steel (Iwase 2003) and the alliance between Nippon Steel, Sumitomo Metal Industries, and Kobe Steel to form a second large steel firm in 2003 (Ohashi 2004).

The formation of close investment, technology supply, and sales relationships with Chinese steel firms represents the most important strategic effort to restore the financial health of the two Japanese steel firms. The two remaining Japanese steel firms export millions of tons of steel to China, supply technology and capital to expand steel production in China, and focus on producing and exporting to China higher-quality and higher-value-added specialty steels (Iwase 2003; L. Lewis 2003). Relations between the two major Japanese steel firms and the Chinese steel industry are not entirely complementary, however. Rapidly growing iron ore demand in China and the resulting higher prices led the Japanese steel firms to develop and introduce technologies to utilize lower-quality iron ore with lower iron ore content (56 percent instead of the usual 66 percent iron content) in order to reduce their raw materials costs (Elsham 2004). In Chapter 7 we will return to analyzing this relationship between Japan and China and our fifth research question, how is China utilizing and transforming the Japan-created global raw materials industries to support China's rapid development?

These strategies helped the restructured and consolidated firms in the Japanese steel industry survive this decade of crisis by partnering with more competitive firms. However, these firm strategies did nothing to resolve Japan's broader domestic economic crisis that began in the 1990s, a period in which much of the rest of the world economy grew rapidly, most notably in China and the United States. We will return to this question of decline and the steel industry in Chapter 7.

Ships, Shipbuilding, and MIDAs

All of these innovations in steel production led to larger-scale and increased distance across the needed spaces. The cost of distance offsets the savings of processing steel. This contradiction between economies of scale and diseconomies of space generates state-sector-firm collaboration to design and implement more efficient transport technologies, more effective transport infrastructures, and the incorporation of ever broader spaces as potential sources. These transport technologies required and promoted larger transport scale.

The technical achievements and scale increases in steel production and their development over time both required and provided the means for increased fuel efficiency of transport. Because hull size increases arithmetically but cargo volume increases geometrically, moving a much larger capacity ship requires only a relatively small increase in fuel consumption, dramatically reducing fuel used per ton of cargo moved. Size of ship, or scale of transport, is inversely related to fuel usage. The advances in steel quality associated with scale-dependent fuel economies of scale in smelting contribute to the tensile strength requirements of the hulls of larger ships

TABLE 3.3
Average Distances in Major Bulk Trades, 1976
(in nautical miles)

	Japan	Europe	North America	World Average
Iron ore	6,140	4,300	2,970	5,000
Coal	6,240	3,020	—	4,660

SOURCE: Drewry 1978b:1.

and to the capacity of the boilers and engines to withstand the temperatures and the pressures that increase in order to increase the efficiency of transfer from heat energy to mechanical energy.

The transport strategy developed via the coordinated efforts of MITI, the ExIm Bank, and the Japanese shipping, shipbuilding, and steel firms allowed Japanese steel firms to create large economies of scale in bulk shipping to dramatically reduce production costs of steel in Japan and to capture all of these benefits for themselves, rather than sharing them with coal- and iron ore–producing firms and exporting regions.

The tremendous distances that Japanese raw materials imports traveled relative to European and North American imports and relative to the world average created a strong incentive for efforts to reduce raw materials transport costs, as table 3.3 shows. This spatial disadvantage, created by the U.S.-determined unavailability of nearby supplies of iron and coal in China, would have made Japan uncompetitive in raw materials–based industries under the existing technological conditions of the 1950s.

After the end of World War II, initial Allied plans for Japan's postwar reconstruction imposed strict limits on the Japanese shipping and shipbuilding industries. However, the Strike Mission of 1947 and the Draper Mission of 1948 recognized the problems that would result from severe restrictions on Japan's shipping and shipbuilding industries, including the major balance-of-payments problems accruing from dependence on expensive foreign shipping, as well as the high cost to the United States of continuing to support Japan in the absence of the recovery of Japan's shipping and shipbuilding industries. The shift in U.S. policy in the late 1940s to favoring the reconstruction of Japan as a geopolitical bulwark in Asia led to the elimination of externally imposed restrictions on Japan's shipping and shipbuilding industries (Chida and Davies 1990:62–65).

At the same time, the Japanese government developed its strategies for the reconstruction of the nation. The Priority Production System regulation of December 1946 identified several key industries as the leading sectors in which to concentrate resources. A variety of laws encouraging shipping and shipbuilding took effect in the late 1940s, including the Programmed Shipbuilding Scheme of 1947 to support the growth of both shipping and shipbuilding. The program sought to speed the construction of shipping to ease the severe postwar shortage based on government provision of low-cost financing to private shipping firms. Funding initially came from the Rehabilitation Finance Bank and then, after 1953, from the Development Bank of Japan. The Korean War provided important benefits to Japanese shipowners and especially to Japanese shipyards because of the increased freight rates and demand for ships during the period (Chida and Davies 1990:66–86).

The Programmed Shipbuilding Scheme shaped and drove the growth of Japan's shipbuilding industry. Chida and Davies (1990:89–90) summarize the program as follows:

> After taking into account the state of the economy and the estimated demand for tonnage, the Government decided upon the level of output and the types of ships that would be required during the following year. It then loaned the necessary funds at a less than commercial rate of interest . . . to some of the firms that wished to order appropriate ships. The amount of loan allocated to individual ships varied according to the type of vessel, but never covered the full cost. The extent of the borrowing that was permitted was also altered from year to year, but in any event the balance had to be found by the companies themselves. While accumulated reserves might sometimes be used, the usual practice was to secure a further loan to cover the balance from the city banks with which respective firms had close connections. These were so conservative in their attitude to shipping that they were unwilling to lend unless part of the price of the ship had already been met from public funds. . . . there can be no doubt that these arrangements made a great contribution to the development of Japan's shipping industry. It is extremely difficult to compare this assistance with that given by other maritime nations to their shipping industries, but it is reasonable to suggest that the Japanese were not disadvantaged! Of even greater importance, perhaps, . . . was the way in which the Scheme allocated its resources. Loans were granted in such a manner as to ensure that the composition of the fleet was best suited to the needs of the economy. This enabled the Government to provide a vital if unintentional overview of the situation—something which does not appear to have occurred in other countries.

This government direction and subsidization reflects the importance of transport as a strategic component of both raw materials access and economic development efforts on the part of the Japanese government. This tightly coordinated system of state-sector-firm relations explicitly sought to balance the interests of shipbuilding, shipping, and steel firms and broader industrial and societal interest in low-cost raw materials imports and industrial export transport, with the state as arbiter of this dynamic tension. This system allocated scarce Japanese capital resources to supply low-cost transport without wasting resources on the notoriously cyclical shipbuilding industry, a delicate balancing act of restricting capacity and output in pursuit of broader state developmental goals.

In addition to government support through financing, government support for research and development on ship construction also played a critical role in the postwar era, most importantly via the agreement signed between the Japanese government and the U.S. shipping firm National Bulk Carriers (NBC) in 1951. The booming ship construction market led NBC (owned by U.S. shipping magnate D. K. Ludwig) to search for a former naval shipyard to utilize for civilian shipbuilding, especially for large-scale petroleum tankers (Todd 1991:13). NBC investigated a number of former naval shipyards in Germany and Japan and selected the Kure naval shipyard in Japan.

The terms of the agreement between NBC and the Japanese government on the ten-year lease (later renewed until 1962) required that "while NBC was to construct ships for its own purposes as and how it wished, as much Japanese steel as possible was to be utilized. Of even greater long-term significance was the insistence that all types of Japanese shipbuilders and engineers were to have free access to the establishment and were to be permitted to examine all aspects of its building system" (Chida and Davies 1990:112). In addition to promoting the consumption of Japanese steel, this new shipyard developed the technological and organizational innovations that made Japan the world's leading shipbuilder, based on a set of globally unique lease terms intended to transfer advanced technology to Japan and to train Japanese engineers and managers at no cost to Japanese firms or to the Japanese government. This created both a free training institute and a free source of imported shipbuilding technology, one of the most important organizational and institutional innovations in the Japanese economy, creating a linchpin for making shipbuilding a generative sector.

Beginning in the early 1960s, Japanese shipyards began introducing a number of technological innovations of their own, based on the experience and technology introduced to Japan by NBC, including the replacement of labor with machines in the hull construction and fitting-out departments, rationalizing the designing of ships, and introducing "section" or "block" building and welding that allowed the development of new larger shipyards with more efficient layouts permitting the construction of larger ships. All of these improvements increased labor productivity, reducing the amount of labor required to build each ship and increasing the competitiveness of Japanese shipbuilding relative to the more labor-intensive methods that remained in use much longer in other nations (Chida and Davies 1990:91; Yamamoto 1980:165).

For example, during the 1980s, Japanese labor requirements for building a 62,000-dwt bulk carrier fell from 380,000 hours in 1981 to 170,000 hours in 1991 (UNCTAD 1992:39).

The high wages of shipyard workers made labor saving a critical issue in Japan; during most of the postwar era, shipyard workers earned the highest wages in Japan (Chida and Davies 1990). As was the case in the steel industry, heavy industrialization based on raw materials increased domestic consumption in Japan both directly and indirectly through workers' wages (Tilton 1996:41), providing a market for the industrial products that utilized steel and other processed raw materials.

These technological and organizational improvements in Japanese shipyards during the 1950s and especially the 1960s gave Japanese "shipbuilders sufficient economies of scale that they could lead the world in the new technology" of building larger and larger oil tankers demanded after the closing of the Suez Canal and as the distance between oil extracting regions and their customers increased (Chida and Davies 1990: 98–99). Japanese shipyards pioneered the increasing scale of shipbuilding. A Japanese shipyard built the first large (130,000 dwt) oil tanker in 1962, and continued to lead the way in increasing scale, reaching 480,000 dwt in the early 1970s (Sasaki 1976:8). Japanese shipyards pioneered similar innovations in bulk carriers, launching the world's then largest ore carrier at 224,000 dwt in 1983, with a fuel consumption of 6 kilograms per ton of cargo, versus 10 to 11 kilograms for conventional 130,000-dwt bulk carriers (*Zosen,* May 1983:28). In order to build these large ships, Japanese shipbuilding firms constructed fifteen shipyards between 1964 and 1976 with the ability to build ships between 300,000 and 1 million dwt (Nagatsuka 1991:14–15).

The tremendous expansion of the size of bulk carriers and of the number of Japanese-owned bulk carriers from the 1960s onward resulted from the Japanese government policy of linking the steel and shipbuilding industries (Chida and Davies 1990:119). The shipbuilding industry used 35 percent of all heavy steel sheet (Yamamoto 1980:164), providing a large market for a major steel product. As the result of these technological innovations and the tremendous demand in Japan for bulk shipping, "Japan then emerged as the world leader in the production of very large vessels and subsequently dominated the market for oil tankers and ore-carriers. The timing of this development was particularly fortuitous for Japan as it occurred just as a boom began which required substantial numbers of large tankers" (Chida and Davies 1990: 133). This boom in fact rested largely on Japan's rapid economic growth and the huge volumes of imported iron ore, coal, oil and other raw materials on which this growth depended.

The Japanese government also provided financing on concessionary terms for the export of Japanese-built ships through the Export-Import Bank of Japan. Additionally, the government during the 1950s provided funding for the modernization of the Japanese steel industry, with one important result being the reduction in the cost of steel plate used in shipbuilding, making Japanese ship exports much more cost competitive (Chida and Davies 1990:108–9).

With this support from the Japanese government, the Japanese shipbuilding industry increased from only 15.6 percent of world production (829,000 tons) in 1950 to 43.9 percent in 1965 (5.4 million tons) and peaked at 18 million tons in 1975, 50.1 percent of world production. The Japanese shipbuilding industry became the largest in the world in 1965 and produced about half of total world output from the mid-1960s through the mid-1980s (Nagatsuka 1989:17). Shipbuilding remained one of Japan's most important export industries from the 1950s through the 1980s (Chida and Davies 1990:106), and Japan is still one of the world's three largest shipbuilding nations today.

The Japanese shipbuilding industry also became more concentrated in the early 1960s with the formation of IHI through the merger of two of Japan's largest shipbuilders and the formation of Mitsubishi Heavy Industries through the merger of three firms in 1964. These and other major shipyards also developed close relationships with smaller shipyards, increasing the coordination of the industry and reducing competition between shipbuilding firms (Chida and Davies 1990:168–72).

The Japanese shipbuilding industry provided a new tool for Japan's iron ore access strategy during the 1980s via the construction and employment of ore-bulk-oil carriers and bulk carriers exceeding 300,000 dwt. These large ships allowed Japanese steel firms to expand their iron ore supply relationship with Brazil with the opening of the Carajás mine, the world's lowest-cost iron ore producer, 12,000 miles from Japan. This new strategic element resulted from learning from experiences in the coal and iron ore trade with Australia, Canada, Brazil, and South Africa and from experiences in managing long-distance shipping of oil. This learning led to the expansion of Japanese transport networks beyond the relatively short 3,600-mile haul from Australia to 12,000-mile coal and oil shipment.

Lowering costs on these even longer hauls required another dramatic increase in scale from ships at 100,000 to 200,000 dwt to those exceeding 300,000 dwt. Oil tankers reached this scale by the early 1970s, but iron ore, with a stowage factor of 0.5 cubic meters per ton, more than twice as dense as crude oil (1.2 cubic meters per ton) and almost three times as dense as coal (1.4 cubic meters per ton) (Stopford 1988:255), presented a tremendous technical challenge. The technological advances in ship construction and in the quality, weight, and size of steel plate and beams, most notably the mass production of high-tensile steel due to this demand from shipbuilding, allowed Japanese shipbuilding firms first to build larger oil tankers and then to build ore-bulk-oil and larger dedicated bulk iron ore carriers.

The prosperity of the Japanese shipbuilding industry during the 1960s and early 1970s came to an abrupt end after Nixon's decision to abandon the gold standard in 1971, the oil crisis of 1973, and the ending of fixed foreign exchange rates. The industry entered a prolonged period of depression (Chida and Davies 1990:138–39) as the industry's global competitiveness steadily declined. The crisis led Japanese shipbuilders to reduce shipyard capacity in two stages (the first in 1980 and the second in 1988) from 9.8 million gross tons per year in 1975 to 4.6 million gross tons per year. The firms sought to improve profitability and end the tremendous losses that resulted from shipyards' competing with one another in a situation of excess capacity and low demand, which often led to ships being sold below their costs of production (Nagatsuka 1989:8–9). The crisis in shipbuilding also reduced the shipbuilding labor force from its peak of 273,900 in 1974 to only 84,600 in 1988 (Nagatsuka 1989:24).

In many ways, the shipbuilding industry provides the clearest example of the rapid collapse of Japan's post–World War II political economy in the face of rising domestic costs and increasing global competition from nations seeking to emulate Japan's development model, most notably South Korea and China. The formerly world-leading Japanese shipbuilding industry failed to maintain its global competitiveness, despite repeated state-sector-firm interventions and billions of dollars of assistance, leading to the decline of many areas dependent on the industry. The success of the shipbuilding industry created vested interests in both firms and labor in maintaining their positions, even in the face of increasing international competition, weakening the dynamic tension of state-sector-firm relations that had supported the industry's growth. Simultaneously, Japan's economic ascent created opportunities for new, lower-cost competitors to enter the industry because of the demand for ships during boom periods in the global economy. These new entrants modeled their state policies, technologies, and organizational strategies after those in the Japanese shipbuilding industry in hopes of emulating Japan's success. In this new global industry, largely created by Japan's economic ascent, Japanese shipbuilding firms became progressively less competitive because of Japan's success and the loss of dynamic tension in the industry in Japan.

Shipbuilding served as a key generative sector in the Japanese government's postwar development plans. The industry consumed huge quantities of Japanese steel and other inputs; was one of the most important export industries in Japan for many years; served as a model for the import, adaptation, and improvement of industrial and organizational technologies; and provided the increasing scale of ships needed by

Japanese shipping firms to import huge volumes of raw materials for the Japanese steel mills. These ships linked massive exporting and importing systems in the steel industry with their rapidly increasing scales of operation. Just as in earlier periods in Holland, England, and the United States, shipbuilding created a tremendous range of material, economic, organizational, and technological linkages to other industries and served as a generative sector for almost three decades after World War II.

Linking the Internal and External Dimensions

Our goal in this chapter was to address our first question, what drove Japan's rapid economic ascent? The steel and shipbuilding industries based in the MIDAs and the pattern of state-sector-firm relations to fund and assist this model of development drove Japan's internal development in a wide range of industries linked directly and indirectly to these generative sectors. The pattern of state-sector-firm relations and other elements of Japan's postwar political economy developed in these generative sectors provided the foundation for Japan's rapid economic growth from the 1950s through the 1980s.

The economic stagnation that began in the 1990s also affected the steel industry. The industry entered what one analyst called "its first consolidation and realignment" (Wu 2001:13.7) during 2001, with several alliances and mergers between steel firms to reduce excess capacity. These alliances and mergers created two new, stronger steel firms that remain global leaders, with one of them, JFE Holdings, earning a profit of more than US$2.5 billion in 2005 (Fackler 2005).

The broader economic crisis and the problems of the steel industry, combined with a series of studies since the late 1980s that claim that Japanese steel prices are among the world's highest (Peters 1988:538; Tilton 1996:171), led some analysts in their search for explanations of these problems to criticize the steel industry as a costly and inefficient sector, perhaps even since its phenomenal growth began in the early 1950s (Calder 1993; Katz 1998:95–96; Tilton 1996:169–77).

This surprising reinterpretation of the role of the steel industry in Japan's economic ascent argues that, because the pattern of state-sector-firm cooperation kept domestic steel prices above what the market would have set, the steel industry hampered Japan's economic development. This narrow focus on prices that have certainly not been set in a competitive marketplace ignores the developmental benefits of the allocation of resources to the steel industry and its workers. High steel prices provided the capital for investment in larger- and larger-scale blast furnaces, basic oxygen furnaces, continuous casting, and other technological innovations; provided the funds for investing in shipbuilding, shipping, and other linked keiretsu firms; paid high wages that created a middle-class consumers' market in Japan; and created a stable political economy for more than four decades—all fundamental parts of Japan's rapid ascent.

Ironically, from the perspective of the United States, to whose steel industry these authors implicitly compare Japan's "poorly functioning" steel market, the strongest argument against this portrayal of the Japanese steel industry as uncompetitive is the alleged "dumping" of Japanese steel exports in the U.S. market at less than the Japanese market price. It is quite likely that the "dumping" prices have been profitable for the Japanese steel firms, given their tremendous economies of scale, although these sales are less profitable than higher-priced domestic sales. Japanese steel exports were not sold at a loss to benefit U.S. consumers, drive U.S. steel firms out of business, or for any reason other than to make a profit from the very high degree of international competitiveness (until at least the early 1990s) of Japanese steel production because of the industry's economies of scale, relatively new MIDA plants, and its very low raw materials acquisition and transport costs. The pattern of state-sector-firm relations created in the steel industry during the late 1940s and 1950s created problems for Japan today, but these problems are of relatively recent vintage. The steel industry from the 1950s through the 1980s drove Japan's economic ascent, rather than hindering it, as this reinterpretation implies.

However, this does not explain how the two key raw material ingredients for these industries and all resulting products, coal and iron, arrived in Japan at costs low enough to make Japanese industries and products the most competitive in global markets. In the following two chapters, we analyze the Japan-driven globalization of these two previously localized industries and how the coordinated efforts of Japanese firms, industry sectors, and the Japanese state combined to drive down the cost of moving ever greater volumes of these raw materials thousands of miles to Japan, the essential elements of the cumulative sequential increases in scale of this phase of globalization that underlay Japanese dominance of world trade.

CHAPTER FOUR

Creating Japan's Coal-Exporting Peripheries

Creating a New Model of Raw Materials Acquisition

The Japanese steel mills and the Japanese state, with the initial support of the United States, constructed and then progressively reconstructed a model of raw materials access in coal that required complex processes of learning and negotiation with potential coal-exporting nations and firms, and developing and repeatedly reworking a system of state-sector-firm coordination in Japan in response to conditions in the world economy and in trading-partner nations. Exporting firms and states repeatedly sought to improve their terms of trade for coal exports, and the Japanese steel firms and the Japanese state repeatedly used their evolving pattern of state-sector-firm coordination to respond to these efforts and to restructure the globalizing coal industry in ways that supported Japanese development and progressively reduced the cost of importing coal into Japan. Exporting firms and states and global market conditions made creating and maintaining low-cost, secure access to millions of tons per year of metallurgical coal very difficult, making the successes of the Japanese steel mills and the Japanese state both remarkable and critical to Japan's sustained economic ascent.

As with steel, we locate the Japanese solutions to coal procurement within these technological and scale imperatives of competition at the world-historical moment of Japan's ascent. Our explanation of Japan's rapid ascent to dominance of world steel production focused largely on domestic dynamics and consequences. This international aspect of ascent in the world-system hierarchy emphasizes intercore competition, even while it emphasized the importance of cheap, steady access to foreign sources of raw materials. The existing hegemon's systems of acquisition of foreign raw materials and, more generally, of capital accumulation and global inequality, in place by the mid-1900s, relied on U.S.-based transnational firms and their wholly owned subsidiaries around the world

In contrast to the U.S. model, the Japan-driven model of raw materials access, cap-

TABLE 4.1
Japanese Coal Production, Imports, and Consumption
(in millions of metric tons)

	Domestic Production	Total Imports	Coal Consumption
1930	31.4	2.9	34.3
1940	57.3	6.9	64.2
1950	38.5	0.8	39.3
1961	54.5	11.2	65.7
1970	44.1	50.2	94.3
1980	18.1	68.3	86.4
1990	8.3	103.6	111.9
2000	2.5	124.1	134.5
2003	0	175.6	175.6

SOURCES: IEA 1992, 1998, 2002; *Japanese Economic Statistics*; *Japanese Industry* 1968:34; SCAP, SCAP Natural Resources Section 1949; USBM/USGS *Minerals Yearbooks*.

TABLE 4.2
Japanese Steel Production
(in thousands of metric tons)

1950	4,838
1960	22,186
1970	93,518
1980	111,629
1990	110,000
2001	102,866
2005	112,720

SOURCES: Japan Iron and Steel Federation; USBM/USGS, *Minerals Yearbooks*.

ital accumulation, and global inequality relies on trade via transfers between joint ventures, partnerships in long-term contracts, and other mechanisms that link firms (Harvey 1995). The Japanese steel firms developed this model to overcome the problems of capital shortage and obstacles to Japanese foreign direct investment.

Obtaining metallurgical coal and iron ore at costs low enough to make Japanese steel production globally competitive presented key challenges for Japanese economic development. The rapid economic development of Japan after World War II entailed a rapid growth in Japanese demand for coal. Japan historically produced a significant amount of coal from domestic resources, but the growth of demand coupled with the exhaustion of many coal deposits, the lack of large domestic coking coal resources, and government recognition of the increasing noncompetitiveness of high-cost Japanese coal mines necessitated a growing role for imported coal (table 4.1). Metallurgical coal demand rose rapidly throughout the postwar era in Japan, mainly due to the rapid growth of the Japanese steel industry (table 4.2).

Material Characteristics and Japanese Coal Access Strategies

Scale-dependent technologies and organization to lower the cost of steel require cheap, steady flows of raw materials. Raw materials must flow at volumes and physico-chemical compositions appropriate to the technology of operation of different types of smelters and to the quality demands of consumers. Early iron and steel plants used far more charcoal and then coal than iron ore, so owners tended to locate blast furnaces as near the coal mine as possible (Isard 1948). Steady reduction of the proportion of coal to iron ore progressively weakened this connection (Harris 1988; Isard 1948, 1954; Pounds and Parker 1957), but coal transport continues as a main factor cost and as a potential source of savings in producing low-cost, high-quality steel.

The Japanese steel industry's technological and organizational strategies continued the historical trend of efforts to decrease the amount of coal used per unit of steel (Koerner 1993:67). Improved control over the chemical and physical processes of pig iron and steel production simultaneously reduced fuel costs and produced stronger steel. Less coal is used to make more high-quality steel, and a smaller quantity of this higher-quality steel performs the same work. These interacting processes combine in reducing total coal consumption (Isard 1948; Pounds and Parker 1957).

The physical and chemical complexity and diversity of the biological and geological processes that form coal complicate its extraction and transport. Coal, a type of carbonaceous rock, forms by the accumulation of plant material in a variety of wet environments. The amounts of pressure and heat applied to the forming coal determine its quality: greater amounts of heat and pressure produce higher-quality coal. In mountainous areas, geologic forces simultaneously produce very high-quality coal and make it difficult for humans to extract the coal because of the depth of the overburden covering the coal and the frequently sharply angled and broken coal seams resulting from the formation of the mountains (McGraw-Hill 1992:47–48). The coal must then be transported across difficult mountainous terrain to consumers, another expensive operation. Thus, geology that leads to high-quality coal creates cost-increasing topography.

Multiple types of vegetation provided the original material for coal. These different vegetable species were preserved in a wide variety of environments, soil types, and humidities. Different geological processes provided varying degrees of the heat and pressure that concentrated the carbon and other combustibles into a form capable of storing the great amounts of energy per unit of matter that makes coal so useful in metallurgy. These differences create widely diverse types and qualities of coal, with different proportions of moisture, sulfur, carbon, and volatile elements. This diversity makes blending of coals to achieve precise quality control possible, but techno-logically and operationally very challenging.

In contrast, large level deposits in relatively flat areas typically consist of one or a few veins that many be many meters thick. These deposits, although often of lower quality, form in areas where relatively inexpensive open-pit methods can be used to extract the coal (McGraw-Hill 1992:47–48), making lower-quality coal much cheaper to extract but often less useful for steel production. The economies of scale possible from large-scale surface mines made them extremely attractive to the Japanese steel mills with their rapidly increasing scale of blast furnaces during the 1960s and 1970s.

Handling coal through multiple loadings and unloadings can pulverize the coal, and long-term storage can cause coal to combust spontaneously. The physical, chem-ical, and topographic characteristics of metallurgical coal fit more easily with the smaller loads and shorter hauls that fit river- and lake-based iron and steel industries, such as in the United States and Western Europe. In order to establish a steel indus-try of unprecedented scale using ocean-based sources, the Japanese steel firms and the Japanese state needed to invent and coordinate new blast furnace firing techniques with solutions to the peculiar handling and storage problems that coal posed for ocean transport in very large ships.

Further, river- and lake-based systems historically fitted their blast furnaces to the characteristics of particular coal deposits. U.S. and European blast furnace operation in the 1950s depended on highly skilled and experienced labor to achieve consistent quality of output. Japanese steel plants so increased the scale of smelting, in combi-nation with the distance and international boundaries between smelters and their coal sources, that the Japanese needed to devise technologies and organizations that fitted different types of coal to standardized blast furnace operation. They achieved this by developing new ways of blending coal to very precise specifications, including the incorporation of computer controls. This technology required the Japanese steel firms to control precisely the type and quality of coal coming from each separate source. They gained this control by negotiating new forms of international contracts with their multiple sources. They devised these techniques in order to "stretch" very expensive U.S. metallurgical coal with lower-grade Australian coal, but ultimately they perfected and extended what they had learned so as to blend a "universal" coal from multiple global sources.

The precise specifications of metallurgical coal restrict the numbers of available deposits and make access far more problematic. To be competitive, a steel industry must have access to good metallurgical coal. The U.S. steel industry's access to huge volumes of very high-quality Appalachian coal resolved the coal quality issue for the United States. However, the very high cost of transporting this Appalachian coal to

Japan, the major source in the years immediately following World War II, made total reliance on this source uneconomic, while few similar high-quality coals existed in other areas of the world and commanded a price premium.

The Japanese steel mills worked to develop process control technologies that allowed the blending of a variety of coals with different properties to create a mixture that could meet the needs of the growing scale of blast furnaces in Japan. During the late 1950s and early 1960s, the Japanese steel mills blended high-quality U.S. metallurgical coal with a range of coals from Australia. However, labor strife in Australia and the continued high cost of importing U.S. coal because of limitations on the size of ships that could load at Hampton Roads, Virginia, led the Japanese steel firms to search for alternative coal sources. The Japanese perfected the negotiating strategies and improved the transport technologies that gave them access to Australia and then created arrangements with major new sources in southeastern British Columbia and in other nations.

The capital investments needed for the mining and transport of these precisely specified coals from multiple sources greatly exceeded what the Japanese steel mills could finance through direct investments. In overcoming their capital shortage, Japanese firms used long-term contracts, state-sector-firm associations, and joint ventures in the process of revising and perfecting contractual forms that the Australian and U.S. firms and states initially required. They developed strategies and bargaining skills that devolved much of the capital risk onto the individual exporters. International contracts and large-scale shipping required diplomatic and financial support from the state and depended on joint ventures between competing Japanese steel firms. The need for extensive interfirm collaboration for the diplomatic, financial, and technical innovations that supported this collaboration extended and deepened the generative dynamic of the Japanese steel industry.

Creating the Initial Formulation of the New Model in Australia

Obtaining access to Australian coal in the late 1940s and early 1950s became the first major step in creating the raw materials supply system to sustain Japan's economic ascent. The U.S. State Department, U.S. Military Occupation Forces in Japan, the Japanese steel firms, and the Japanese state worked together initially to buy Australian coal indirectly, via U.S. military procurement channels, and then to establish direct short-term and then long-term supply agreements with Australian coal producers.

Japanese steel-based development plans depended on finding a way to stimulate and organize extraction and transport from a diversity of new sources, some as yet undiscovered, on adapting and diffusing new technologies of iron and steel production, and on revolutionizing the technology and lowering the costs of coal transport. These tasks required organizational, strategic, economic, and geopolitical innovations from the Japanese state, Japanese financial institutions, and the Japanese steel, shipbuilding, and shipping firms. These innovations transformed coal from one of the world's most regional industries, with only 132 million tons traded internationally in 1960 (almost all within the same geographic region), into one of the most global industries, with 494 million tons traded internationally in 1997 (see table 4.9).

In the process of making it global, the Japanese steel firms and the Japanese state also made it more competitive, and so lowered its costs. Japanese long-term contracts, joint-venture investments, and ocean transport innovations transformed Australia into the world's largest metallurgical coal exporter and Japan's most important source of metallurgical coal. The Japanese strategies first developed to foment Australia-Japan coal trade reduced the real cost per ton of metallurgical coal imported into Japan from US$86.65 in 1959 (in 1992 dollars) to US$43.63 in 1998 (see table 4.5).

For the steel industry, bulk, weight, and distance create most of coal's transport cost, but interrupted supply creates even greater costs because of high capital costs of unused capacity and operational inefficiencies of unexpected changes in coal types. The Japanese steel firms had to gain access to metallurgical coal from reliable sources. They also had to overcome the resentments and distrusts carried over from Japan's aggressive raw materials diplomacy and conquest before and during World War II. They then had to develop ocean shipping technology in the form of huge bulk carriers that could transport coal and iron ore to Japan at low cost. Finally, they had to convince local and international firms and local governments to develop specific mines, railroads, and ports and to commit a specified amount of coal to Japanese steel firms. Japanese firms complemented these internationally focused efforts with systematic attempts to reduce the amount and the cost of coal used per ton of steel.

The search for sources of coking coal for the steel industry became the pioneering effort in establishing Japan's raw materials access strategies based on state-sector-firm cooperation and support from the existing hegemon. Repeated cooperative efforts by the U.S. and Japanese governments in the late 1940s and early 1950s failed to adequately reintegrate Japan into the Southeast Asian economy due to political and military conflict in the region, anti-Japanese sentiment, European colonial powers' resistance to a loss of trade with their Asian colonies, and other Asian nations' nationalist efforts to promote development (Borden 1984:115–212). The Japanese steel mills needed an alternative to very high-grade but very expensive U.S. metallurgical coal nearer to Japan.

In the late 1940s, the supply of thermal coal for residential heating and electricity generation for homes and industries, on the one hand, and the need for metallurgical coal for the steel industry, on the other, constituted the most pressing issues facing the U.S. Occupation Forces and the Japanese government. During the late 1940s and the 1950s, coking coal imports came almost exclusively from the United States; the United States supplied 81 percent of Japan's metallurgical coal needs between 1949 and 1959 (see table 4.3). U.S. metallurgical coal CIF, or Cost, Insurance and Freight (the total cost of buying the coal and shipping it to Japan), in Japan in 1959 cost US$18.94, while Australian metallurgical coal cost only US$13.95, a savings of 26 percent (see table 4.4). Much of Japan's steam coal imports also came from the United States, again despite the high cost of long-distance transport and the need to pay for these imports in scarce dollars. However, because metallurgical and thermal (also termed steam) coal are both forms of bituminous coal and form via similar processes, these two types of coal often occur in the same geologic formation and even in the same mine. This natural characteristic meant that one region's coal deposits could potentially supply the coal needed for both heat generation and metallurgical processing.

Gaining access to the metallurgical coal needed for steel production faced a wide range of obstacles. No well-developed world market for metallurgical or steam coal in the late 1940s and early 1950s existed on which Japan could rely for spot purchases of rapidly growing amounts of coal. No coal firms planned exploration or mine development anywhere in the world that could meet Japan's growing coal needs. Known reserves in existing coal-producing regions could not meet projected demand growth, creating a need to bring new mining regions into production. No shipping technology adequate to move tens of millions of tons of coal and iron ore thousands of miles to Japan existed. Japan's actions in World War II made Japan extremely unpopular with other Pacific Rim nations, making nations in the region unwilling to allow either Japanese direct investment or trade with Japan. Additionally, from the end of World War II until the early 1970s, Japanese firms and the Japanese economy as a whole lacked the capital resources necessary to supply large-scale foreign investment in raw materials extraction (Anderson 1987; Ozawa 1986), with strict government controls on foreign exchange and investment activities in place throughout the period. In short, the prospects for acquiring access to coal and other raw materials during this period appeared quite dim. The Japanese steel mills and the Japanese government in the 1950s did, however, have three tools to solve this problem: extensive experience blending low-quality domestic coal with high-quality U.S. coal in blast furnaces to reduce costs, strong support from the U.S. government for Japanese industrialization, and a coastline amenable to ocean shipping.

The eastern coast of Australia, only 3,600 nautical miles of sailing distance from

TABLE 4.3
Japanese Metallurgical Coal Import Volume
(in millions of metric tons)

	Australia	United States	Canada	South Africa	China	Former USSR	Total
1956	0.02	2.4	0	0	0.5	0.07	3
1957	0.2	3.5	0	0	0.3	0.2	4.3
1958	0.2	2.5	0.005	0	0.1	0.3	3.2
1959	0.4	3.1	0.08	0	0	0.3	3.9
1960	0.9	4.3	0.4	0	0	0.4	6.2
1961	2	5.3	0.5	0	0	0.8	8.6
1962	2.6	5.4	0.5	0	0.2	1	9.6
1963	2.9	5.1	0.6	0.0	0.1	0.9	9.6
1964	4.5	5.4	0.7	0.0	0.2	0.8	11.7
1965	6.5	6.6	0.8	0.0	0.4	1.1	15.5
1966	7.5	7.2	0.8	0.0	0.6	1.3	18.0
1967	8.5	11.0	0.8	0.0	0.6	2.2	24.0
1968	11.8	14.7	0.9	0.0	0.1	2.4	30.9
1969	15.5	19.1	0.9	0.0	0.0	3.1	39.9
1970	15.0	25.9	4.3	0.0	0.0	2.5	48.8
1971	16.6	18.5	7.8	0.0	0.0	2.4	45.4
1972	20.6	15.5	7.7	0.1	0.0	2.4	48.5
1973	24.8	15.4	10.3	0.1	0.1	2.6	55.8
1974	22.8	25.5	9.6	0.2	0.0	2.9	62.6
1975	21.7	22.4	9.3	0.2	0.0	3.0	61.0
1976	26.3	14.5	8.4	1.4	0.0	3.2	64.3
1977	27.0	14.4	11.4	2.7	0.0	2.7	59.3
1978	24.2	10.0	10.9	2.4	0.0	2.2	50.9
1979	27.0	14.0	9.8	2.4	0.0	1.9	56.7
1980	25.9	19.4	10.8	2.8	1.0	1.9	62.2
1981	29.2	21.8	9.3	2.7	1.1	1.1	65.3
1982							
1983	28.2	14.8	10.4	3.1	1.5	1.5	59.7
1984	29.7	15.1	15.2	4.6	1.3	1.6	67.9
1985	30.1	12.8	17.2	4.6	1.2	2.8	69.2
1986	27.9	11.5	15.9	5.2	1.2	4.2	66.4
1987	28.6	8.9	15.4	4.2	1.3	5.2	63.9
1988	28.9	12.8	18.4	3.9	1.3	5.2	71.1
1989	30.0	10.1	17.7	3.5	1.2	5.5	68.7
1990	29.6	9.6	17.6	3.4	1.3	5.5	67.6
1991	35.7	9.9	17.5	3.3	1.7	3.7	74.5
1992	32.2	9.1	14.1	3.3	1.6	2.7	64.5
1993	32.9	8.4	14.5	2.8	1.6	2.9	65.0
1994	31.2	6.8	15.3	3.1	1.7	2.9	63.2
1995	31.6	7.6	15.1	3.2	2.2	3.0	65.4
1996	31.7	5.8	15.9	2.7	3.1	2.8	65.5
1997	33.1	5.0	16.0	2.2	3.1	2.4	65.4
1998	31.6	4.6	15.2	1.9	3.0	2.3	62.8
1999	37.9	2.1	13.6	0.5	2.4	2.2	63.2
2000	40.7	1.0	12.1	0.3	3.3	2.4	64.7
2001	36.8		9.5		5.6		57.2

SOURCES: All data for 1963–68, 1977, and South Africa, China, and former U.S.S.R. 1963–77 estimated from Panda 1982:96 and USBM/USGS, *Minerals Yearbooks;* IEA 1983:176 for 1978–81; IEA 1992:302 for 1983–91; IEA 1995:I; IEA 2001:II.

the coast of Japan, provided a potential solution to both needs. Both kinds of coal existed in Australia, most of it undiscovered. The Australian state and mining firms active in Australia lacked incentives to explore for it. However, Australian firms and the state governments of New South Wales and Queensland in the early 1950s sought ways to increase steam coal exports to generate export revenues, economic growth, and employment and resolve a crisis of excess capacity and declining production and employment (Fisher 1987; Panda 1982).

The Australians distrusted Japanese reliability and did not plan to export metallurgical coal, the type of coal critical to Japan's steel industry and therefore its heavy-industry-based development plans. From 1951 onward, U.S. State Department and other government officials in Australia promoted the idea of exporting metallurgical coal to Japan. The United States actively supported World Bank loans for Australian coal mines (Whittington 1953b). U.S. diplomats also consulted extensively with Australian businessmen and politicians known to favor expanded mining and export of Australian coal (Lee 1952; Smith 1952; Whittington 1953a, 1953b).

These U.S. efforts to gain Japanese access to Australian metallurgical coal finally succeeded when the United States devised a means of avoiding the politically sensitive problem of exporting to Japan. The Japanese Procurement Agency, a part of the U.S. Army occupation government of Japan, contracted for 100,000 tons of coking coal from Queensland in 1953 (Lee 1953a). Delivery began in 1955 and opened the door for constructing a new coal-supplying periphery for Japan. The U.S. government, pursuing its Cold War goal of rebuilding Japan, used its considerable economic and political leverage to win over a potential raw materials exporter; to appeal to citizens and firms interested in exporting raw materials, the United States funded politically acceptable forms of trade relations that did not initially involve foreign direct investment by Japanese steel firms. The Japanese steel firms and MITI watched and learned well.

This export of metallurgical coal in 1955 set an important precedent for Australian exports to Japan. Australian mining firms became willing to consider exports to Japan because of decreasing domestic demand for coal due to the substitution of petroleum in electricity generation, locomotive power, and furnace oil (Fisher 1987; Peterson 1955). The Australian national government and the state government of New South Wales sought to resolve the crisis of excess capacity in the state's coal industry via negotiations between the Joint Coal Board (a joint agency of the national and New South Wales governments created to deal with the "coal problem"), the U.S. military, the U.S. State Department, and the Japanese government to sell steam coal to Japan (Fisher 1987). The interests of the U.S. and Japanese governments and Japanese steel mills in rebuilding Japan's economy centered on metallurgical coal, and this goal quickly displaced the initial Australian goal of steam coal exports.

By 1959 the Japanese steel mills and Australian coal mines signed contracts to export 3 million tons per year of metallurgical coal from New South Wales during the first five years of the 1960s (Fisher 1987:172–73). Australian exports increased to 6.6 million tons in 1965, 16.5 million tons in 1970, and 24.9 million tons in 1973 (see table 4.3). The market opportunity in Japan and the support from the U.S. and Australian governments and the World Bank led Australian and foreign mining firms to invest in exploration in Australia, resulting in the discovery of huge new volumes of metallurgical coal reserves.

These initial sales to Japan in the mid-1950s opened the door to another major development in the Australian coal industry: the rapid growth of Queensland as a coal-producing and coal-exporting state. As early as 1953, the Japanese government engaged in negotiations supported by the U.S. government to buy coal from Queensland because of the huge potential in that state for metallurgical coal production via lower-cost surface mining (Lee 1953a). One U.S. government official argued in 1953 that the development of the Blair Athol metallurgical coal mine and the railroad infrastructure needed to export the coal depended on signing a long-term contract with Japan, because this would provide the incentive for American mining firms, including potentially the Utah Construction Company, to invest in this and other metallurgical coal deposits. Another U.S. official stated that the Australian government did not want Japanese equity investment in the mine, but might consider Japanese funding for capital equipment from Japanese trading firms and the Japanese ExIm Bank, with a further possibility of the World Bank investing US$20 million (Lee 1953b). A shortage of pounds sterling in Japan to pay for metallurgical coal imports could be overcome by arranging "a 'switch deal' under Section 550 of the Mutual Security Act, whereby we [the United States] might supply surplus cotton to Australia (chargeable to the Japanese program) and turn over the pound proceeds to Japan to help them buy Australian coal" (Lee 1953b:3).

As the result of this encouragement, Queensland developed rapidly as a coal-producing state, eventually surpassing New South Wales. This rapid growth created ongoing concerns beginning in 1970 about competition between producers in the two states and the ability of the Japanese steel mills to play the producers off against one another to buy coal more cheaply (Fisher 1987:186).

Changing technological and economic conditions in resource-rich Australia and extensive efforts by the existing hegemon thus helped to pave the way for the establishment of a long-term supply relationship between Japan and Australia. As a result, the Australian coal industry experienced a growth period from 1961 through 1982

(Fisher 1987:180). The Japanese steel firms exploited this situation by identifying firms and state governments most favorably disposed to promoting coal exports. As these individual actors became more invested in exports, they and their competitors increased political pressure and capital commitment to natural resource exports to Japan. The cumulative impacts of these processes in the late 1940s and 1950s created a new raw materials supply relationship critical to Japan's rapid economic ascent during the 1960s and early 1970s.

Refining and Expanding the Coal Access Strategy, 1960–1973

The Japanese successes at inducing new mines snowballed. Between 1955 and 1965, Japan's share of total Australian coal exports increased from a mere 4.4 to 94.4 percent (Raggat 1968:335), making Australia extraordinarily dependent on Japan as the purchaser of almost all of Australia's coal exports. Long-term contracts between the Japanese steel mills and Australian and transnational coal-producing firms formalized and expanded the initial trade fomented by SCAP, the U.S. State Department, and the World Bank. These contracts supported the development of a rapidly growing number of metallurgical coal mines during the 1960s and early 1970s (Frost 1984:51; Koerner 1993:77; Panda 1982:94; W. Scott 1979:15).

The Moura metallurgical coal mine in Queensland, opened in 1961, began the transition from exporting mainly from existing mines to developing new mines dedicated to export to Japan via long-term contracts (Koerner 1993). Theiss Brothers, a Queensland company, developed the initial project and signed a long-term contract for exporting 184,000 tons per year (increased to 500,000 tons in 1962) to Japan. Two other firms soon became partners in the mine (Frost 1984; Koerner 1993): Peabody Coal from the United States, diversifying its mining operations into a rapidly growing producing area, and Mitsui, a Japanese trading company seeking to guarantee long-term supplies of metallurgical coal, the first and only Japanese direct investment in Australian mining, smelting, and refining by 1964 (McKern 1976).

The partners, led by majority-owner Peabody, confronted a serious problem: a lack of transport infrastructure at the Queensland government-owned port of Gladstone and a Queensland government-owned railroad line that could not carry enough coal to meet the expanded demand of 1.5 million tons per year by 1968 (an amount doubled again by the end of the 1960s). The national government lent Queensland A$400,000 in 1962 to improve the Gladstone harbor, but the railroad problem required a private solution: Peabody Coal paid A$13 million of the A$15 million cost of a new rail line as advance freight charges (Frost 1984; Koerner 1993), although McKern (1976:70) reports that the company paid only A$14.8 million of the A$27.5

million cost of the railway. The Moura mine became a template for state-firm cooperation in funding the provision of infrastructure to support coal exports.

Moura also established another important characteristic of Japanese investment in Australian resources: "its extraordinary low rate of profit return, averaging about 2 per cent or less. This is because Japanese investors have not been primarily motivated by profit. . . . their main motivation has been to secure assured supplies of low-cost high-quality raw materials and to seek markets for Japanese capital equipment" (Panda 1982:128). The mine paid royalties of A5¢ per ton and freight charges varied from A$2 to A$3 per ton depending on volume (McKern 1976:70). Later agreements with the Japanese steel mills were not as generous to the mining firms involved (McKern 1976:70).

Another U.S. firm, Utah Development Corp., undertook the largest expansion of Queensland's metallurgical coal capacity during the 1960s. After signing an initial contract for 1.3 million tons per year of coal over ten years from its Blackwater mine project, Utah provided an A$5 million refundable shipment guarantee to enable the Queensland state-owned railroad to upgrade the rail line to Gladstone, and Utah built its own spur to its mine site. This mine paid a higher freight rate on a ton-mile basis; the Queensland government used these higher freight rates to capture a greater share of the rent from coal export than just that from the royalty (Frost 1984; McKern 1976). In 1965 Utah signed a contract for 22.4 million tons of coal to be exported to Japan over ten years (McKern 1976:217), paying the same A5¢ per ton royalty as Moura, but a higher freight rate (McKern 1976:70–71).

At its Goonyella mine, Utah Development and its Japanese partner in Central Queensland Coal Associates (CQCA), Mitsubishi, contracted to export 85 million tons of coal between 1971 and 1983, built their own coal port at Hay Point, and paid tonnage guarantees (Frost 1984) equivalent to the cost of the line (McKern 1976:71) to the Queensland state-owned railroad, which built a 201-kilometer rail line for A$37 million. This rail line also served three other mines developed by CQCA during the 1970s. Other firms also built their own railroad spur lines connecting their mines to the main line in the early 1970s (Frost 1984). By 1989 CQCA owned five of the nine largest coal mines in Australia, with capacities ranging from 5.4 to 6.6 million tons per year each. Utah opened a total of five new mines in central Queensland between 1967 and 1976 with a capacity of 17 million tons per year based on long-term contracts and, in most mines, minority (15 percent in the mid-1970s) Japanese investment (Koerner 1993). An Australian subsidiary of British-owned RTZ, CRA, in the 1960s bought the Blair Athol mine, the first mine developed with U.S. and World Bank support in the 1950s to supply the Japanese market (Dyster and Meredith 1990:247).

In New South Wales, both the state-owned Joint Coal Board mines and foreign-owned coal firms developed export capacity at existing mines during the 1960s. Clutha Development (100 percent owned by Daniel Ludwig, the U.S. shipping magnate who operated the NBC shipyard in Japan discussed in chapter 3), bought several existing mines, mainly to export coal to Japan. Two Australian subsidiaries of British mining companies, RTZ and Consolidated Goldfields, also bought mines during the 1960s, mainly with the goal of exporting to Japan (McKern 1976:68).

The long-term contracts signed during the 1960s typically covered 10 to 15 years of specified annual quantities of coal, with a plus or minus 10 percent option for the buyers with six months' notice. These contracts "carried no provision for price negotiations but included escalation clauses which allowed producers to pass on virtually all increases in cost to the buyers" (Panda 1982:97). The Japanese steel mills could adjust for fluctuations in demand via the 10 percent option, and the Australian coal producers sought to adjust to these fluctuations by developing alternative spot sales markets (Panda 1982:97). Australian coal saved the Japanese steel firms money in comparison with more expensive U.S. coal; the average CIF savings per ton ranged between US$3.85 and US$14.25 between 1960 and 1972, a savings range of 22 to 53 percent (this average does not take into account quality differentials; see table 4.4).

These contracts with Australia did not seek to minimize costs during this period, as evidenced by the escalation clauses. These clauses provided an incentive and guarantee to mining firms in Australia to undertake these capital intensive investments that allowed Japan to diversify away from its dependence on the United States. Australia and the United States competed for market share leadership in coal exports between 1965 and 1975, but Australia has remained the single largest exporter of metallurgical coal to Japan since 1975 (see table 4.3).

Several important differences between coal production in Queensland and in New South Wales emerged by 1970. The government of New South Wales played a much larger role in the industry as a direct producer of coal and as a manager of trade via the Joint Coal Board (Fisher 1987). The two most important coal producers, the Joint Coal Board and BHP, both based in New South Wales, increased their coal output and investment during the 1960s (Dyster and Meredith 1990:246) but still declined in relative importance as new firms entered the industry. The majority of coal production in New South Wales came from higher-cost underground mines (the maintenance of employment in these higher-cost mines caused the "coal problem" of the 1940s and 1950s), whereas most coal production in Queensland came from much lower-cost surface mines (Fisher 1987). New South Wales also charged a much higher per ton royalty than did Queensland; during the 1960s, New South Wales charged up to A25¢ per ton royalty on metallurgical coal for export, while Queensland charged royalties of only A5¢ per ton (McKern 1976:72).

TABLE 4.4
Average CIF Values of Metallurgical Coal Imports to Japan
(in US$ / metric ton)

	Australia	United States	Canada	South Africa	China	Former USSR	Average
1963	13.39	17.79	14.46	0.00		14.57	16.80
1964	13.24	18.21	14.42	0.00		14.52	15.70
1965	13.42	18.48	14.34	0.00		14.54	15.70
1966	13.06	18.57	14.36	0.00		14.46	15.71
1967	13.01	18.67	15.00	0.00		14.34	15.56
1968	12.95	18.79	15.34	0.00		14.09	15.99
1969	13.60	19.51	15.72	0.00		14.48	16.69
1970	15.42	26.26	16.60	0.00		15.75	21.32
1971	16.07	27.47	20.04	0.00		18.37	21.36
1972	17.47	28.88	21.07	17.28		19.52	21.97
1973	21.48	33.42	22.88	19.31		21.29	25.64
1974	32.87	74.45	35.20	40.47		39.49	50.99
1975	44.02	70.22	54.03	44.89		53.87	56.16
1976	51.91	70.41	60.58	42.06		55.52	59.09
1977	54.06	72.37	58.80	42.73		54.94	59.06
1978							
1979							
1980	59.59	81.27	62.16	53.14	55.81	58.10	66.40
1981							
1982	68.22	83.96	70.77	67.17	68.64	71.02	74.42
1983	63.36	78.82	70.16	57.88	56.10	59.98	67.76
1984	59.04	70.94	69.53	50.98	52.16	52.25	63.09
1985	54.36	68.67	67.51	49.62	51.17	54.69	59.77
1986	52.82	64.71	66.65	46.99	47.22	52.73	57.42
1987	48.27	64.05	65.43	43.35	43.31	48.63	53.97
1988	48.30	60.34	67.37	42.55	46.05	50.14	55.05
1989	52.58	63.34	69.73	47.68	52.08	54.65	58.39
1990	55.27	66.90	71.27	50.11	54.38	57.45	60.72
1991	56.64	66.16	71.85	51.94	53.22	56.86	60.61
1992	53.55	63.68	70.98	52.36	51.66	55.80	57.86
1993	51.49	61.82	67.12	46.78	50.52	54.37	55.39
1994	47.89	59.34	64.65	46.93	47.03	51.80	51.91
1995	51.15	61.37	64.49	49.54	49.49	54.81	55.03
1996	54.07	61.05	64.44	50.94	51.88	57.21	56.39
1997	52.73	61.24	64.84	49.64	49.98	57.09	55.19
1998	49.47	59.53	59.73	47.06	46.78	54.63	50.98
1999	41.83	55.79	51.05	39.74	40.01	45.17	42.95
2000	39.01	52.69	45.46	39.99	37.12	43.62	39.46

SOURCES: IEA 1992:307 for 1983–91; IEA 2001:I.74 for 1980, 1982, 1992–2000; Panda 1982:101 for 1963–82.

Coal producers in the two states competed for Japanese coal export contracts, often leading to severe price competition that benefited the Japanese steel mills (Fisher 1987:186; Koerner 1993), an outcome (first recognized in the early 1970s) that led to lower prices for Australian coal than for U.S. coal, even after adjustment for quality differentials (McKern 1976:184); this problem continues today.

The Queensland surface mining firms and the state of Queensland effectively sacrificed an important share of the differential rent from their more favorable natural mining conditions and resulting higher labor productivity and lower costs in an on-going effort to gain market share and earn a higher total volume of profit via expanded production, rather than maximizing rent. This strategy benefits Japanese steel mills and helps ensure the maintenance of long-term excess capacity in the metallurgical coal industry. The microeconomic logic is clear: lower-cost producers expand production because their marginal costs are lower than competitors. This strategy ignores the consequences for industry structure of this seemingly rational behavior in the face of a strategically acting cartel of buyers (the Japanese steel mills): the Japanese steel mills signed long-term contracts and made small equity investments with low profit potential to ensure steady, long-term supplies of low-cost coal that simultaneously provided a lever to drive down market prices (e.g., the 50 percent real reduction in metallurgical coal import costs CIF to Japan) and secured more favorable contract terms with other producers. This diversification strategy in turn provided a lever to secure more favorable terms with the Australian producers, who continue to follow a standard but badly flawed microeconomic strategy of expanding production in the vain hope of forcing higher-cost producers out of the industry.

The coal producers in New South Wales negotiated an important change in their coal contracts in 1970, providing for yearly pricing negotiations. The large Queensland coal companies considered this too risky and instead continued to rely on informal annual discussions about prices without altering other contract terms during most of the 1970s (Panda 1982:97). This contractual change sought by the New South Wales coal firms eventually became increasingly problematic for the coal producers and advantageous for the Japanese steel firms. The Japanese steel firms, supported by the Japanese government, undertook an intensive campaign of bringing new suppliers in other countries into production in the 1970s and 1980s to reduce their dependence on Australia and increase their bargaining power in negotiations with their Australian suppliers.

During this same period between 1960 and 1973 and at the same time that Australia-Japan metallurgical coal trade expanded so dramatically via long-term contracts, the Japanese steel mills began efforts to further diversify their sources of supply using the Moura model. The Soviet Union supplied between 5 and 10 percent of Japanese metallurgical coal imports between 1958 and 1973, and Poland, China, South Africa, Taiwan, and West Germany also exported small amounts to Japan during this era. The most important diversification effort, however, focused on western Canada, an effort that increased Canada's share in Japanese imports from 0.1 percent in 1958 to 19 percent by 1973 (see table 4.3).

The Japanese steel mills' interest in western Canadian metallurgical coal resulted from a combination of three factors: the continued rapid growth of Japanese metallurgical coal demand, the desire to diversify supplies away from dependence on Australian sources frequently threatened by labor strife, and the high-quality metallurgical coals produced by the mountainous topography and geology of western Canada. This coal could be transported via existing rail lines to the west coast of Canada. Large-scale transport required developing two new deepwater ports, one at Vancouver and the other just south of Vancouver at Roberts Bank on an artificial island.

Canada already had a long history as a coal producer, similar to Australia prior to Japanese involvement. However, Canadian anthracite and bituminous coal production declined from 16 million tons in 1949 to only 9 million tons in 1969. Coal mining in western Canada first became a possibility in 1885 with the discovery of coal in the Elk Valley along the Fording River, the site of several current major mines, and the first coal mining took place in the late nineteenth century. The Canadian Pacific Railroad Syndicate conducted much of the initial exploration and staking of claims in the region in the first years of the twentieth century; the syndicate's holdings would eventually become a Canadian Pacific coal mining subsidiary, Fording Coal. At the end of the 1960s, the Canadian Pacific used the geological evidence collected at the beginning of the century as the basis for new investigations whose favorable results led to the signing of one of the first long-term contracts with the Japanese steel mills (*Free Press*, June 23, 1991:14).

Coal production in British Columbia faced total extinction by the early 1960s, a crisis of even direr proportions than the "coal problem" in New South Wales. The signing of three-year contracts in the mid-1960s for 1 million tons per year between the Japanese steel mills and a longtime local coal company owned mainly by investors from Seattle, Crowsnest Industries, demonstrated the high quality and large amounts of coal available in the region. In the late 1960s, Kaiser Resources (a partner in an iron ore mine in Australia that already supplied the Japanese market) bought this mine and signed a long-term contract with the Japanese steel firms in 1968, beginning a new boom in coal production in western Canada (Coal Task Force 1976:21). Kaiser Resources, a subsidiary of U.S.-based Kaiser Steel Corporation (66.6 percent of equity) and its joint-venture partners Mitsubishi Corporation and the Japanese steel firms (total of 33.4 percent of equity) signed a fifteen-year contract for 5 million tons per year of metallurgical coal (Koerner 1993:77). By 1991 this joint-venture Balmer mine became the largest coal mine in the world (MEMPR 1992:33).

This initial investment in Canada, while relying on a long-term contract to supply metallurgical coal to Japan, also exposed a trading company and the Japanese steel companies to a larger share of the financial risk of the project than the Australian Moura and Utah model. Given the fact that the Japanese steel mills accepted a significant share of the equity risk in the Balmer mine, the existence of a long-term contract for supplying the Japanese steel mills, and the generally favorable coal prices during the 1970s, the Balmer mine earned significant profits (*Canadian Mines Handbook / Canadian Mining Handbook, 1980 – 81* 1980:137).

The Japanese steel mills signed long-term contracts with three new open-pit mines in western Canada soon after. These three mines, Luscar, Smoky Hills, and Fording River, all followed the Australian post-Moura and post-Utah model, with the Japanese role limited to the long-term contract, and all began production between 1969 and 1972 (*Canadian Mines Handbook / Canadian Mining Handbook, 1993 – 94* 1993: 219 – 20, 317 – 18; Fording Coal 1993).

These long-term contracts in Australia and Canada embodied the state-sector-firm coordination so critical to the development of the Japanese steel industry. The long-term contracts linked all the Japanese steel mills, putting them on an equal footing in terms of coal access and cost, and providing an important mechanism for MITI to coordinate steel capacity and production.

Long-term contracts, limited equity investments, and supply diversification strategies gained access to coal sources in Australia and Canada, but this coal then needed to be moved to the new steel mills in the MIDAs in Japan. The Japanese steel firms' agreements with Australian coal mining firms and state governments in Australia depended first on the construction of rail links from the mines to the coast. The Japanese used long-term contracts and their own projections of rapid growth of consumption in Japan to encourage mining. They then used the prospect of mine traffic and stimulated competition between different states to induce the state governments to invest in railroads and ports to support these mines. Once one state agreed to do so, mine operations put pressure on other state governments to follow suit. The Queensland state-owned railroad used loans and advance freight payments from the mines to build the rail infrastructure (Frost 1984:49 – 53).

Railroads built to export mineral production must articulate with maritime transport. This requires construction of appropriate port facilities. Vessel size offers the greatest savings in the next stage, ocean transport of exported coal, and the Japanese steel firms required large ports to handle such vessels. Prior to the 1960s, the combination of the relatively low price of coal and the high cost of transporting such a high-volume and low-value cargo greatly restricted the coal trade. The Japanese achieved significant reductions in ocean freight rates by designing, constructing, and promoting the use of large capesize bulk carriers. The dramatic growth in ship capacity made economically possible the rapid increase in international trade in coal since the early 1960s. Japanese shipyards produced a very large share of the new, much larger ships that carry coal around the world, while long-term contracts for and sometimes small equity investments in new mines by Japanese firms stimulated the construction of many new large ports in many areas of the world.

In 1979 the cost of building a coal-loading port of 20 to 25 million metric tons per year throughput capacity was estimated in 1979 U.S. dollars to be $6 to $8 per ton, or $120 million to $200 million, while operating costs typically totaled 5 to 10 percent of the total capital investment (WOCOL 1980:178). Japanese-led globalization of coal markets and Japanese-led increases in dry bulk cargo ship sizes directly determined the scale and design of these ports. These high port throughputs typically require only one or two berths because their equipment loads very large ships very rapidly. This scale of ports effectively limits them to serving only very large bulk shipments. The low value-to-volume ratio and the very large quantities of coal needed to fill these large ships makes a high rate of port throughput essential, while the characteristics of coal make the fastest bulk handling methods available (e.g., the piping of liquids such as petroleum or the pneumatic loading of grains and very fine ores) unsuitable for coal handling. Instead, lumpy coal must be loaded using a combination of dumping railroad cars and conveyor systems to load ships.

Competitive global access to coal, therefore, requires large ports and efficient loading systems in both exporting and importing countries. The Japanese aggressively initiated such projects at home and abroad, but paid only for the domestic ports. Mining companies often built and operated the port facilities in both Queensland and New South Wales, as was the case for the Moura, Blackwater, Goonyella, and other Queensland mines developed during the 1960s; in some cases, state governments built and operated ports (Frost 1984; IEA 1992:109; Tex Report 1994a:552–55). Japanese diplomatic efforts and mining company pressure induced state governments to build other ports, including Abbot Point, Dalrymple Bay, Auckland Point, and Clinton (IEA 1992:109).

In Canada, a privately owned railroad firm, the Canadian Pacific Railroad, and the formerly national-government-owned Canadian National Railway built railroad links to the coal mines, gaining in return large volumes of coal export traffic. Investments totaling hundreds of millions of dollars during the 1980s led to "the creation of one of the world's most advanced coal-hauling systems especially designed for long distances and mountainous terrain" (Coal Association of Canada 1993:41). As one Canadian National executive stated, "our costs per ton per kilometer are among the lowest in the world" as a result of this integration of loading, railroad, and unloading facilities (Coal Association of Canada 1993:41). This highly efficient coal hauling system required the overcoming of a number of significant natural obstacles to cross the mountainous terrain of southern British Columbia, including filling in a swamp and the construction of the longest railway tunnel in the Western Hemisphere at a total cost of C$500 million (George 1991:18–21). One industry publication noted that "at almost $15 million a kilometer ($24 million a mile), it may be the most expensive section of railway track in the world. But, it's worth every last nickel, says the railroad" (*CoalTrans*, January–February 1993:29).

Two coal ports opened in 1970 to export coal from southeastern British Columbia and Alberta, Neptune Terminal in Vancouver and Westshore Terminal south of Vancouver at Roberts Bank. The Canadian government reclaimed the land for both ports, although the mining companies built and owned the ports themselves. The location of Westshore Terminal exposes ships loading there to the weather, resulting in berthing costs twice as high as at the very sheltered Neptune Terminal in Vancouver harbor. However, the sheltered Vancouver harbor restricts the size of the cargo that can be loaded onto large bulk carriers there; very large bulk carriers sometimes top off cargoes partially loaded at Neptune Terminal at the more accessible Westshore Terminal (interview with Neptune Terminal Executive, September 30, 1993).

Westshore Terminal represents a social solution to the lack of a naturally produced larger capacity port site in southern British Columbia near existing rail infrastructure: an incredibly expensive artificial island built at Canadian government expense makes possible large-scale exports of coal to Japan at a higher in-port but lower overall voyage cost because of the economies of scale in ocean bulk shipping. These economies of scale for Japanese consumers who purchase the coal FOB (Free On Board, a cost that includes buying the coal from the mine and shipping it to the port) could only be captured, however, via Canadian government subsidization of port construction. In order to take advantage of the naturally produced coal wealth of southeastern British Columbia, the Canadian government spent a huge amount of money to build the artificial island in the hopes that this would make it possible to earn export revenues, create jobs in the mining region, and produce higher tax receipts from production and exports. A very significant share of the benefits from the construction of the island accrue to Japanese firms and consumers and not to Canada.

To create a third secure source of metallurgical coal, the Japanese steel mills signed a long-term contract in 1971 to import 3 million tons per year of metallurgical coal for twelve years from South Africa from 1975 to 1987. This contract provided the basis both for the dramatic expansion of coal mining capacity in South Africa and for the construction of a rail line to the coast and a new coal port at Richards Bay by the South African government (IEA 1987:9–10) at a cost of US$800 million (Sullivan 1981:114). The mining companies received very favorable tax treatment: the mine was not taxed until the capital investment was recovered. The major mining companies operate the port, but the national government owns the port (IEA 1987:9–10). South Africa's role in the world coal industry expanded significantly during the late 1970s and early 1980s.

The Japanese steel mills, with the assistance first of SCAP and later of the Japanese state, thus devised a model of long-term contracts to guarantee long-term secure access to metallurgical coal from Australia that could be transferred to other regions. This new model accommodated the resource nationalism of host nations. It fundamentally altered the nature and composition of the world metallurgical coal industry, transforming metallurgical coal flows from domestic movement from captive mines to their steel mill owners to transoceanic trade flows governed by long-term contracts. Domestic and transnational firms assumed the capital cost and risks of opening up previously unexploited metallurgical coal deposits. Deposits that had not even been explored for earlier because of the tremendous distances between these deposits and potential markets suddenly became highly attractive. The Japanese steel mills used the market opportunities in Japan, long-term contracts, and small equity investments as tools to induce mining firms in Australia and Canada to invest repeatedly in creating excess capacity in the world industry, driving down prices and the production costs of the Japanese steel mills. The Japanese steel mills refined this model during the 1970s and early 1980s in ways that made these long-term contracts and the newly globalized coal industry even more favorable to the interests of the Japanese steel mills.

The Oil Price Shocks and Metallurgical Coal, 1973–1985

The oil price shocks of 1973–74 and 1979–80 affected the metallurgical coal and steel industries and the Australia-Japan coal relationship in contradictory ways. On the positive side from the Australian perspective, coal prices increased as part of an oil-led increase in energy prices. The average CIF metallurgical coal price in Japan in real terms (in 1992 U.S. dollars) increased from US$80.14 in 1974 to US$162.76 in 1975 (see table 4.5), motivating intense efforts by the Japanese steel firms to reduce coal costs. Further, firms, governments, and international organizations, led by the newly formed International Energy Agency, projected dramatic increases in coal demand after the first and especially the second oil price shock (Fisher 1987). These projections caused an upsurge in coal investment globally and in Australia.

On the negative side for both Australian coal producers and the Japanese steel mills, coal production costs increased because of general inflation in wages and prices. Further, inflation and currency instability made long-term contractual relations acrimonious. In relation to Australia-Japan coal trade during the early 1970s, "Japanese

TABLE 4.5
Japanese Metallurgical Coal Prices
(in US$ / metric ton CIF in January)

	Average	1992 US$/ton
1959	18.00	86.65
1960	17.23	81.76
1961	16.99	79.75
1962	16.93	78.54
1963	16.26	74.50
1964	15.79	71.43
1965	15.73	70.05
1966	15.44	66.74
1967	15.67	65.91
1968	15.88	64.06
1969	16.34	62.50
1970	20.16	72.86
1971	21.53	74.60
1972	21.90	73.50
1973	21.33	67.40
1974	28.16	80.14
1975	62.43	162.76
1976	58.49	144.24
1977	58.68	135.84
1978	59.75	128.52
1979	61.16	118.22
1980	62.75	106.86
1981	68.71	106.02
1982	74.97	109.01
1983	73.66	103.79
1984	62.87	84.94
1985	62.17	81.07
1986	58.90	75.36
1987	55.35	68.36
1988	53.94	64.03
1989	57.27	64.83
1990	59.37	63.76
1991	61.87	63.73
1992	59.17	59.17
1993	58.45	56.76
1994	51.77	49.03
1995	54.47	50.17
1996	56.68	50.73
1997	55.51	48.52
1998	50.74	43.63
1999	42.95	
2000	39.46	

SOURCES: Tex Report 1994a; U.S. EIA 2006.

buyers tended to take unfair advantage of the oversupply situation by enforcing not only tonnage but also price reduction, without paying sufficient regard for long-standing contractual provisions for the well being of the overall business relationship" (Panda 1982:98).

Conflict increased in the Australia-Japan metallurgical coal relationship during the mid-1970s during the Whitlam Labor government. Previous governments in the 1950s and 1960s promoted domestic and foreign investment in raw materials for export as an economic development strategy (see, e.g., *Engineering and Mining Journal*, January 1970:69–72, for a statement from the Gorton government in the late 1960s; McKern 1976 for an overview of government minerals policy from the 1940s through the 1970s). The growth of Australian coal exports, concerns about the adequacy of returns to Australia, and concerns about the rapid expansion of foreign ownership of Australian minerals led the Whitlam government to undertake a variety of measures to increase Australia's benefits from the coal trade via a policy of resource diplomacy (McKern 1976; Panda 1982:11–17). The federal government intervened in the 1974 coal price negotiations and forced a 19 percent price increase over what the Japanese steel mills and Australian coal producers had negotiated. In 1975 the government sought another large price increase, conducted government-led negotiations in Japan that increased Australian coal export tonnage (but at a lower price than that paid for U.S. imports, angering the Australian coal producers), and imposed an excise tax of fifty cents per ton on coal exports as part of efforts to impose export controls and regulate export contracts for minerals (Anderson 1987; Fisher 1987:188–91; Panda 1982:99–100).

The Whitlam government lost power in December 1975 in a controversial political maneuver when the political opposition blocked the federal government's spending ability in response to a plan to borrow funds from Arab oil-producing states to buy a share of Australia's minerals industries. The largely ceremonial governor-general then dismissed the prime minister, appointed the opposition leader as prime minister, and called an election (*Chicago Tribune* 1991:10), a move called a coup d'etat by one Australian analyst (Fisher 1987:191). Australian resource policies did not change significantly in the late 1970s and early 1980s, except to impose a more systematic form of export controls over coal and iron ore in 1978 that required firms to gain approval for the basic parameters of their export contracts from the federal government before entering into negotiations with customers, a requirement opposed by the state government of Queensland (Anderson 1987; Bambrick 1980:167–68). These policies encouraged the Japanese steel mills to further diversify away from high rates of dependence on Australian coal and other resources because of the at least partially successful efforts of these policies to improve Australian producers' negotiating position via government coordination (Anderson 1987; Fisher 1987:191; Koerner 1993; Panda 1982:17).

Despite these conflicts, the expansion of coal production for export to Japan continued during the 1970s and early 1980s. Between 1972 and 1975, the Japanese steel firms and Australian coal mines signed long-term contracts for a total of 238.9 million tons (Australian Bureau of Mineral Resources, Geology and Geophysics 1977:17;

Frost 1984; USBM/USGS 1973b:497, 1974b:527). In 1980 these parties signed contracts for another 100 million tons, and the Japanese steel firms signed contracts in Canada for another 46.5 million tons (USBM/USGS 1981b:578). Australian ports lacked capacity to meet increased demand for coal exports during the late 1970s and early 1980s, and the state governments of Queensland and New South Wales and the coal mining firms planned to spend US$800 million to increase coal port facilities (Sullivan 1981: 113–14). A new coal terminal in Newcastle, New South Wales, opened in 1984 at a cost of US$238 million for the first stage, designed for loading on ships up to 180,000 deadweight tons (dwt) (*Coal Age,* November 1986:58–60). Port Warratah Coal Services, a 70–30 Australian-Japanese joint venture, linked the coal producers, their Japanese partners, and the Joint Coal Board (Sullivan 1981:114).

In Queensland, the companies that owned four of the mines in the Bowen Basin developed a new coal terminal at Hay Point. The Queensland government owned the terminal and paid a large share of the $250 million cost, but a consortium of the mining companies managed the port (*Bulk Systems International,* May 1985:55–59; Sullivan 1981:114). At Gladstone, port capacity at Clinton was expanded by a new $400 million loading facility and the port was deepened to accept 120,000-dwt ships (Sullivan 1981:114). These investments in ports for which we have been able to obtain data total US$1.058 billion just during the late 1970s and early 1980s. Including the costs of earlier developments and further expansions in the past two decades, the total investment in ports by state governments probably totals US$2–3 billion.

The increase in demand for Australian coal initiated a process of restructuring in the Australian coal industry. BHP, one of Australia's largest industrial and mining firms, bought Peabody Coal's share of the company that owned the Moura mine in the late 1970s (W. Scott 1979:15) and the coal mines owned by Utah Development in the early 1980s (IEA 1984:8), making BHP the leading coal-exporting firm in Australia. The Japanese trading companies and steel mills also increased their role in the Australian industry (IEA 1984:8). Mitsubishi acquired 40 percent of Hogan and Gorman Pty. Ltd., owner of the Ulan coal deposits, in 1979 (W. Scott 1979:13).

Australia-Japan coal negotiations in the late 1970s changed one of the most important provisions of the long-term contract arrangement: "in July 1978, Japanese steel mills threatened to cut purchases of coal substantially unless the Australian companies gave up the inclusion of escalation clauses in the sales contracts. . . . Japan argued that Australian sales prices were not moderate enough to justify escalation clauses. It was also argued that cost increases should be shared equally between the buyer and the seller. Escalation clauses held out disadvantages to local consumers as they had to pay for higher costs facing the producers and in many cases the higher costs were the result of the producer's own inefficiencies. It was also argued that escalation clauses encourage uncompetitiveness of the Japanese steel industry, which in turn would cause hardship for the Australian coal industry" (Panda 1982:100). Metallurgical coal export contracts shifted during the early 1980s away from base price plus escalation to regular reviews of prices and quantities, including annual price negotiations. Many of these contracts have no price, no contract provisions, which in effect render the contracts short-term, because failure to agree on a price frees the buyer from the obligation to purchase any coal from the producer. This shift to annual price negotiations opened the door for the Japanese steel mills to take full advantage of the excess capacity that their long-term contracts and equity investments during the 1970s, 1980s, and 1990s created.

Most important, the two oil price increases and their resulting impacts on world economic growth by the early 1980s produced sharply divergent results for Australian coal producers and the Japanese steel mills. Demand for metallurgical coal fell far below projections (Fisher 1987:192) because of global recessions of mid-1970s and early 1980s due to energy price increases. This development led to a sharp increase in excess capacity based on overly optimistic projections of coal demand by the IEA in the early and mid-1980s (Fisher 1987:195–201) and set the stage for the conflictual relations between the Japanese steel mills and their suppliers in Australia, Canada, and other nations over the past two decades, as the Australian state and coal producers expanded production to meet wildly overoptimistic demand forecasts (Fisher 1987:201–4).

Other analysts, including Barnett (1985), Koerner (1993), and other Australian researchers, argued that the Japanese steel mills sought explicitly to foment excess capacity at least since the early 1980s: "it is also possible that the supremacy of the Queensland prices in 1983 and 1984 is yet another reflection of the Japanese strategy of paying relatively high prices in the early years of new projects. The overall Japanese strategy seems to be aimed at maximizing the supply sources of coal and their preferential pricing has certainly encouraged the development of new mines" (Barnett 1985:446). Diversification efforts at very high initial prices also characterized the next round of Japanese long-term contracts in western Canada, further exacerbating the problem of excess capacity in the globalized coal industry.

At the end of the 1970s, the Japanese steel firms returned to western Canada in search of additional supplies of metallurgical coal. Long-term contracts brought five more Canadian metallurgical coal mines into production between 1981 and 1984. These five mines exhibited two distinct patterns of Japanese involvement. One mine, the Line Creek mine, followed the earlier pattern in which the Japanese steel mills signed only a long-term contract (MEMPR 1992:37). The second pattern involved both long-term contracts and direct Japanese investment in these mining projects. The Greenhills mine included both a long-term contract with the Japanese steel firms and joint-venture ownership involving several Japanese firms and Pohang Iron and Steel Corporation of South Korea (*Canadian Mines Handbook / Canadian Mining Handbook, 1980–81* 1980:137). The Gregg River Mine in Alberta involved a private Canadian firm (60 percent equity) and a consortium of Japanese firms (40 percent equity) (*Free Press*, June 16, 1991:2).

Japanese policies of supply diversification and long-term contracts also created a new mining area in northeastern British Columbia. These two new mines, Quintette and Bullmoose, produced high-quality metallurgical coal (MEMPR 1989:17). However, the naturally produced mining conditions of this high-quality coal made mining extremely difficult, because these "coal seams are in many places highly disturbed by thrust faults, normal faults and intense folding. In almost every case it is almost impossible to lay out a comprehensive mining pattern to enable maximum extraction rate to be achieved" (Ball 1976:580). These challenging coal seam characteristics presented huge and costly problems for mining in northeastern British Columbia, especially the Quintette mine.

The total cost of developing the Quintette and Bullmoose mines in northeastern British Columbia, including infrastructure, totaled US$1.9 billion, with the Canadian and British Columbian governments contributing US$1.2 billion of the total (IEA 1984:18). These coal mines required the construction of lengthy new railroad connections, upgrading of existing railroad main lines, and the construction of a new port, all funded by the Canadian federal government and British Columbia's provincial government. The provincial government provided US$500 million for the construction of the B.C. Rail line connecting the mine to existing rail lines and US$95 million for the construction of the town of Tumbler Ridge in the mine area, out of its total US$700 million contribution. The Canadian federal government spent US$500 million, including US$235 million to upgrade the existing federally owned Canadian National Railway lines and US$230 million to build the government owned Ridley Island coal port (USBM/USGS 1988b:11, A-6).

The government of British Columbia provided a huge operating subsidy for coal transport from the mines. In order to recover the capital and financing costs of the provincial government's US$500 million contribution, the freight rate for the total 250-kilometer trip would have needed to be more than US$16 per ton, rather than the US$4.85 ton rate agreed on as part of the negotiations for the mine. The federal government's interest in building a major new Pacific coast port to relieve the burden on the already extremely busy Vancouver port and the provincial government's interest in stimulating economic development in remote northeastern British Columbia and in creating additional revenue for provincially owned B.C. Rail, in addition to both governments' interest in promoting exports and the creation of jobs and tax revenues, led to the provision of tremendous subsidies to these projects for exporting coal to Japan.

South African coal exports to Japan also increased during the late 1970s and early 1980s. The Richards Bay coal terminal grew rapidly from a relatively small port into one of the world's largest coal-exporting ports; by 1992 Richards Bay had an annual capacity of 53 million tons per year, could accept ships of 190,000 dwt, and had a 5-million-ton stockpile capacity (IEA 1992:112). The initial Japanese long-term contract in 1971 brought on stream this major port serving one of the world's major metallurgical- and steam-coal-exporting nations. Another important function of the port developed in the late 1970s: topping off capesize ships that could load only around 60,000 tons of cargo in the United States at Hampton Roads, Virginia, to full loads for the voyage to Japan. This helped to reduce the cost of importing high-quality U.S. coal by lowering the overall cost per ton by using larger ships. Further, in 1984 one large South African mining company, Gencor, succeeded in negotiating an agreement to ship its coal to Japan CIF, referred to as "something of an industry breakthrough" (*Bulk Systems International,* March 1984:19). This highly unusual agreement resulted from the Japanese steel mills' extensive efforts to diversify sources of supply during this era. Trade sanctions against South Africa during the late 1980s, however, hindered the ability of South African coal mining firms to export to Japanese and other global markets.

The Japanese steel mills sought to expand metallurgical coal supplies from the Soviet Union in the early 1970s. In 1974 the Japanese steel mills and the Soviet Union formed a joint venture for a surface mine in eastern Siberia at a cost of US$450 million to export 8 million tons per year of metallurgical and steam coal to Japan, and Japan helped fund the development of a new coal port on the Pacific Ocean (IEA 1984:25–27). The Japanese steel mills also sought to expand metallurgical coal trade with China in the early 1980s, including funding the modernization of two coal ports (IEA 1984:23).

By 1982–83 the world steel industry had a high degree of excess capacity, as did the world metallurgical coal industry (Fisher 1987:216). However, foreign direct investment by the Japanese steel mills and Japanese trading companies continued to expand during this period. In 1975, 18.9 million tons of coking coal imported into Japan (31 percent of total Japanese imports) came from mines involving Japanese equity participation; this increased to 30.2 million tons (40.8 percent) by 1988.

Despite the difficulties of the period between 1973 and 1985, the new mines built and contractual patterns established during this period created a global industry that greatly benefited the Japanese steel mills and the Japanese economy.

Restructuring, Excess Capacity, and Expansion in a Mug's Game, 1985–2006

In Australia, despite the steady decline in real coal prices (from US$109.01 CIF in Japan in 1959 to US$43.63 in 1998 in constant dollars; see table 4.5), Australian and transnational mining firms continued to expand investment in and capacity for metallurgical coal exports. One of Australia's largest firms, Broken Hill Proprietary (BHP) consolidated its position as a leading coal and mining firm (Dyster and Meredith 1990:285). BHP bought several smaller coal mining firms over the past two decades, including the purchase of QCT Resources in a partnership with Mitsubishi at a cost of US$894 million in 2000 (Lyday 2001:1), and the purchase of Billiton's coal operations in 2001, consolidating its position as the world's leading exporter of metallurgical coal with 30 percent of the global export market (Platts 2002).

Other restructurings of Australia's metallurgical coal industry occurred in recent years. After Shell's coal mining subsidiary steadily expanded its holdings in Australia in the 1980s and 1990s, Shell sold it to Anglo American for US$850 million in 2000 (Lyday 2001:1), creating a new leading metallurgical coal exporter. In another major ownership change, Rio Tinto, already a leading coal exporter, bought the Australian mines of Peabody Group for US$555 million in 2000 (Lyday 2001:11); Peabody had been one of the earliest entrants into the Australian coal export business to Japan in the 1960s. Rio Tinto also bought Arco Resources' Australian mines in 1999 (Wyatt and Nakamoto 2000). Other major takeovers during 1999 included RAG of Germany's purchase of Portman Mining's Burton mine and Glencore's purchase of Cyprus Coal of Australia (Wyatt and Nakamoto 2000). In 2002 Xstrata of Switzerland purchased Glencore for US$2.5 billion (Wallace 2002), making Xstrata a leading coal exporting firm in both Australia and South Africa.

This extensive process of ownership restructuring created four major metallurgical coal producers, BHP, Rio Tinto, Xstrata, and Anglo American, and one significant medium-size producer, MIM Holdings. In the face of this consolidation and effort to improve the coal exporters' bargaining positions, the Japanese steel mills increased their reliance on smaller independent Australian coal-exporting firms, including Macarthur Coal, Centennial Coal, and Austral Coal (Heathcote 2002:41). Macarthur announced plans to open three new metallurgical coal mines within four years (*AAP Newsfeed* 2006). This clearly reflects Japanese strategies since the 1970s of bringing new producers into operation in order to reduce the bargaining power of existing large suppliers.

This ownership restructuring did not slow the development of new mines in Australia, despite the financial difficulties of many coal mining firms. Australia's position overall as the world's lowest-cost metallurgical coal exporter and the weak Australian dollar combined to make Australian mining firms attractive takeover targets (Wyatt and Nakamoto 2000). In Queensland during 2000–2001, twenty major mine expansions and new mines were under development or in the planning phase, and nine firms were engaged in a variety of exploration activity (Queensland Department of Natural Resources and Mines 2001:4–13). In New South Wales, thirteen new mines or major expansions opened or were underway during 2000–2001 (Haine 2001:654). In 2002, seven more mine projects totaling 27 million tons of capacity were completed, and another twenty-five coal projects totaling 116 million tons of capacity were planned for completion between 2003 and 2007 (Chadwick 2002:106).

Lower production costs in comparison to other major coal producers provided the main incentive for Australian metallurgical coal producers to expand production. In 1985 Barnett (1985b:468) estimated the break-even cost for new Queensland coking coal mines at US$38.80 FOB, new southern British Columbia mines at US$57.10, the Bullmoose mine in northeastern British Columbia at US$62.60, the Quintette mine in northeastern British Columbia at US$79.40, and U.S. Appalachian medium volatility coal producers at US$63.00 and low-volatility producers at US$58.00.

In western Canada, coal mines opened in the early 1980s restructured and merged repeatedly during the past fifteen years in the face of low prices and excess capacity. A Canadian mining company, Teck Corporation, took over the Quintette mine after the project accumulated a C$700 million debt (*Elk Valley Miner,* July 23, 1991:15), but Teck could not return the mine to sustained profitability and closed the mine in 2000. At the Bullmoose mine, also majority owned by Teck, restructuring efforts returned the mine to profitability after the dramatic price declines of the 1980s, but the exhaustion of economically recoverable reserves meant that the mine closed in 2003.

The ending of trade sanctions against South Africa in 1991–92 allowed South African coal mining firms to greatly expand exports to Japan and other markets. South African mining companies historically produced coal at very low cost and used this cost advantage (*CoalTrans,* September–October 1992:50) and transport cost advantages of a large-scale port located on a major sea route to Asia to restore its role in the Japanese and world coal markets.

In response to this global metallurgical coal overcapacity, the world's two largest metallurgical coal exporters, BHP in Australia and Fording Coal in Canada, successfully cooperated to force up coal prices in the mid-1990s, despite the consumer market power held by the Japanese steel firms. The Japanese steel firms responded swiftly to the sharp price increase in 1995 by imposing a new pricing mechanism called the "fair treatment system" during contract negotiations for the 1996 fiscal year. The fair treatment system called for prices to be linked to the coal quality requirements of individual Japanese steel mills and for the details of the contract negotiations to remain confidential.

The Japanese firms argued "that prices could be negotiated to better reflect the value-in-use for specific quality specifications and hence improve the efficiency of price formation" (Swan, Thorpe, and Hogan 1999:17). However, "given that coal prices and other contract details remain confidential both during and after the price negotiations, it is unlikely that the efficiency of the market has been enhanced with the introduction of the fair treatment system" (Swan, Thorpe, and Hogan 1999:17). These researchers found in their econometric modeling of the relationship between coal quality and prices that the fair treatment system actually weakened the relationship between coal quality and price in these contract negotiations. In other words, the fair treatment system accomplished the opposite of what the Japanese steel firms said it was intended to do by tying prices more closely to coal quality. The fair treatment system instead reduced the ability of coal sellers to gather market information and especially to have any opportunity to work cooperatively because of negotiating secretly and individually with the still-coordinated Japanese coal buyers.

Export coal prices fell dramatically in the late 1990s as a result. Canadian coal export prices fell from C$52.80 in 1997 to C$50.50 (US$33.09) in 1998 (*Coal Age*, February 1, 1998:11) and to C$41.45 (US$27.19) for Fording Coal's exports in 1999 (*Coal Age*, February 1, 1999:13). The president of the Coal Association of Canada called this price cut "a reduction of historical proportions. . . . We haven't seen a price cut of this magnitude before" (*Coal Age*, February 1, 1999:13). New mines were delayed, hundreds of employees laid off, and some mines simply closed (*Coal Age*, April 1, 1999:11; June 1, 1999:7). In Canada, a major restructuring consolidated all existing metallurgical coal mines in the hands of one company, a joint venture between Teck and Fording Coal, in an effort to increase market power and prices (Hayes 2004; *Platts Coal Week International* 20003; Schmidt 2003).

Intense global competition and excess capacity fomented by Japanese long-term contracts lower raw materials prices and reduce or eliminate rents (as demonstrated by the halving of real costs of importing coal into Japan between 1959 and 1998 mentioned earlier), putting intense pressure on exporting firms to reduce costs or face bankruptcy. The resulting restructuring from the late 1980s through the early 2000s bankrupted firms, closed mines, and devastated communities.

The growth of Chinese steel production and consumption that created new opportunities for the Japanese steel mills also transformed the gloomy situation of coal-producing firms and regions. Rapidly growing metallurgical coal consumption by

China's steel industry transformed China from a metallurgical coal exporter to an importer in the early 2000s, a process furthered by the unreliability of Chinese coal-exporting firms that often fail to meet export contract commitments, forcing buyers to look for other sources (*Global News Wire* 2005). Chinese coal imports soaked up existing excess coal capacity and stimulated a huge investment rush in Canada, Australia, and other coal mining regions (Morrison 2004). With metallurgical coal contract prices in 2004 and 2005 exceeding US$100 per ton and spot prices exceeding US$150 per ton, the highest level in twenty-two years (AME 2004a; Wailes 2004), coal firms are reopening mines closed because of uncompetitively high costs in northeastern British Columbia and are investing in previously economically unattractive mining projects around the world, including in western Canada (Hayes 2004; Morrison 2004; Pine Valley Mining Corp. 2005; Wailes 2004; Western Canadian Coal 2005).

The China-driven boom in the coal industry provoked a variety of strategic responses by the two major Japanese steel firms. The Japanese steel mills forged even closer relations with RTZ, a major Australian supplier of both coal and iron ore, with the goal of guaranteeing long-term supplies by expanding existing mines and developing new mines devoted to the Japanese market (*AAP Newsfeed* 2003; *Asia Pulse* 2004; *JCN Newswire* 2004a) and with Anglo Coal in Australia as well (*Skillings* 2005). The Japanese steel mills also signed a new ten-year, 25-million-ton contract with Elk Valley Coal Corporation of Canada, the partnership between Teck and Fording (*Coal Age*, November 2005:6). Nippon Steel and POSCO of South Korea also invested US$25 million each to buy 2.5 percent ownership stakes in the Elkview coal mine in southeast British Columbia owned by Elk Valley Coal to ensure long-term coal supplies (*CoalTrans* 2005:8). The Japanese steel mills are also seeking to establish new supply relationships with mines in Indonesia and China (Pearson 2003).

These Japanese strategies and the opening of a number of new mines helped push down prices slightly for 2006–7. The Japanese steel mills sought a price decrease of 30 percent (*AFX News* 2006), but the large coal producers in Australia negotiated a price decline of only 8 percent (from US$125 per ton FOB to US$115) (McCloskey 2006:44).

Despite these Japanese steel mills' strategies to maintain control over the coal industry, most firms involved in the coal industry are increasingly shifting their focus to China. BHP Billiton, a leading global coal and iron ore exporter, CVRD, a global leader in iron ore, and Anglo American, a leading coal exporter, all invested in coal mining and coke production in China during 2004–5 (AME 2004b; Ng 2005). The continuing rapid growth of Chinese steel production makes this strategy a sound idea in the context of China's rapid economic ascent.

Consequences for Coal-Producing Regions

The access strategies developed by the Japanese steel mills and the Japanese state to acquire coal in increasing volumes at progressively lower cost critically supported the success of the steel and shipbuilding generative sectors and the broader process of Japanese economic ascent. In order to do this, the firms and states of coal-exporting regions paid the costs of building this global coal mining and transport system. Exporting states and firms all justified their investments as promoting local and national economic growth and capturing the benefits of raw materials industries domestically.

The huge costs and increasingly large and sophisticated technological and organizational systems of coal mining and transport could not be supported by existing impoverished raw materials peripheries in Asia, Africa, or Latin America. Instead, the Japanese steel firms and the Japanese state relied on creating relationships via long-term contracts and, at times, limited equity investment in partnership with large mining firms and the national and regional governments of nations that were part of the core or semiperiphery of the capitalist world-economy. National governments in Australia and Canada (as well as in Brazil, a key component of Japan's iron ore periphery) all emphasized domestic industrialization of raw materials and, at times, extensive resource nationalist efforts to capture the benefits of raw materials exports. Long-term contracts seemed to respect resource nationalist goals of domestic control, particularly in comparison to the wholly owned subsidiary model utilized by U.S. mining firms. Transferring the costs of creating this coal supply system to exporting states and firms resulted in a restructuring of the capitalist world-economy, with relatively highly developed raw materials exporters transferring an important part of their wealth to support Japanese industrialization. Regions within these advanced nations, such as the coal mining regions of New South Wales and Queensland in Australia and British Columbia in Canada, became disarticulated from their domestic national economies and tightly integrated into Japanese industrial systems that articulated these new raw materials peripheries with the Japanese steel, shipbuilding, and steel-consuming industries. This domestic disarticulation and integration into Japan's industrial system imposed heavy costs on these peripheries, as we show in this section.

Surface mining on a large scale to supply major customers such as the Japanese steel companies is much more capital intensive than underground mining methods. In Australian underground mining, labor costs ranged from US$6.00 to US$7.00 per short ton of raw coal, or 30 to 48 percent of total cost in the late 1980s; capital costs were only 15 to 21 percent of total costs. Surface mining, in contrast, is much less la-

TABLE 4.6
Australian Coal Mining Employment

	Number of Employees
1961	17,235
1965	15,394
1970	17,057
1975	21,505
1980	27,600
1985	31,900
1990	29,600
1995	25,800
2000	17,555
2001	18,316

SOURCES: Fisher 1987:185; New South Wales 2002; Queensland 2001:58.

bor intensive, with labor costs per ton of US$2.06 or 13.3 percent of total costs, while capital costs were 39 percent of total production costs per ton (U.S. Department of Commerce 1989:30–52). Surface mining operations in Australia, Canada, the United States, and other nations to supply the Japanese market thus employ only relatively small numbers of workers to produce millions of tons per year for export, placing an important limit on the number and value of consumption linkages from these mines, as table 4.6 shows for Australia.

Even in the most competitive exporter, Australia, work force downsizing and mine closures continued to harm coal mining workers and their communities (Grundy 2001:35). The increase in real terms in per worker costs from A$71,2000 in 1990 to A$108,200 in 2000 (Curtotti and Maurer 2001:640) justified work force reductions from the coal mining firms' perspective. In a nation with a very strong union system that historically exercised a great deal of political power and had been such a potent force that the Japanese steel mills feared overreliance on Australian coal, the shift toward a neoliberal political economy during the 1990s had devastating impacts on coal industry unions. Institutional changes that opened the door for enterprise bargaining and the weakening of industrial unions in the late 1980s and early 1990s led to a progressive weakening of coal mining unions and their loss of power in negotiations with the coal mining firms and increasing labor flexibility and control over workers by firms. Political and business elites justified these changes to increase labor productivity and reduce labor costs as increasing Australia's international competitiveness in coal and other industries (Bowden 2001; Waring and Barry 2001).

These changes also dramatically reduced the economic development benefits of coal mining as they forced down wages, reduced employment levels, and disrupted rural coal mining communities. One of the most important developmental linkages from the coal industry to the rest of the Australian economy, high wages paid to growing numbers of coal miners from the 1950s through the 1980s, declined dramatically. This reduced the benefits to Australia and the Australian people of extracting millions of tons per year of coal for export to Japan.

The large-scale coal transport system developed by the Japanese steel mills also limits the gains to exporting regions from involvement in the industry. From the Australian perspective, the combination of a long-standing system of FOB contracts for coal exports to Japan from Australia and CIF shipments to Europe from Australia is the exact opposite of the situation that would best serve Australia's interests. Barnett (1985:446–47) notes that:

> Mr. John Doherty, General Manager, Coal BP Australia has long maintained that this FOB-CIF basis is back to front to the optimum for Australia. He maintains that a supplier should sell CIF into the markets in which he has a freight advantage, for Australian coal this is the Asian market, and sell FOB into markets where he has a freight disadvantage, for Australian coal this is the European market. To benefit from this marketing pattern the supplier would need to be a price taker in the CIF market, in this case Japan, and a price setter in the FOB market, in this case Europe. It also follows that for this pricing structure to evolve it would be desirable if the seller was a minor supplier into the CIF market and the major supplier into the FOB market. However, for the Australian coal industry the market situation is the reverse of this ideal situation. A truly competitive market would see all coal sold on a CIF basis with the delivered price for similar quality coal being uniform in any particular market, and the price level in each market would be determined by the combination of FOB port and transport costs for the marginal supplier into each market. The coal trade with Japan does not meet these conditions. . . . the USA price of US$84.6 per ton CIF Japan is by far the highest, which is to be expected as the freight cost is the highest and the coal is the best quality. The range in the actual FOB prices, which range from US$68.7 per ton for U.S. coal to US$56.1 per ton for South African coal, probably reflects coal quality rather than the true marginal worth of the coal to Japan. For example, the Canadian and Australian hard coking coals are of quite similar quality and the FOB prices are similar. If this assumption is correct it indicates that, relative to the USA coal CIF prices, the Canadian coal was underpriced by US$8.6 per ton, the Australian coal by US$12.0 per ton and the South African coal by US$4.4 per ton.

Clearly, FOB shipping contracts and resulting Japanese control over shipping redounded very strongly to Japan's benefit in the course of the Australia-Japan coal trade over the past three decades.

While the pattern of coal supply relationships suited Japanese needs and initially allowed Japan to resume trade with Australia despite Australian antipathy toward Japan, this transfer of capital costs and risks proved quite deleterious to these exporting firms' and nations' interests in the long term, even though the original idea for these long-term contract arrangements came from the Australians (Priest 1993:20–25). Koerner found that "Pacific metallurgical coal markets have suffered significant distortion as a result of the resource procurement strategies of the Japanese steel industry establishment" (1993:79). The Japanese steel mills' joint negotiating strategy resulted in a bilateral monopoly, precluding competition on the demand side, whereas on the import side Japan's diversification strategy led to destructive competition between firms, state governments, and coal-exporting nations. Additionally, "the substantial transport component of delivered cost creates a situation of bilateral monopoly bargaining over the distribution of locational rents" (Koerner 1993:79), while the knowledge asymmetry between Japanese and suppliers' negotiators similarly favored Japanese interests. Koerner (1993:79) estimates that the producer surplus lost to Australian coal producers on the 365 million tons of metallurgical coal exported to Japan from the early 1960s to the end of the 1980s totaled US$3.6 billion in 1987 dollars. From 1994 through 2004, coal firms in New South Wales averaged an annual profit of only 7 percent (Goldsmith 2004:20). As another analysis of the Australia-Japan coal supply relationship concludes, "as long as Australia fails to receive a fair price for the energy resource that made the 'Japanese miracle' possible, it will never have a relationship of maturity and respect with Japan" (Botsman, Evans, and Millis 1994:4).

In our own calculation of the rent forgone by Australian coal producers and the Australian state and national governments, we compared Australian coal prices CIF in Japan with those for coal from the United States in order to estimate how much it would have cost the Japanese steel mills to have continued to rely on the United States for its coal imports, as they did in the 1940s and 1950s. On this basis, the loss to Australia in current dollars totaled more than US$10.8 billion between 1963 and 2000; in constant 1992 dollars, the total is more than US$18.8 billion (see table 4.7). This forgone rent accrued to the Japanese steel mills, steel consumers, and purchasers of products made from Japanese steel over the past four decades, conferring an important increment to firm profits and Japan's global competitiveness and representing a significant loss of mining firm profits and state revenues in Australia.

Huge investments in railroad and port facilities, typically by national and state governments in areas such as Australia, Canada, and the United States, made coal available at competitive prices to Japanese consumers and imposed additional costs and risks on exporting regions. Without these investments, Japan could not acquire enough metallurgical coal to permit the rate of growth of its steel industry in the post-

TABLE 4.7
Average CIF Values of Metallurgical Coal Imports to Japan
(in US$ / metric ton)

	Australia	United States	Difference	Australian Imports to Japan (in million tons)	Rent Forgone (in US$ millions)
1963	13.39	17.79	4.40	2.9	12.76
1964	13.24	18.21	4.97	4.5	22.365
1965	13.42	18.48	5.06	6.5	32.89
1966	13.06	18.57	5.51	7.5	41.325
1967	13.01	18.67	5.66	8.5	48.11
1968	12.95	18.79	5.84	11.8	68.912
1969	13.60	19.51	5.91	15.5	91.605
1970	15.42	26.26	10.84	15.0	162.6
1971	16.07	27.47	11.40	16.6	189.24
1972	17.47	28.88	11.41	20.6	235.046
1973	21.48	33.42	11.94	24.8	296.112
1974	32.87	74.45	41.58	22.8	948.024
1975	44.02	70.22	26.20	21.7	568.54
1976	51.91	70.41	18.50	26.3	486.55
1977	54.06	72.37	18.31	27.0	494.37
1978				24.2	
1979				27.0	
1980	59.59	81.27	21.68	25.9	561.512
1981				29.2	
1982	68.22	83.96	15.74		
1983	63.36	78.82	15.46	28.2	435.972
1984	59.04	70.94	11.90	29.7	353.43
1985	54.36	68.67	14.31	30.1	430.731
1986	52.82	64.71	11.89	27.9	331.731
1987	48.27	64.05	15.78	28.6	451.308
1988	48.30	60.34	12.04	28.9	347.956
1989	52.58	63.34	10.76	30.0	322.8
1990	55.27	66.90	11.63	29.6	344.248
1991	56.64	66.16	9.52	35.7	339.864
1992	53.55	63.68	10.13	32.2	326.186
1993	51.49	61.82	10.33	32.9	339.857
1994	47.89	59.34	11.45	31.2	357.24
1995	51.15	61.37	10.22	31.6	322.952
1996	54.07	61.05	6.98	31.7	221.266
1997	52.73	61.24	8.51	33.1	281.681
1998	49.47	59.53	10.06	31.6	317.896
1999	41.83	55.79	13.96	37.9	529.084
2000	39.01	52.69	13.68	40.7	556.776
Total					10870.939

SOURCES: IEA 1992:307 for 1983–91; IEA 2001:I.74 for 1980, 1982, 1992–2000; Panda 1982:101 for 1963–82.

war era. Although the governments and state-owned firms in raw materials regions collected taxes and revenues from these exports, and domestic and transnational firms sometimes profit from these exports, these firms and governments also bear a disproportionate share of the risks involved in making possible Japan's tremendous economic growth following World War II. The Japanese steel mills transferred a large share of the burden for meeting their coal needs to the raw materials–extracting periphery, allowing the Japanese steel mills to devote their resources to modernizing their own plants in order to compete very effectively in the world market.

The costly burden of providing subsidized rail infrastructure created ongoing losses and inefficiencies for state-owned railroads in Australia. Total public support for railroads in Australia between 1990 and 1999 was estimated at A$32 billion, while operating losses during this period just in New South Wales and Victoria totaled almost A$7 billion (Owens 2002:5, 9). The inability to resolve these problems led to the restructuring of the Queensland state-owned railroad to allow access by privately owned firms that can now compete for coal hauling and other freight contracts (Queensland Department of Natural Resources and Mines 2001:3). New South Wales, the other major coal-producing state, also restructured its state-owned railroad to allow private train operators to compete for freight contracts (Owens 2002:5–6). Freight rates in New South Wales fell by an estimated 25 percent as the result of restructuring (Curtotti and Maurer 2001:642). However, safety and financial problems continue to plague the restructured industries (Owens 2002:7).

Restructuring and privatization are changing the Australian port industry as well. The Queensland government leased the state-owned Dalrymple Bay coal port to a private firm (Queensland Department of Natural Resources and Mines 2001:3), effectively transferring a heavily subsidized port facility worth several hundred million dollars to a private operation. Port costs are estimated to have fallen in real terms from US$3.37 a ton in 1994 to US$1.70–2.60 a ton in 2000 (Curtotti and Maurer 2001:643).

Royalties provide another important developmental impact of mining. In New South Wales, surface mines pay A$2.20 a ton and underground mines pay A$1.70 a ton. In Queensland, all mines pay an ad valorem royalty of 7 percent (Hogan and Donaldson 2000:525). Total mineral royalties for all types of minerals between 1969 and 1997–98 in Australia totaled A$68 billion (Hogan and Donaldson 2000:526), but coal royalties made up only a very small share of total state receipts in the two largest coal-producing states, 1 percent of total state revenue in New South Wales and 2.9 percent in Queensland (Hogan and Donaldson 2000:526).

Even with the dramatic price increases in metallurgical coal since late 2003, Australian coal firms confront two cost challenges: the sharply rising value of the Australian dollar relative to the U.S. dollar (in which coal prices are denominated) raises their production costs (Syddell 2003), and the state government of New South Wales increased its per ton royalty on coal to 5–7 percent of the pretransport price, rather than the previous A$1.70 per ton for underground coal and A$2.20 per ton for surface mines. Australian coal firms argued in mid-2004 that, at coal prices of US$50 per ton, the new royalties would cause losses, job cuts, and firms to shift investment to neighboring Queensland (*Coal Age,* June 2004:7). The doubling and tripling of metallurgical coal prices during 2004 and 2005, however, mean that paying the royalties will be less burdensome for the coal firms and, more significantly, that state revenues will likely increase from A$200 million in 2003 (*Coal Age*, June 2004:7) to A$600–800 million or more, capturing a much larger share of the value of exported coal in the exporting region.

The Balmer mine in southeast British Columbia presents the single most striking example of the risks for raw materials–extracting nations of becoming part of Japan's raw materials periphery. Its profitability during the 1970s made it an attractive prospect for Kaiser Steel to sell first half and then all of its shareholding in the mine and its wholly owned subsidiary, the Roberts Bank coal terminal, to the provincial government of British Columbia. The provincial government sought to increase the economic and developmental benefits of exporting coal via a policy of resource nationalism.

The provincial government subsequently sold shares in the firm to the public on the Vancouver Stock Exchange with the intention of spreading the benefits from this profitable business throughout the province. The firm, Westar Group, attracted a large number of small investors, many of whom sank their life savings into this investment in a highly cyclical industry (*Business in Vancouver*, September 28–October 4, 1993:9). The price declines and excess capacity of the late 1980s created severe financial difficulties for Westar Mining, the coal mining joint venture, whose losses totaled C$107.4 million between 1987 and 1991 (*Westar Mining Annual Report, 1991:* 22). Declining Japanese prices for metallurgical coal from the Balmer mine and the newer Greenhills mine, the increasing financial costs of production resulting from the rising value of the Canadian dollar relative to the U.S. dollar (in which sales were denominated), and severe operational problems at the Balmer mine because of the decline of the main coal seam also contributed to these financial problems (*Westar Mining Annual Report, 1991:* 3,6). These financial losses, combined with a badly mismanaged investment in North Sea oil, forced Westar Mining into bankruptcy in 1992 and forced the sale of its two mines (*Business in Vancouver*, September 28–October 4, 1993:9; *Canadian Mines Handbook / Canadian Mining Handbook, 1993–94* 1993:357).

As a result, many small investors in British Columbia lost their savings, and the small mining communities of Fernie, Sparwood, and Elkford around the Balmer mine experienced both employment problems and problems in collecting taxes owed by the mines (*Elk Valley Miner*, May 28, 1991:7; *Free Press*, June 9, 1991:1). The Japanese steel firms, partners in Westar Mining, allowed Westar Mining to go bankrupt without offering the relatively small amount of capital needed (estimated at C$75 million over five years in 1991) (MEMPR 1992:34) to recuperate the Balmer mine, with devastating consequences for the Canadian small investors and mining communities that had shared the risk of providing the Japanese steel firms with an essential raw material for twenty-five years.

This presents an opportunity for examining why the Japanese joint-venture partners did not act to help keep Westar Mining solvent. Because the increasing operational difficulties at Balmer were known to the Japanese steel firms, because the Japanese steel firms were already paying higher than market prices for metallurgical coal from the new mines in northeastern British Columbia, because the long-term contracts expired soon anyway, and because there was a situation of persistent chronic overcapacity in the world metallurgical coal market as the result of heavy investments geared toward supplying the Japanese market, the Japanese steel firms had no incentives to act in the way another investor in a joint venture that was losing money but that could be resuscitated with new investments would have done—that is, to invest new capital in order to overcome the mining difficulties encountered at Balmer. The history of Balmer and Westar Mining clearly demonstrates both the potential rewards (the profitability of the 1970s) and the tremendous difficulties (the disaster of the early 1990s) involved in dealing with Japanese firms as long-term contract customers and even as equity investors.

Although the coal industry is typically seen as a low-technology holdover from an earlier era, in western Canada and in most other mining areas supplying the global coal industry created by Japan's economic ascent, the coal industry is both technologically sophisticated and highly productive. Increasingly large-scale and often computer-controlled mining equipment (Downing 2002) made the coal mines of British Columbia the world leaders in productivity per employee in the coal industry (see table 4.8). These gains in productivity as part of broader restructuring efforts in Canadian coal mining firms became key elements in the struggle of these firms and the re-

TABLE 4.8
British Columbia Coal Productivity and Employment

	Coal Produced per Employee (in tons)	Total Employment
1960		1,182
1965		649
1970	· 1,881	1,275
1975	3,230	2,763
1980	2,997	3,612
1985	3,885	5,821
1990	4,310	5,654
1995	6,451	3,800
2000	8,941	2,925
2001	9,230	2,869

SOURCE: British Columbia Ministry of Energy, Mines and Petroleum Resources: www.em.gov.bc.ca/Mining/MiningStats/33employcoal.htm.

gion's governments, communities, and workers to remain competitive in this global industry.

In response to the lower prices and intense global competition in the late 1990s, a new round of restructuring began in Canada. Even at the most productive and competitive mine in western Canada, Fording River, where productivity increased from 1,600 employees in 1977 producing 3 million tons of coal (1,875 tons per employee) to 825 workers producing 9 millions tons in 2002 (10,909 tons per employee) (Ednie 2002:13), low prices led Fording to cut another 15 percent of its work force in early 2003 (*Platts Coal Week International* 2003:9).

Some analysts estimate that western Canadian coal mining firms are the most productive overall in the world because of high labor productivity and continuous technological innovation (Downing 2002), although Australian analysts argue that Australian productivity is 13,000 tons per employee (Commonwealth of Australia 2001:3). However, these productivity levels could not counteract negative world market conditions in the late 1990s and early 2000s fomented by the Japanese steel mills. New mines were delayed, including Fording's long-anticipated Cheviot project (*Platts Coal Outlook* 2003:8; Schmidt 2003), hundreds of employees laid off at other mines, and some mines simply closed (*Coal Age*, April 1, 1999:11, June 1, 1999:7; Downing 2002). Other firms sought to use the industry's economic difficulties as an opportunity to acquire assets at low cost (Frank and Heinzl 2002; Heinzl 2002).

The China-driven boom in coal demand, prices, and coal mining firm profitability since 2003 led to new investment in coal mining in western Canada. The mines in southeastern British Columbia, now owned by a partnership of Fording Coal and Teck Corporation, responded to the boom by increasing output from existing capacity by hiring temporary and permanent workers, many of whom had been laid off during previous rounds of restructuring in the area or after the mine closures in northeastern British Columbia. The partnership, the Elk Valley Coal Corporation, had been formed to consolidate ownership, rationalize operations, lower costs, and negotiate more effectively with the Japanese steel mills than had been the case during the earlier period of fragmented ownership of mines in the area. Fording Coal's profits rose from C$150 million in 2004 to C$834 million in 2005 (*Canadian Press Newswire* 2006b). The other partner in Elk Valley Coal, Teck, earned record profits of C$1.35 billion in 2005, double the C$617 million of 2004 (Wong 2006).

However, the partnership has been reluctant to invest in new capacity because of concerns about potential future financial problems that would result in the next downturn in the industry. As a result, the firm initially hired workers as temporary contract employees at lower wages, fewer benefits, and no long-term security when the current boom began, restricting the benefits to the area's communities of the boom. Many of these temporary workers became permanent employees by 2005, but the rational firm strategy in light of the long history of boom and bust cycles in the coal industry constricts the local developmental impacts of the region's largest industry during the current boom.

High coal prices have led to a boom in coal mining investment in northeastern British Columbia, the area where the high-cost Quintette and Bullmoose mines closed a few years ago. Three new firms opened new mines in the area in 2005 and 2006: Northern Energy and Mining, Pine Valley Mining (a partnership with Mitsui Matsushima of Japan), and Western Canadian Coal Corporation (*Canadian Corporate Newswire* 2006a; *Canadian Press Newswire* 2006c; Pine Valley Mining 2005; Western Canadian Coal Corporation 2006). Two other firms will open new mines in the area soon, Hillsborough Resources and West Hawk Development Corporation (*Canadian Corporate Newswire* 2006b; *Canada Press Newswire* 2006a). Another mine nearby in Alberta that was closed due to high costs and low profitability in the 1990s has also been reopened (*Canadian Corporate Newswire* 2006d). In southeastern British Columbia, a new coal mine is expected to open in 2007, owned by yet another new entrant into the industry (*Canadian Corporate Newswire* 2006a).

These seven new entrants are undermining the concentration of ownership and exports built by the Elk Valley Coal partnership in their effort to increase prices and profits. The huge profits available with coal prices exceeding US$100 per ton offer tremendous short-term profit potential, but this investment rush will lead in the medium and long terms to a new situation of excess capacity and low prices, with the attendant harm to coal-producing regions, firms, states, and populations.

Despite the impressive gains in labor productivity, the social return on extraction in the region for the firms involved and for the region as a whole remain relatively small, while consumers of the region's coal captured most of the gains through the mechanism of lower real prices for metallurgical coal. The situation of excess capacity in the world metallurgical coal industry that developed largely in response to Japanese long-term contracts and Japanese investment in the expectation of rapidly growing demand for metallurgical coal led to an important transfer of value from producing firms, regions, and laborers, whose wages should have increased at a rate commensurate with the dramatic increase in labor productivity.

The disastrous western Canadian experience with Japanese investment and long-term contracts during the 1990s may be a portent of the future for other extractive regions that export natural resources to Japan: when natural and market conditions turn against a particular extractive region, often due to the strategic actions of the Japanese state and Japanese firms to reduce their raw materials costs, the economic and social impacts of Japanese reaction and adaptation to these changed conditions may be devastating. The current boom in demand and prices based on the Chinese steel industry is improving conditions in coal-producing regions somewhat, but the current investment rush may create the same problem of excess capacity within a few years.

Japanese Coal Strategies and Their Consequences

This Japanese coal access strategy dramatically restructured and globalized the coal industry. Conventional wisdom assumes that rapidly expanding demand stimulates exploration and may lead to dramatic revision upward of known reserves. The incorporation of new sources involves far more than market forces. Exploration requires faith in cross-national respect for and transparency of rules. Exploration is not the most costly stage of most mineral extraction, but it is the most risky because of the high likelihood of failure. Without guarantees of rights to reserves, companies will not prospect. The Japanese state and Japanese steel mills convinced initially recalcitrant foreign countries to promote exploration.

These Japanese efforts resulted in the tremendous increase in known reserves of coal. In 1962 the World Power Conference estimated total world coal reserves (anthracite, bituminous, sub-bituminous, and lignite) at 572.7 billion metric tons (Brubaker 1967); by 1989 British Petroleum estimated that world total coal reserves were 1,174 billion short tons (IEA 1990:279), or more than twice as large, despite world coal production from 1962 to 1989 of 97,881 million metric tons.

Japanese access strategies transformed world coal trade as well. While world hard coal production increased by 77 percent between 1960 and 1990, world hard coal exports increased even more rapidly, by 202 percent. The share of hard coal production exported also increased significantly, from 6.7 percent in 1960 to 11.5 percent in 1990.

As table 4.9 shows, world coal trade is geographically concentrated: only three countries exported 53 percent of world total hard coal exports in 1960, 67 percent in 1981, 63 percent in 1990, and 54 percent in 2000. While the United States remained an export leader throughout the period, the identities of the other two world leaders changed between 1960 and 1981, with Australia and South Africa replacing the U.S.S.R. and Poland; Australia by 1990 became the world's leading hard coal exporter on the basis of the coal supply relationship with Japan.

The volume of world coal trade as measured by the ton-miles traveled by oceanborne coal trade and by the average distance traveled by each ton of exported coal from the exporting to the importing country also increased dramatically, as table 4.10 shows.

The ton-miles traveled by oceanborne coal exports increased between 1966 and

TABLE 4.9
World Hard Coal Trade
(in millions of metric tons, with % of total in parentheses)

	1960	1970	1981	1990	2000
World exports	132.0		271.6	398.8	573.6
United States	34.8(26)	65	102.1(38)	96.0(24)	53.0 (9.2)
Australia	1.7 (1)	19	51.0(19)	106.1(27)	186.8(32.6)
Canada	0.9 (1)	4	15.7 (6)	31.0 (8)	31.7 (5.5)
South Africa	1.0 (1)	1.3	29.2(11)	49.9(13)	69.9(12.2)
Colombia	0 (0)	0	0 (0)	13.9 (4)	34.5 (6)
Former USSR	14.7(11)		22.0 (8)	28.1 (7)	30.5 (5.3)
Poland	21.0(16)	29	15.0 (6)	18.0 (5)	23.7 (4.1)

SOURCES: Gordon 1987:48; IEA 1982, 1992, 1998.

TABLE 4.10
*Oceanborne Coal Trade Measured
by Distance Traveled*

	Billions of Ton-Miles	Average Distance Traveled per Ton
1966	226	3,705
1970	481	4,762
1976	591	4,653
1980	952	
1990	1,849	
2000	2,509	4,800

SOURCES: *Fearnleys Review* 1991 cited in UNCTAD 1992:3; *Fearnleys
World Bulk Trades* 2001:24–25.

1991 by 743 percent. This indicates both the dramatic expansion of oceanborne coal exports from new coal-exporting countries, including Australia, South Africa, Colombia, and Indonesia, and the increase in the average distance each ton travels; this distance increased by 25.6 percent between 1966 and 1976. In the second half of the twentieth century, coal increased faster than any other major cargo in terms of ton-miles in international seaborne trade (*Fearnleys Review* 1991 cited in UNCTAD 1992:3). This increased coal trade underlay Japanese industrial ascendancy and resulted from specific Japanese strategic actions in both coal mining and transport.

Without dramatic changes in the world coal and shipping industries, driven by Japanese raw materials access strategies, the Japanese steel industry could never have become the world's leading steel industry and a generative sector for the Japanese economy. We have estimated the cost and equipment requirements of transporting 99.2 million tons of metallurgical and steam coal imported into Japan during 1991 from its four largest coal suppliers, Australia, the United States, Canada, and South Africa, comparing transport in the 25,000-dwt ships of 1966 with 125,000-dwt ships of 1991. The cost in 1980 U.S. dollars would be $985 million using the smaller ships, but use of the larger ships reduces the total cost to $353 million, a saving of 64 percent. Using a smaller number of larger ships also reduces transaction, loading, and route management costs. Japanese coal importers almost always take delivery of coal FOB from the exporting port and arrange shipping themselves, reducing their shipping expenses through the use of associated shipping lines or the chartering of outside ships in periods of low freight rates. This strategy produces a striking physical advantage in moving the 469 billion ton-miles of coal transport in larger ships. With 25,000-dwt ships, at any point in time there would be 412 ships on the world's oceans either heading toward or away from Japan in the coal trade; using 125,000-dwt ships, this number falls to only 83. This 80 percent reduction in the number of ships in the Japanese coal trade clearly represents a significant reduction in port congestion at both ends of the coal supply chain.

While this example is extremely hypothetical, the point is clear: transport innovations greatly reduced the transport costs of coal and increased Japanese competitiveness. Chapter 6 examines in greater depth the "virtuous circle" of steel, shipbuilding, and shipping as generative sectors of the Japanese economy.

The experience gained from accessing coking coal in Australia with minimal Japanese capital investment laid the foundation for the tremendously successful program for diversifying sources whose capital expenses were largely met by exporting states and firms: the "ABC policy (Australia, Brazil, and Canada) . . . a term applied to describe this approach, and to recognize the need for vigilant management of security of supply, quality, and delivery. . . . the strategy has been clear: supply basic intermediate feedstock materials to downstream assembling and processing manufacturing industries at the lowest possible cost" (McMillan 1985:79–80). This model, in various forms and combinations (Ozawa 1986), since the late 1940s provided the material foundations for Japan's economic ascent. The challenge of gaining access to Australia's metallurgical coal began a learning process for the Japanese state and the Japanese steel mills on how to create the raw materials supply relations to support industrialization. Australia became the first major raw materials supplier directly dependent on Japanese markets; Brazil and Canada became during the 1960s the other two major pillars of Japan's raw materials supply chains. Locationally, topographically, and politically, these countries presented very different sets of problems and opportunities for Japanese raw materials access strategies. In learning how to respond to and exploit these differences, the Japanese state and Japanese firms developed highly useful flexibility and agility that later served them well in other countries.

In summary, the Japanese steel mills and the Japanese government, with initial support by the existing hegemon, the United States, restructured the world metallurgical coal industry to supply low-cost metallurgical coal to Japan, while transferring the vast bulk of costs and risk to mining firms and state and national governments in Australia and, later, in Canada, South Africa, and even in the United States itself. The new combination of large-scale mines and large-scale transport facilities, while reducing the cost per ton of production and transport, greatly restricted the markets available for these mines' production, because these low costs depend on the utilization of large ships that can berth only in a very small number of ports outside Japan. The coordination of Japanese steel firms in negotiating prices for metallurgical coal, the high capital costs of these mines that make sales even at a loss essential in order to service high debt loads, and the construction of dedicated infrastructure by extractive states and firms all combine to give Japanese steel firms tremendous advantages in bargaining over purchase terms with coal producers. This restructuring of the world coal industry provided a fundamental material and economic pillar of Japan's rise as an industrial power and challenger to U.S. economic hegemony.

In the late 1990s the efforts by the leading Canadian and Australian coal-exporting firms to take advantage of their dominant supplier positions via coordinated bargaining again challenged Japan's power in this relationship. The coal-exporting firms had learned from the Japan-driven process of globalization and flexibility and sought to take advantage of a new negotiating strategy. The Japanese steel mills and the Japanese state responded quickly and very effectively to this challenge. The current China-driven boom in the coal industry creates new challenges for the Japanese steel mills, but, based on past experience, the Japanese steel mills may be able to overcome these challenges as well.

The restructuring and reworking of the model of raw materials access pioneered in the coal industry represents an incredibly sophisticated process of learning and adaptation to changing and often adverse conditions by Japanese firms and the Japanese state via restructuring one of the world's most localized industries into one of the most truly global industries. The globalization of industries and markets means that successful ascendant economies have to be more astute, learn more about more diverse places, create tighter coordination on the importing side, and more generally create a model of state-sector-firm coordination that is much more complex than in earlier historical cycles. The challenges confronting China, the most important case of economic ascent in recent years, to replicate and expand upon the Japanese model are thus even greater than those overcome by Japan during the post–World War II era.

CHAPTER FIVE

Replicating Japan's New Model in Iron Ore

Iron Ore and the Japanese Steel Industry

The Japanese steel industry in the late 1940s and early 1950s confronted the same problem with iron ore that it did with coal: how to gain access to and transport to Japan large quantities of bulky, low-value ore. For the first fifteen years after World War II, however, no easy solution could be found. Japanese iron ore production provided only a tiny part of this rapidly growing demand, and iron ore imports expanded rapidly (see table 5.1). As discussed in chapter 3, scrap steel outweighed iron ore as the "raw material" for Japanese steel production until the early 1960s. Shortages and quality limitations of scrap, combined with U.S. efforts to encourage and help fund the development of an iron ore–based integrated steel industry in Japan (Tiffany 1988), pushed the Japanese steel firms toward increased reliance on iron ore imports. The Japanese steel firms relied on a diverse set of six suppliers in Asia, Latin America, and Africa with widely varying iron ore qualities and relatively expensive extraction and transport costs during the 1940s and 1950s. This complex and difficult-to-manage system would be radically transformed during the mid-1960s.

To secure supplies of iron ore, the Japanese steel mills and the Japanese state gradually replicated the strategies and trade relationships developed to resolve the challenge of coal supplies. The Japanese state and steel mills promoted exploration of new areas, pushed new transport technologies and infrastructure, and devised new contractual and rent forms that significantly reduced their equity participation and capital risk. As in the coal trade, their emerging strategy tended to create competition between suppliers within a market characterized by excess capacity. This essentially prevented large mining firms from restricting supply in order to keep ore prices high. The Japanese state and steel mills devised strategies and instruments to restructure the world industry and its transport characteristics so that they revolved around and favored Japanese steel mills and MIDAs. These strategies reduced Japan's real average

TABLE 5.1
Japanese Iron Ore Production and Imports
(in millions of tons)

	Iron Ore Production	Iron Ore Imports	Annual Rate of Import Growth	Iron Ore Net Import Dependence Ratio
1946				
1947	0.3	0		0
1948	0.3	0		0
1949	0.3	0.5		63
1950	0.4	1.6	220	80
1951	0.8	1.5	−6	75
1952	0.6	3.1	107	84
1953	0.7	4.8	55	87
1954	0.9	4.3	−10	83
1955	0.9	5	16	85
1956	0.9	5.5	10	86
1957	1.1	7.9	44	88
1958	1.3	9.5	20	88
1959	1.1	7.6	−20	87
1960	1.4	10.5	38	88
1961	1.6	14.9	43	90
1962	1.6	21.2	41	93
1963	1.4	22.4	6	94
1964	1.4	26.3	17	95
1965	1.4	31.2	19	96
1966	1.4	39	25	97
1967	1.4	46.1	18	97
1968	1.3	57	24	98
1969	1.3	68	19	98
1970	1.1	83	22	99
1971	0.9	102	23	99
1972	0.8	115	13	99
1973	0.8	112	−3	99
1974	0.6	135	21	99.6
1975	0.4	142	5	99.7

(continued)

iron ore costs CIF from US$49.80 per ton in 1964 (in 1998 dollars) to US$24.44 per ton in real terms in 2000 (see table 5.2). The consequences for Japan's iron ore peripheries, as in the case of coal, included initial booms in production, exports, employment, and other measures, but in the long run they brought low prices; negative returns for firms, communities, and states from large investments in mines and infrastructure; declining employment; and a variety of other problems.

In this chapter, we again focus on our second and third questions, this time in relation to Japan's creation of its iron ore peripheries. How did Japan globalize the world economy in support of its rapid economic growth, and what are the consequences of the new forms of global inequality created by this globalization? Japan's technical, financial, and diplomatic strategies to cheapen access to and transport iron ore global-

TABLE 5.1
Continued

	Iron Ore Production	Iron Ore Imports	Annual Rate of Import Growth	Iron Ore Net Import Dependence Ratio
1976	0.4	132	−7	99.7
1977	0.5	134	2	99.7
1978	0.5	133	−1	99.6
1979	0.4	115	−14	99.7
1980	0.4	130	13	99.7
1981	0.3	134	3	99.8
1982	0.3	123	−8	99.8
1983	0.2	121	−2	99.8
1984	0.2	109	−10	99.8
1985	0.2	125	15	99.8
1986	0.2	125	0	99.8
1987	0.2	115	−8	99.8
1988	0.2	112	−3	99.8
1989	0.06	123	10	99.9
1990	0.03	128	4	99.9
1991	0.02	125	−2	99.9
1992	0.02	127	2	99.9
1993	0.03	114	−10	99.9
1994	0.006	115	1	99.9
1995	0.003	116.1	1	99.9
1996	0.003	120.4	3.7	99.9
1997	0.003	119.2	−1	99.9
1998	0.004	126.6	6	99.9
1999	0.002	120.8	−4.6	99.9
2000	0.002	120.1	−1	99.9
2001	0.002	131.7	9.7	99.9
2002	0.001	126.3	−4.1	99.9
2003		129	2.1	

SOURCES: Tex Report 1994b; USBM/USGS various years a.

ized the world economy and exacerbated global inequalities, particularly in Australia and Brazil, Japan's two largest suppliers of iron ore. We also address our fifth research question, how is China utilizing and transforming the Japan-created global raw materials industries to support China's rapid development?

The Material Characteristics of Iron Ore

As with coal, material properties of iron ore shape technologies, social organization, cost and optimal scale of iron ore extraction and transport, and thus the most effective strategies for cheap procurement. In a few deposits, the crude ore hauled from the mine to the processing plant requires only minimal crushing and screening to concentrate the ore by eliminating waste materials, producing direct-shipping ore. The Japanese system of ocean-based global sourcing and transport innovation elim-

TABLE 5.2

Japanese Iron Ore Price CIF Overall Average

(in US$ / metric ton)

	Current Value	1998 Value
1946	3.01	25.1
1947	3.44	25.1
1948	3.88	26.2
1949	4.46	30.5
1950	4.92	33.2
1951	5.4	34
1952	6.21	38.1
1953	6.81	41.5
1954	6.76	41
1955	7.21	44
1956	7.68	46
1957	8.1	46.8
1958	8.27	46.7
1959	8.48	47.4
1960	8.35	45.9
1961	9.13	49.6
1962	8.82	47.4
1963	9.22	49
1964	9.46	49.8
1965	9.25	47.7
1966	9.5	47.7
1967	9.64	47
1968	9.78	45.9
1969	10.15	45.13
1970	10.39	43.62
1971	10.92	43.96
1972	12.09	47.12
1973	12.75	46.77

(*continued*)

inated the cost constraints of distance to these rare deposits, so their share of imports to Japan and in world trade steadily increased. In most mines, however, mine site beneficiation (increasing the iron content, reducing the amount of waste material, and producing uniformly sized ore) requires a variety of physical processes, depending on the chemical and physical characteristics of the ore and the cost and local availability of water, power, and other inputs in the purification process. This beneficiation produces iron ore concentrates (Bolis and Bekkala 1987:10–11). The Japanese early on devised joint ventures that obliged the mining company as exporter to undertake the costly investments in and operations of beneficiation.

After beneficiation, the ore is shipped to a blast furnace, often hundreds or thousands of miles away, for processing into pig iron. Iron ore particles of less than one-quarter inch in diameter (termed fines) require a further processing step of agglomeration (increasing particle size by combining these small particles) to permit their use in a blast furnace, either at the mine site or at the blast furnace. The first method

TABLE 5.2
Continued

	Current Value	1998 Value
1974	15.5	51.24
1975	19.44	58.89
1976	22.56	64.6
1977	25	67.26
1978	27.74	69.32
1979	30.79	69.16
1980	34.48	68.22
1981	37.46	67.14
1982	38.68	65.33
1983	46.31	75.78
1984	39.92	62.66
1985	38.58	58.47
1986	34.22	50.88
1987	29.64	42.52
1988	28.33	39.04
1989	31.31	41.18
1990	30.89	38.54
1991	30.11	36.03
1992	28.58	33.21
1993	25.79	29.11
1994	25.16	27.67
1995	27.73	29.66
1996	28.9	30.03
1997	29.92	30.39
1998	31.16	31.16
1999	26.77	26.19
2000	25.81	24.44

SOURCES: Tex Report 1994b; USBM/USGS various years a.

of agglomerating iron ore fines, sintering, requires burning fines, coke, and lime or limestone in a plant adjacent to a blast furnace, because sinter is brittle, deteriorates when handled, and allows the blast furnace and steel plant to capture and reuse steel plant dust and coke breeze in the sintering plant (Bolis and Bekkala 1987:11; Manners 1971:171–72).

In contrast to sintering, pelletizing takes place near the mine by combining fines with a binding agent and then hardening in a furnace into pellets with 60 to 65 percent or more iron content. Hard pellets are very easy to transport long distances to blast furnaces (Bolis and Bekkala 1987:11). U.S. Steel originally developed pelletizing technology to counteract the declining quality of domestic ore, particularly the taconite ores from the Mesabi Range (Manners 1971:161–62). Japanese and Western European companies benefited enormously from U.S. Steel's investments in developing these technologies and applied them to many of the newly established deposits of much higher initial quality and therefore lower processing costs than U.S. Steel's Mesabi ore.

This wide variation in ore characteristics and the resulting technological requirements of extracting, concentrating, and agglomerating the ore mean that the costs of production of iron ore mines and their associated processing facilities vary enormously. Natural conditions and the expensive technologies required to overcome less favorable natural characteristics critically determine choice of deposits for mining firms and levels of rent for exporting states. Japanese competitiveness increased as negotiators for their firms and state agencies mastered the subtleties, complexities, and skills of devising favorable long-term contracts that devolve as much of the cost as possible on exporters. Their success in reducing transport costs broadened the number of sites they could exploit, effectively globalizing their supply and strengthening their bargaining position with different potential suppliers.

The process of combining fines into pellets provides part of the necessary energy via an exothermic reaction (production of heat energy by the reaction itself), thus requiring only very limited energy inputs of either fuel oil or natural gas. The dramatic increases in fuel prices during the 1970s led to a stagnation in the volume of pellet production in core countries because of increased energy costs. However, some peripheral and semiperipheral nations, most notably Brazil and other Latin American nations, continued to increase pellet production because of the higher value added of pellets in comparison to iron ore (Bolis and Bekkala 1987:11). This value added by pelletizing created an incentive for states in extractive regions that sought to promote development to invest in capital and energy intensive pelletizing, reducing the capital costs and energy needs at Japanese steel mills. What appears as a significant forward linkage that exports a more valuable partially processed product from the perspective of an extractive state simultaneously externalizes capital and energy costs from the perspective of the Japanese state and Japanese steel firms, lowering their production costs and enabling their blast furnaces to operate more efficiently and produce lower-cost steel. The rapid growth in Japanese joint ventures in Latin American iron mining coincided with those countries' emerging cost advantage in pelletizing.

Iron ore mining offers tremendous opportunities for economies of scale. Few iron ore mines of more than 1 to 2 million tons per year existed in 1950, whereas by 1965 mines in Minnesota and the U.S.S.R. extracted 25 million tons per year of crude ore that were beneficiated to extract 11 million tons per year of ore for shipment to blast furnaces (Manners 1971:159–60). The largest iron ore mines today in Australia and Brazil produce 35 to 50 million tons of ore per year. New technologies for saving fuel via increased scale of blast furnaces also created incentives for increasing the scale of mines, because operational efficiencies of blast furnaces and quality control both increase when only one or a small number of predictable-quality iron ores are used in each batch of pig iron. The scale economies available in the pelletizing process further contributed to the increase in the scale of mining. The economic benefits available from operating combined large-scale mines and pelletizing plants (Manners 1971:164–65) further add to the pressures to increase the size of the total operation.

Since the 1960s, these economies of scale increased dramatically as the size of excavators, trucks, and other equipment increased. Increasing size of machinery and vehicles reduces labor costs. It also reduces congestion and waiting time at the mine wall, on the narrow roads circling upward out of the pit, and on loading docks. Because scale of operation and rate of throughput must be compatible at all stages of the operation, scale economies at one stage often dictate scale increases through all stages. The combined pressures for increased scale of extraction and transport drove capital costs up dramatically. Only large reserves of ore promised sufficient time of extraction to amortize these investments. The need for large deposits reduced the number of attractive sites for exploration. With fewer possible sites, average distance to the industrial countries increased, enhancing the importance of scale in transport. Although a significant number of small mines operate around the world, major iron ore mines increased in scale over the past thirty years by a factor of 30. Large-scale mines now dominate iron ore extraction. Indeed, export to distant international markets, including Japan, virtually excludes small mines because they cannot supply enough raw material fast enough to fill the large trains and ships whose economies of scale made long-distance trade possible.

These increasing economies of scale in mining and beneficiation made mining companies increasingly unwilling to invest the large sums needed to build these facilities without assurance of long-term markets, given the dramatic shift in the industry away from the earlier U.S. vertically integrated mine to the steel mill model. This in turn created tremendous incentives for iron ore consumers who did not own their own captive mines and who had previously purchased large volumes of iron ore through yearly contracts to negotiate long-term contracts that mining firms could use as security to obtain the large bank loans needed to finance these mines. The Japanese steel mills found long-term contracts especially attractive, because they already depended on long-distance imports from a diverse set of suppliers, as did Western European steel firms, whose import dependency increased rapidly. Buyers and sellers had to work out the form of these contracts, however.

Manners (1971:169) concludes that overall "the gains [from these long-term contracts] were mutual. And simultaneously with the lessening of the risks taken by the mining industry, both the proportion of ore sold on the open market and the medium-term flexibility of ore movements was significantly reduced." These long-term contracts with the Japanese steel firms did at least temporarily reduce the market risks for mining companies, but in the long run they increased the investment and price risks to mining firms and imposed tremendous economic and environmental costs on the host countries. This process would focus, as it had in coal, on the development of a raw materials trade relationship between Australia and Japan.

Patching Together an Iron Ore Supply System, 1946–1959

The Japanese steel mills and the Japanese state faced similar challenges to those for metallurgical coal in their efforts to gain access to supplies of imported iron ore after World War II. Prior to World War II the Japanese tried to establish a trade relationship with Australia to acquire iron ore. The key effort focused on a major foreign investment by the Nippon Mining Company in 1936 of £450,000 in the Yampi Sound Mining Company to develop the Koolan Island iron ore deposits in Western Australia, with the ore to be shipped to Japan in Japanese ships. However, on May 19, 1938, the Australian government ordered a total embargo on iron ore exports from Australia to any other nation. While the Australian government publicly claimed that the embargo resulted from the need to preserve the limited amount of Australian iron ore resources for its domestic steel industry, Japan's imperial expansion plans created fear on the part of the Australian government that the plans included southward expansion to include Australia (Blainey 1969; Panda 1982:60–61).

This sudden elimination of a major potential source of iron ore forced the Japanese government to focus on exploration and development of iron ore within the boundaries of the Japanese empire, including in the Yangtze region of China, the Philippines, French Indochina, Malaya, Korea, Manchukuo, and in Japan itself. These sources and scrap provided the major sources of steel raw materials during World War II (Panda 1982:59–62).

After World War II, given Japan's limited domestic iron ore reserves, the Japanese steel industry required imported steel scrap and new foreign sources of iron ore. As in metallurgical coal, the United States provided a significant share of Japan's imports during the early period. In 1948 the United States supplied 400,000 tons of iron ore to Japan and helped arrange for imports of 250,000 tons each from Brazil and the Chinese island of Hainan (USBM/USGS 1949a:659). During the early and mid-1950s, East and Southeast Asia remained Japan's major sources of iron ore, with mines in New Caledonia and Malaya that supplied Japan during World War II reactivated in the late 1940s (USBM/USGS 1949a:659, 1950a:628) with assistance from the United States, including the provision of modern mining equipment (USBM/USGS 1951a:624).

The U.S. government supported the creation of supply arrangements with mining companies in the Philippines, India, Thailand, Pakistan, Hong Kong, Canada (from Vancouver Island and Texada Island in British Columbia), and in the Portuguese colony of Goa in the early 1950s (USBM/USGS 1951a:641–42, 1954:570). In the case of Goa in 1951, the ExIm Bank of Japan provided partial funding, the bank's first overseas investment (Ozawa 1986:605). In 1951 Japan imported a total of 3.3 million tons of iron ore from the United States (1.0 million tons), the Philippines (938,000 tons), Malaya (775,000 tons), Goa (270,000 tons), Hong Kong (171,000 tons), Canada (103,000 tons), and India (93,000 tons) (USBM/USGS 1954a:566). Production for export in India expanded particularly rapidly with financial support from Japan (USBM/USGS 1955a:578), and India remains one of Japan's largest iron ore sources. A variety of government-owned, locally owned, British, and U.S. mining companies operated these mines (USBM/USGS 1956a:576).

By the end of the 1950s, Japanese steel firms also began to acquire iron ore from even more distant sources, including Peru via a Peruvian-Japanese joint venture (USBM/USGS 1957a:610), Chile (with support from the Mitsubishi group) (USBM/USGS 1959a:552), and Brazil (Panda 1982:63–67; USBM/USGS 1957a:611). CVRD, a state-owned company formed in 1942 to take over iron ore mines in Minas Gerais state owned by British mining companies, became the most important partner for the Japanese steel mills in Brazil. The U.S. and British governments supported the nationalization with the goal of promoting steel production in Brazil and iron ore exports to the United States and Great Britain during World War II. The U.S. government provided US$14 million from the U.S. Export-Import Bank to support the mechanization of mining. However, disputes between U.S.-appointed and Brazilian directors of the new firm and a lack of funding made the growth of iron ore mining very slow during the 1940s, especially after the end of the war and a return to reliance on domestic captive iron ore mines in the United States.

The Korean War boom in the early 1950s allowed the Brazilian government and CVRD to raise prices unilaterally from US$8 to US$14 per ton for exports to the United States, providing the funds for rapid expansion of mining and infrastructure. In the late 1950s, CVRD began negotiating with the Japanese steel mills, the world's fastest-growing market, for iron ore sales, and sought other markets as well. CVRD signed its first long-term contracts with the Japanese and European steel mills in 1963, and CVRD established its shipping subsidiary, Docenave, in 1962 in order to reduce its shipping costs and increase its competitiveness in the Japanese market. In conjunction, CVRD used these long-term contracts to develop the port of Tubarao into what soon became one of the world's largest iron ore–exporting ports and increased iron ore mining capacity to 6 million tons by 1962 and to 20 million tons by 1967. The Brazilian military government that seized power in 1964 promoted mining and raw materials exports as development strategies, and CVRD became one of Brazil's leading exporters (Raw 1987:6–15), a position it maintains today.

TABLE 5.3
Japanese Iron Ore Imports by Source
(in millions of tons)

	Total Imports	Australia	Brazil	India	Canada	United States	Chile	Peru	Venezuela	Hong Kong	Malaysia	Philippines	Goa	South Africa	Angola
1950	1.5	0	0	0.1	0	0	0	0	0	0	0.5	0.6		0	0
1951	3.1	0	0	0.09	0.1	1	0	0	0	0.2	0.8	0.9	0.3	0	0
1952	4.8	0	0	0.4	0.7	1.3	0	0	0	0.1	0.9	1.2	0.4	0	0
1953	4.3														
1954	5	0	0	0.5	0.5	0.3	0	0	0	0.09	1	1.3	0.5	0	0
1955	5.5	0	0.009	0.9	0.5	0.3	0	0	0	0.1	1.6	1.6	0.4	0	0
1956	7.9	0	0.048	1	0.3	1	0.012	0.3	0.082	0.1	2.4	1.5	1.1	0.012	0
1957	9.5														
1958	7.6	0	0.046	1.2	0.5	0.5	0.017	0.1	0.004	0.1	2.4	1	1	0.002	0
1959	10.5	0	0.2	1.7	0.7	0.5	0.07	0.1	0.03	0.1	1.2	1.9	0	0.2	0
1960	14.9	0	0.4	2	1	0.8	0.3	0.7	0	0.1	5.4	1.1	2.6	0.4	0
1961	21.2	0	0.4	1.6	1.2	0.9	2.4	2.4	0	0.1	6.4	1.3	3.5	0.4	0.02
1962	22.4	0	0.5	1.7	1.6	1	2.8	2.4	0	0.1	6.4	1.3	2.8	0.6	0.02
1963	26.3	0	0.5	4.9	2	1.7	3.6	2.9	0	0.1	6.5	1.4		0	0.05
1964	31.2	0	0.5	6.9	1.7	2	5.3	2.7	0	0.1	6.3	1.5		1.1	0.079
1965	39	0.1	0.8	7.7	1.8	2.4	6.8	3.9	0.1	0.1	6.5	1.4		2.1	0.2
1966	46.1	2	2	10											
1967	57	8	2	11											
1968	68	14	2	13											
1969	83	23	4	14											
1970	102	37	7	16											
1971	115	46		17											
1972	112	48	9	18											
1973	135	64	13	19											
1974	142														
1975	132	62.3	23.1	16.5	3.8	0	7.9	2.7	0	0	0.1	1.5		1.7	1.4

Year											
1976	134	56	24	17							
1977	133	64	27								
1978	115	53	21	14							
1979	130	55	26	17							
1980	134	57	23	16							
1981	123	55	27	16							
1982	121	54	27	16							
1983	109	50	24	15							
1984	125	59	29	16	3	4.8	1.4	0	0	3.9	5.7
1985	125	53	28	19	3.1	4.8	1.4	0	0.014	3.7	6.5
1986	115	43	25	21	2.4	4.8	1.5	0.1	0.05	3.6	5.6
1987	112	48	28	20	2	4.6	1	0.5	0.06	4.6	5.5
1988	123	53	29	22	2	4.8	1.2	0.5	0.04	4.3	5
1989	128	55	30	20	2	5	1	0.8	0.04	4.8	4.9
1990	125	56	29	22	2.2	3.4	0.5	1.5	0.07	5.2	4.7
1991	127	57	29	19	1.4	4.4	0.6	1.8	0.06	4.6	5
1992	114	54	27	16	1.2	3.2	0.7	1.5	0.012	3.7	4.2
1993	115	54	28	17							
1994	116.1	55	28	16							
1995	120.4	59	28	18							
1996	119.2	60	26	16							
1997	126.6	65	29	17							
1998	120.8	54	26	16							
1999	120.1	66	24	15							
2000	131.7	71	27	17							
2001	126.3	70	25	16							
2002	129										

SOURCES: Tex Report 1994b; USBM/USGS various years a.

By 1960 Japan's major iron ore suppliers in order of importance were Malaysia, India, Peru, Brazil, South Africa, and Chile. Japan's total iron ore imports increased from 3.35 million tons in 1951 to 14.97 million tons in 1960 (see table 5.1) due to the rapid growth of the Japanese steel industry. Imports from all six nations continued to grow during the 1960s (see table 5.3), but managing these diverse, distant, relatively small, and high-cost sources was difficult and expensive. Moreover, the costs of transporting iron ore from these areas to Japan were very high. One Japanese cement manufacturing firm in 1957 made the first significant effort in iron ore to resolve the transport cost problem: the firm contracted to build two specialized ore-cement carriers to export cement from Japan to Southeast Asia and then return with cargoes of iron ore for the Japanese steel mills (USBM/USGS 1958a:610). As in the coal trade, this early effort developed into a broader transport strategy during the 1960s. The relationship with the metallurgical coal industry in Australia provided a much more efficient and much less costly raw materials supply strategy, in comparison with this iron ore supply situation, and the Japanese steel mills and the Japanese state replicated this model in iron ore during the 1960s.

Creating an Iron Ore Periphery, 1960–1973

The rapid growth of Japanese steel production during the 1950s and the plans of the Japanese steel firms and the Japanese state for continued rapid growth during the 1960s prompted MITI to develop plans for meeting the projected growth in demand for iron ore imports from 15.3 million tons in 1960 to 44.98 million tons in 1970 (see table 5.4).

Several key points emerge from this plan. First, the Japanese steel mills and the Japanese state regarded the system of relying on a large number of relatively small suppliers as inadequate, particularly since the only large source, Malaya, would decline in absolute terms over the next decade. Second, the plan called for the development of several new sources. Third, the plan called for the development of India and Goa as Japan's largest sources, shipping 10.5 and 7.5 million tons of iron ore, respectively. Most significantly, two nations that eventually became the key iron ore peripheries for Japan, Australia and Brazil, played only minor roles in the plan for 1970.

The Japanese steel mills and the Japanese state implemented a variety of strategies to secure rapidly increasing amounts of iron ore during the 1960s. In Canada, the provincial government of British Columbia in 1960 changed royalty rules and relaxed a requirement that 50 percent of each iron ore deposit be left in the ground as property of the government to supply a hoped-for provincial steel industry in the future (USBM/USGS 1961a:581). This exporting state strategy helped encourage further in-

TABLE 5.4
MITI Iron Ore Import Plan
(in millions of tons)

	1960	1970
Imports from existing mines		
African countries	0.3	2
Brazil	0.3	0.5
Canada	1.13	1
Chile	0.27	2
Goa	2.85	7.5
Hong Kong	0.12	0.1
India	2.2	8.5
Korea, Republic of	0.3	0.2
Malaya	5.36	3
Peru	0.45	3
Philippines	1.47	1
United States	0.53	1
Total	15.28	29.8
Imports from new mines		
African countries	—	1.5
Australia	0	1
Brazil	—	0.5
Chile	—	1
China	0	1
India	—	2
Korea, North	0	1
Peru	—	1
U.S.S.R.	0	2
Venezuela	0	1
Other	—	3.18
Total	—	15.18
Grand total:	15.28	44.98

SOURCE: USBM/USGS 1961a:592.

vestment in iron ore mining in the province throughout the 1960s, based on financial support and contracts with the Japanese steel mills (USBM/USGS 1962a:672). A new mine opened on Moresby Island in 1967 with a ten-year contract with the Japanese steel mills to supply 1 million tons per year (USBM/USGS 1968a:570).

The Japanese steel mills replicated this strategy in several other areas of the world. In India, the Japanese steel mills and the Japanese state provided tens of millions of dollars to support the expansion of iron ore mining and the necessary infrastructure (USBM/USGS 1964a:625), and signed a long-term contract in 1964 with the Bailadila mine for 4 million tons per year for nineteen years (USBM/USGS 1965a:587). In Africa, the Yawata and Fuji steel mills signed a ten-year, 12-million-ton contract in 1964 in Swaziland (USBM/USGS 1965a:588). The Japanese steel mills signed an eleven-year contract for 1.1 million tons per year in Sierra Leone in 1968 (USBM/USGS 1969a:579), and an eight-year contract for 14 million tons in Angola in 1969 (USBM/

USGS 1970a:563) in support of the effort to increase supplies from Africa. The Japanese steel mills also signed contracts for 1 million tons per year of Brazilian iron ore by 1966 (USBM/USGS 1966a:497); CVRD signed a contract for 50 million tons of iron ore in 1969 (USBM/USGS 1969a:575); and MBR, a new Brazilian iron ore mining company, signed a contract for 105 million tons over sixteen years in 1970 (USBM/ USGS 1971a:577). The Japanese steel mills signed the first long-term contract with the U.S.S.R. in 1967 for 4.9 million tons per year over five years (USBM/USGS 1968a:573–574).

U.S. steel firms, including Kaiser Steel and Bethlehem Steel, played important roles as iron ore suppliers to the Japanese steel mills during the 1960s. Bethlehem signed a long-term contract for more than 7.7 million tons of ore from a mine in Chile and sought Japanese equity participation in a proposed mine in Gabon (USBM/USGS 1969a:577).

The total of these contracts, as well as contracts in Australia, reached 81 million tons per year by 1969 (USBM/USGS 1970a:566), 36 million tons more than MITI's plan from 1960, and an increase of 66 million tons in contracted imports between 1960 and 1969, or 440 percent in a decade. By 1970 Japan's iron ore imports totaled 102 million tons, more than twice the planned 44.98 million tons in MITI's 1961 plan. Imports from Brazil totaled 7 million rather than the planned 1 million tons, imports from India totaled 16 million rather than the planned 10.5 million tons, and imports from Australia totaled 37 million rather than the planned 1 million tons. Japan's domestic iron ore production provided only 0.9 million tons, or less than 1 percent of total iron ore demand of 103 million tons (see table 5.3).

Obviously, the growth of Japan's iron ore periphery and its steel industry did not result from precise planning but evolved as an extremely dynamic system that responded to market opportunities, firm recognition of these opportunities, changing political and material conditions in exporting regions, and other changes. The pattern of state-sector-firm relations emerged from a process of learning, cooperation, and conflict that proved able to adapt to often unexpected and initially problematic changes domestically and internationally, not from an all-powerful state. The organizational, technological, and strategic innovations developed in response to these challenges by the Japanese steel mills and the Japanese state drove the creation and evolution of the global iron ore industry.

The Japanese steel firms sought to reduce transport costs in iron ore, as they had in metallurgical coal. In comparison to shipments of oil and coal, however, iron ore's much higher density made using larger-scale ships more difficult for iron ore because of the much greater stress on ship hulls holding iron ore. Japanese shipyards first built specially designed and strengthened bulk carriers capable of hauling much denser iron ore during the 1960s, including four iron ore ships exceeding 50,000 deadweight tons (dwt) designed to make twelve round trips per year from Long Beach, California, to Japan to haul iron ore mined by Kaiser Steel in California (USBM/USGS 1964a:614). In the late 1960s, Japanese shipyards built several specialized iron ore carriers of 100,000 to 125,000 dwt, and later built specialized oil–iron ore carriers of 100,000 to 200,000 dwt that reduced costs by conducting triangular trades of oil and ore in the late 1960s and early 1970s (USBM/USGS 1968a:569).

These large carriers dramatically reduced transport costs by the late 1960s and early 1970s. A long-term contract between CVRD and Fuji Steel called for a reduction in freight costs from US$7.34 per ton for shipment in 50,000-dwt ships to US$5.28 per ton for 105,000-dwt ships (USBM/USGS 1969a:575), a savings of 28 percent per ton by doubling ship size. This also shows the ability of the Japanese steel mills to capture the same economies of scale in the transport of iron ore that they had in metallurgical coal. Combined carriers of 200,000 dwt put into operation on the Brazil-Japan iron ore route reduced costs per ton to US$3.15 (USBM/USGS 1970a:562), thus cutting transport costs by another 40 percent, or a total reduction of 57 percent in comparison with 50,000-dwt ships. The Japanese steel mills placed orders for more than forty combined carriers exceeding 250,000 dwt by 1971 (USBM/USGS 1972a:591).

Another key recurring issue in the iron ore industry also appeared in the early 1960s: concern about excess capacity in the rapidly developing global iron ore industry. The USBM/USGS noted in 1964 (1964a:617) that "a large surplus capacity to produce iron ore existed throughout the world, and buyers were interested in only the highest grade, best structure ore or iron ore agglomerate. The potential market for these high grades continued to exceed the supply. Consequently, there existed the seeming enigma of great expansion plans in an oversaturated environment in most iron-ore-producing areas." This seemingly contradictory situation, large investments in new mining capacity even during times of excess capacity, became a hallmark of the global iron ore industry because of the strategies of the Japanese steel mills and the Japanese state to encourage the development of new sources in order to strengthen their bargaining position, as they had in metallurgical coal.

The most important change in Japan's iron ore importing after World War II occurred with the lifting of the Australian embargo on iron ore exports in December 1960. Japan's mining firm partners in the coal trade in Australia, other Australian and transnational mining firms, and the state government of Western Australia sought to end the ban on iron ore exports during the 1950s. The Western Australian government started a small high-grade charcoal iron industry in 1948. As awareness grew of the existence of significant iron ore resources in the state, the Western Australia government began to negotiate with the Japanese steel mills in 1957 to export iron ore. However, the national government refused to authorize exports because of its increasingly outdated concerns about a lack of iron ore for the domestic steel industry (Hughes 1963:183).

The Western Australia government and some Australian business interests, led by the Australian firm of Duval and Company, campaigned for several years to promote iron ore exports (Hughes 1963:183). However, the end of the ban on exports occurred only after the Western Mining Company and Broken Hill Proprietary Company (two Australian-owned companies), the Western Australia state government, and a coal mining company all announced discoveries of significant tonnages of iron ore, alleviating concerns about domestic shortages. The lifting of the ban on exports ended what Blainey (1969:348) considered a paradoxical situation for Australia: "in years when many Australian economists and politicians were justifiably perturbed that the nation's exports were increasing too slowly, iron ore offered a valuable treasury of export income. The treasury, however, was locked."

The national and state governments began opening the door to increased export revenues from iron ore cautiously at the end of 1960. This opening exploded into an iron ore exploration and development boom during the 1960s. A Western Australia rancher discovered the Hamersley deposits in the 1950s but kept them secret until the export ban ended. The rancher then revealed the deposits to a partnership of Conzinc Rio Tinto of Australia (later renamed CRA), a semi-independent Australian subsidiary of RTZ of Great Britain, and Kaiser Steel of the United States, firms that were already partners in developing the bauxite deposits at Weipa in the region. The exploration rush resulted in the discovery of other massive deposits, revealing hundreds of millions of tons of iron ore reserves (Blainey 1969:349–51; Hughes 1963:183–88).

A change of government in Western Australia in 1961 greatly advanced these companies' interests in iron ore mining for export. The new government sought to promote development through raw materials extraction and processing in the region, with government approval of iron ore exports conditioned on investments in local iron and steel processing (USBM/USGS 1964a:627). Several other iron- and/or coal-producing states, including South Australia, Queensland, and New South Wales, also promoted this policy during the 1960s, often via threats of the creation of state-owned steel firms to challenge Australia's only steel producer, BHP (Hughes 1963:188–89). Changing state government development strategy and the general efforts of the Australian national government to promote the growth of exports further contributed to the tremendous rush of exploration efforts in iron ore.

However, Australian analysts and state and national governments in the late 1950s and early 1960s saw iron ore exports as a means to increase ore supplies to and provide funds for the development of the domestic steel industry. Australian analyses at the time saw Japan as a competitor in the steel industry and sought strategies to increase Australian steel exports, based on their raw materials cost advantage over Japan. Regional governments in Australia promoted exports of iron ore to Japan, just as they had in metallurgical coal in Australia and Canada, with the goal of supporting domestic industrialization of raw materials via export earnings, rather than becoming the focal point and main economic activity of the region. Japanese raw materials strategies effectively trapped these regions in the roles of quarries for Japan, choking off further domestic raw materials–based industrialization in favor of exports. During the 1960s and early 1970s, iron ore and coal exports appeared to offer extremely lucrative long-term contracts for exports to Japan that provided a seemingly secure source of profits for mining firms and sources of employment, local development, export earnings, and tax revenues to regional and national governments. These promised long-term benefits for exporting regions proved far smaller and the costs far higher than anticipated.

In the early 1960s, Australian iron ore producers initially focused on exporting iron ore to Europe, but the long distance and resulting high transport costs made this trade extremely expensive and largely uncompetitive. By offering long-term contracts and credit needed for opening new, and much larger, mines and transport systems, the Japanese contrived to orient most of the greenfield projects toward the Japanese market. By the mid-1960s, Australian iron ore–exporting firms began to focus on the Japanese market because of relative proximity, rapidly growing iron ore demand, and the experiences of some foreign mining firms, including Kaiser Steel, as partners with the Japanese steel mills in coal and iron ore supply relationships in eastern Australia, the United States, Canada, and other nations.

Japan's coal suppliers and other mining firms operating in Australia, confronted with an opportunity to supply Australian iron ore to the world's fastest-growing market, developed a number of large iron ore mines in Western Australia based on long-term contracts, beginning in November 1963 with the Geraldton Mine and quickly followed by many others (McKern 1976:206–16). Other contracts followed, including contracts for a total of 175 million tons of iron ore for delivery between the late 1960s and the late 1980s (USBM/USGS 1965b:588–89) at a total value of more than US$2 billion (USBM/USGS 1966b:475). Total contracted tonnage by 1969 reached more than 750 million tons (USBM/USGS 1970b:564). The Australian mining firm Western Mining and two U.S. mining companies formed a joint venture to build and operate the Geraldton mine. The joint venture paid for the railroad and port infrastructure required for the mine, an important departure from the metallurgical coal model in eastern Australia, where state governments provided railroad and port infrastructure during the 1960s.

One U.K. and two U.S. mining firms formed a joint venture for the second major mine, Mount Goldsworthy; these firms also built their own infrastructure. In contrast to these two mines, the next four iron ore mines developed in Australia (three in Western Australia and one in Tasmania) included the Japanese steel firms or Japanese trading companies as partners: Hamersley, with the Japanese steel mills owning 6.2 percent of the joint venture with one U.S. and one U.K. mining firm and Australian shareholders; Mount Newman, with Mitsui and C. Itoh Japanese trading companies owning 10 percent in a joint venture with one U.S., two Australian, and one U.K. mining firm; Robe River, with Mitsui trading company owning 30 percent of the joint venture with U.S. and Australian mining companies; and Savage River, with Mitsubishi and Sumitomo trading companies owning 50 percent of a joint venture with U.S. and Australian mining companies. Most mines produced very high-quality direct shipping ore exceeding 64 percent iron content, except for Robe River and Savage River, which processed some of their ore into pellets. These ten- to sixteen-year contracts provided a guaranteed market and allowed the rapid expansion of iron ore mining in Western Australia and other parts of Australia.

Most critically for the Japanese steel industry, this exploration and investment by Australian and foreign mining firms revealed the huge iron ore reserves of remote regions of Australia. In 1950 Australia's known reserves totaled only 126 million tons of contained iron ore, a mere 0.5 percent of world reserves (Manners 1971:228). By the early 1990s Australian reserves totaled 10.2 billion tons of contained iron ore, 16 percent of world reserves (USBM/USGS 1992b) and eighty times as large as known reserves forty years earlier, even after the export of hundreds of millions of tons to Japan.

The Japanese trading companies typically handled the logistics of large-scale flows of coal and iron ore as their contribution to the state-sector-firm coordination in Japan. With iron ore deposits located less than 400 kilometers from the west coast of Australia, separated only by a few intervening hills on the gradual downhill railroad journeys, and the coasts of Western Australia and Tasmania amenable to the development of large-scale ports, as eastern Australia was for coal, the Japanese steel firms utilized their large-scale ports in Japan for both coal and iron ore imports. In contrast to the coal mining regions in eastern Australia, however, the iron ore mining companies themselves funded and built this massive infrastructure, which accounted for one-third of the total costs of these mines (McKern 1976:206–16).

The huge scale and costs of these iron ore mines and transport infrastructure made the turnaround time of the massive capital investments in these facilities a critical issue. The Goldsworthy mine produced 5 million tons per year in 1969, so 100,000 tons of iron ore represented 2 percent of the annual production. The mine loaded this week's worth of iron production onto railcars and shipped it to the port over the 3-hour railway journey, loaded it onto a ship in just over two days' time, and shipped it 3,600 miles to Japan in a few days' sailing time (*Skillings* 1969:8), where the steel mills converted it into pig iron, smelted it into steel, and cast it into semifinished products within another three to four weeks. This tightly integrated, large-scale extraction, transport, and processing system made very efficient use of the hundreds of millions of dollars of capital invested in the system by utilizing the latest technologies of mining, rail transport, port facilities, bulk shipping, and steel production in a well-organized system governed by long-term contracts linking the mining company to Japanese steel companies, trading companies, and shipping companies.

These long-term contracts created problems for Australia from the beginning. Even before the Western Australian iron ore mines came into production, mine development costs exceeded estimates by 15 to 30 percent, while contract prices with the Japanese steel mills fell below world market prices. The Australian Foreign Trade Ministry argued in 1965 that "iron ore prices contracted by Western Australian producers were as much as 15 percent below world price levels" (USBM/USGS 1966b:502). One analysis argued that the mining company operators "had one disadvantage in dealing with the Japanese: they competed against one another on price. The result: Japan sewed up one of the best iron-ore import deals in history" (*Business Week*, August 13, 1966:99). Japan's iron ore prices from other sources at the time ranged from 20.5¢ to 26¢ per pound of contained iron, while the Australian contract prices ranged from 14.5¢ to 21¢, with an average of 18¢ per unit of contained ore. Efforts to renegotiate the contracts met only limited success. Other iron ore–exporting countries, most notably India, filed formal protests with the Australian government, and the Australian government subsequently investigated the terms of the contracts (*Business Week*, August 13, 1966:98–100). This disadvantage of uncoordinated negotiations on the exporting end confronting tightly coupled state-sector-firm coordination at the importing end became a hallmark of iron ore–exporting nations' relations with the Japanese steel firms.

One analyst noted in the late 1960s the tremendous influence that Japan's rapidly growing demand for iron ore imports had on the world iron ore market between the early 1950s and late 1960s:

The importance of the Japanese market far exceeded the volume of imports moving into that country. Partly because of the rapid rate of growth of demand for iron ore, but also because of the highly aggressive purchasing policies adopted by their iron and steel industry, the Japanese tended to set the pace and the style of change in the ore markets of the world. Faced with exceptionally high raw-material costs at the beginning of the period, the Japanese steel industry systematically set about to ensure a reduction of its raw-material transport costs. By accepting the responsibility and the economies of long-term and large-scale ore purchases, and by skillful bargaining with its suppliers, Japan by 1965 had established for itself a much admired and an almost enviable position. (Manners 1971:253)

Technological and organizational innovations in transporting iron ore and coal provided the keys to Japan's successful drive to become the world's lowest-cost steel producer.

Australian iron ore exports to Japan increased from nothing in 1963 to 13.8 million tons in 1968, becoming Japan's largest iron ore supplier in only five years. By 1973 exports reached 64 million tons, more than three times greater than Japan's second largest supplier and 56 percent of Japan's total iron ore imports (see table 5.1). Australia remained Japan's largest iron ore supplier throughout the past thirty years, but the Japanese steel firms and the Japanese state embarked on a massive rediversification effort in the late 1970s to lessen dependence on Australia.

Our focus on evolving material process as cumulatively sequential in space and over time allows us to ground comparisons between systemic regimes of accumulation as historical transition and to incorporate within that comparisons of different instances of subordination within a restructured periphery at particular moments in time. Thus we see Canada bound into the formation of new global markets for coal with the same general mechanisms that the Japanese firms and state learned and adapted in Australia, but we can also see how the Japanese adjusted their strategies to the different material and spatial characteristics of the Canadian resources, most notably their far greater distance from Canadian ports, the far rougher terrain between the mine and the port, and then the far greater distance to Japan. These differences enter into both the contractual relations that Japan established with Canadian firms and provincial states and their treatment of these coal exporters once the mines and transport infrastructure were established. The efforts of the Japanese steel firms to diversify their sources of iron ore to Brazil and other nations beginning in the late 1970s similarly reflect these efforts to adapt and adjust access strategies to the material, political, and economic realities of other potential raw materials–exporting regions.

The Iron Ore Access Strategy during Recession and Crisis, 1973–1985

The first oil price shock of 1973–74 initiated a crisis for the world steel industry because of the combined impacts of increased production costs and a long global recession that reduced global steel demand. This long crisis for the steel industry in turn created a severe crisis for the newly globalized iron ore industry after more than two decades of extremely rapid growth. Dramatic annual growth rates of iron ore production and exports were replaced by stagnation and decline, and the entry into operation of new mines built on the basis of expectations of continued rapid growth further exacerbated this crisis. These crises in steel and iron ore created tremendous problems for the Japanese steel mills and for their iron ore suppliers. However, the long-term outcomes for the two partners in the global iron ore industry diverged dramatically, largely as the result of the strategic actions of the Japanese steel mills as they learned from, reacted to, and gradually evolved new strategies for long-term, low-cost access to iron ore.

The high quality, low cost, and proximity of Australian iron ore deposits made Australia Japan's primary supplier once the Japanese learned to negotiate effectively with Australian governments and firms and with the multinational mining companies licensed to operate there. Their experiences with coal, however, showed the Japanese the tremendous advantages of diversifying their sources. It also made them nervous about labor militancy and consequent production stoppages in Australia. The earlier set of diverse suppliers could not, however, provide an adequate solution for this rediversification effort. Malaysia's iron ore exports to Japan ceased by 1972, while Peru's and Chile's export volumes peaked in 1972 and soon fell by 50 percent or more. South Africa's exports increased through 1979 but then declined dramatically, while India's exports fluctuated around their 1973 level for the next twenty years. Only one potential very large-scale alternative source of high-quality iron ore existed: Brazil.

Iron ore prices began escalating rapidly in the wake of the first oil price shock of 1973–74 as energy prices and labor and other costs rose around the world. In 1974 prices for Australian iron ore rose from 16 to 27 percent (USBM/USGS 1975b:659), and prices rose by 15 percent in 1976 (USBM/USGS 1977b:651). A number of iron ore–producing nations, including Australia, Sweden, Peru, Chile, Mauritania, Venezuela, Algeria, Tunisia, Sierra Leone, and India, formed the Association of Iron Ore Exporting Countries (AIOEC) in 1975, with the goal of obtaining higher prices for iron ore. Peru, Venezuela, Mauritania, and Chile all nationalized their iron ore mines during the first half of the 1970s (USBM/USGS 1976b:723–24) in an effort to capture more of the benefits of iron ore exports.

A number of major projects already underway came onstream in the mid-1970s, including a major expansion of mining and exports from South Africa, whose costs had more than doubled, to more than US$1 billion (USBM/USGS 1975b:663). The Mount Wright mine in Canada opened in 1975 (USBM/USGS 1976b:723), Mount Newman Mining in Australia increased capacity to 40 million tons per year in 1976, and other new projects planned to add 35 million tons of capacity in Western Australia at a cost of more than US$1 billion (USBM/USGS 1976b:731). At the same time, some exporters to Japan declined dramatically in importance during this era. Texada Mines in British Columbia ceased production due to the exhaustion of reserves, and production declined in the Philippines as well (USBM/USGS 1977b:655–56).

The Japanese steel mills continued to sign new long-term contracts with existing and new suppliers during this crisis. During 1976 the Japanese steel mills signed contracts for 185 million tons of ore for delivery between 1978 and 1990 with the Hamersley mine in Australia, and for more than 300 million tons with CVRD in Brazil (USBM/USGS 1977a:654). The Japanese steel mills also signed long-term contracts with Companhia de Acero del Pacifico in Chile that brought 3.5 million tons per year of iron ore pellets into the Japanese market for ten years beginning in 1978 (USBM/USGS 1980a:440). The Japanese steel mills also sought to participate directly in the management and operation of their supplying mines during this era, including in the Robe River mine in Australia and in a joint venture with CVRD at the Capanema mines in Minas Gerais, Brazil (USBM/USGS 1977b:632); the mine began producing 10 million tons per year in 1982 (USBM/USGS 1983b:437). The Japanese government also sought to create stockpiles of raw materials in Japan or in supplying nations to ensure stability of supply during the late 1970s (USBM/USGS 1980b:441).

By the mid-1980s analysts of the iron ore industry recognized problems of excess capacity. In 1984 the United States Bureau of the Mines (USBM) noted that "iron ore prices continued to decline, while ocean freight rates remained low. Investments in new facilities also remained relatively low, as overcapacity continued to be a problem in most of the major producing countries" (USBM/USGS 1985b:475). Analysts expected the problem to worsen when CVRD's new Carajás mine, the new Kudremukh mine in India (7.4 million tons per year), and the San Isidro mine in Venezuela (4.9 million tons) entered production in the late 1980s (USBM/USGS 1986b:517).

Brazil offered the Japanese steel mills the opportunity to acquire a large volume of stable supplies of iron ore, but these major reserves of high-quality, low-cost ore with an amenable government and a tractable labor force faced a 12,000 nautical mile journey to Japan. Japanese firms entered into joint ventures and long-term contracts with Brazilian companies in the 1960s, and they established a joint venture in a steel plant greatly desired by a capital-poor and technology-dependent Brazilian state. These relatively small ventures inspired goodwill and trust on both sides. Capitalizing on all of these advantages, however, required a fleet of bulk carriers big enough to cheapen transport between Brazil and Japan. Once the Japanese shipbuilding and shipping companies built this fleet by the early 1970s, however, the Japanese steel mills incorporated Brazil as a major source in their supply network.

The Japanese steel mills eschewed their affinity for dealing with multiple companies by teaming up with CVRD, a Brazilian state-owned mining company, but their base in Australia diminished the risks of this dependency. CVRD sought to expand its market share in iron ore and diversify its markets and lines of operation; CVRD was also willing to invest in large ships and ports. The Brazilian state relied increasingly on CVRD as a major exporter, as a counterweight to the power of foreign mining and minerals-processing firms, as a purchaser of Brazilian-made industrial goods for its operations, and as a source of regional development in the Amazon (Raw 1987:26–29). When the Japanese steel mills used the global steel crisis of the late 1970s and their strong bargaining power to reduce the volume of their iron ore imports from CVRD, CVRD aggressively sought to develop new markets for its iron ore (Raw 1987:33–34).

The Japanese steel firms and the Japanese state developed a raw materials access strategy that guaranteed long-term access to large volumes of iron ore from distant raw materials–rich regions that became highly dependent on trade with Japan. Control over shipping by Japanese importers captured the benefits of an increasing scale of ocean shipping for Japanese firms that consume iron ore: "the facilities and mode of transportation that are uniquely custom-made to fit the specific technical requirements of Japan's logistics alone will give Japan a monopsony position, hindering the entry of other resource-importing nations" (Ozawa 1979:190). Further, in order to reduce the shipping costs on long hauls from Brazil and Australia, many Japanese steel and shipping firms developed triangular trading patterns, often including crude oil transport in ships known as combination carriers or ore-bulk-oil carriers (which means that these ships can carry a variety of bulk raw materials ranging from minerals and grains to liquid petroleum). These triangular trading patterns reduce the amount of time that large bulk carriers spend sailing empty, thereby reducing the cost per ton of transporting iron ore and other cargoes (Penfold 1984). As a result,

> by comparison (with Australia), the ocean transport distance of Brazilian iron-ore to Japan is the longest, and it was thought earlier that this ore would never prove to be competitive. But with the development of so-called triangular transport (that is, oil is first transported from the Persian Gulf to Europe, then the carrier sails in ballast to Brazil in order to load iron-ore destined for Japan), freight costs are lowered significantly thereby enhancing the competitiveness of Brazilian ore. (Kojima cited in Ozawa 1979:190)

These Japanese innovations in raw materials access strategies and transport technologies made iron ore mining firms in Australia and Brazil intense competitors during the past two decades.

Restructuring, Excess Capacity, and Expansion in a Difficult Environment, 1985–2006

The opening of the Carajás iron ore mine in the Brazilian Amazon in 1986 consolidated the power of the Japanese steel mills in the global iron ore industry, greatly intensified competition between mining firms, and increased excess capacity. The Japanese steel mills used the strategies learned and perfected in Australia, but adapted their implementation to the spatial, material, and political realities of Brazil. The Carajás mine, owned by CVRD, a mixed public and private, but very much national, firm until its privatization, quickly became the largest iron mine in the world. The governments of Japan (US$500 million), the United States (US$200 million), and Europe (US$730 million) coordinated by the World Bank (US$304 million), under policies originated because of U.S. concerns in the 1970s to ensure adequate raw materials supplies (see Bunker and O'Hearn 1992; USBM/USGS 1983b:437), provided loans, along with the Brazilian government and Brazilian banks.

In combination with CVRD's mines in southern Brazil, Carajás made CVRD the world's leading iron ore exporter. However, the very difficult global iron ore market had a high degree of excess capacity. The burden of the US$3.2 billion investment in the Carajás mine and railroad, in combination with the preexisting excess capacity in iron ore and the low prices of the 1980s, created serious financial challenges for CVRD that it sought to resolve by increasing production, reaching 44 million tons per year in 1995.

In the case of Carajás, Japan played a far less central role in financing and in contracts than in Australia. The Japanese government and Japanese steel mills used U.S. and European Union interests in the mine to stimulate finance, and then worked to influence the Brazilian national state and CVRD to develop the mine in such a way that it fed into Japanese global sourcing strategies at local cost. CVRD built a much larger and more expensive mine, railroad, and port than initially planned, and it built dedicated oceangoing ships to allow economic shipments of iron ore to Japan. The promise of Japanese long-term contracts led CVRD to expose itself to far greater risks and costs over the much cheaper infrastructure that its original partnership with U.S. Steel had envisioned to barge the ore downriver to the existing port of Belém and then on to the United States in the smaller ships appropriate to regional, rather than global, trade in cheap bulk raw materials (see Bunker and Ciccantell 2005).

Comparison with Australia shows that Japanese strategies in Brazil responded to the topographies and locational characteristics of the Amazon, the far more centrally controlled structure of the Brazilian federal system, the political power of CVRD relative to both the national state and the much weaker Amazonian states, and the greater distance from Brazil to Japan. In order to achieve its own incorporation into Japanese globalizing strategies, CVRD used the national congress and national ministries to undermine local state control over land and taxes. CVRD pushed the establishment of new federal agencies that controlled land use on a military model and promoted national state initiatives that preempted land formerly under local state control. At the same time, it collaborated with Japanese development agencies to promote fiscal incentives that would support the infrastructure required for access to the Japanese market, while manipulating federal decrees that reduced its tax and rent obligations to the local state. In these ways, the Amazon's incorporation into Japan's resource-supplying periphery led to huge capital costs, rent reduction, and impoverishment of local administration (see Bunker and Ciccantell 2005).

The Brazilian government regulated the privatization of CVRD in 1998 to prevent its takeover by one of its main iron ore mining competitors. The winning bidder, Valepar, a consortium that included a Brazilian steelmaker, CSN, a group of Brazilian pension funds, and U.S. Nations' Bank, paid US$3.1 billion for a controlling stake (USBM/USGS 1998b:41.4).

After privatization, CVRD dramatically expanded its ownership of the Brazilian iron ore industry. CVRD sought to increase its profits by consolidating its leading role in the global iron ore export industry. CVRD bought Samitri in 2000 for US$710.5 million, becoming partners in the Alegria mine with BHP, one of its leading competitors (*AFX-European Focus* 2000). In 2001 CVRD bought Socoimex, with 7 million tons per year of iron ore mining capacity; 50 percent of CAEMI, Brazil's second largest iron ore mining firm with a capacity of 27 million tons per year in an arrangement with partner Mitsui for US$280 million; and Ferteco with a capacity of 15 million tons per year for US$650 million (Clifford 2001:10). In 2003 CVRD bought Mitsui's 50 percent of CAEMI for US$426.4 million, giving it control of MBR with an iron ore capacity of 36 million tons per year, and Mitsui in return bought a 15 percent stake in Valepar, CVRD's controlling shareholder, for US$830 million (*Canada NewsWire* 2003; Flynn 2003c). These acquisitions made CVRD Brazil's only major iron ore producer and exporter. CVRD expects its iron ore production to total 300 million tons in 2007, up from 211 million tons in 2004 (*Lloyd's List* 2005a).

CVRD also followed a strategy similar to the major Australian iron ore mining firms during 2002 and 2003, forming much closer relationships with Chinese steel firm Baosteel, including a twenty-year contract for 20 million tons of iron ore (*Business News Americas* 2002a), an amount later increased to 20 million tons per year by 2010 (*Skillings*, June 2004:17); planning to build the world's largest bulk ship of 450,000 dwt to transport iron ore from Brazil to China and coal from China to Brazil (*Business News Americas* 2002d); and negotiating to build a joint-venture steel slab plant to be located in São Luíz (Kinch 2003). CVRD also bought minority stakes in several steel companies that purchase its ore, and formed a joint venture with Nucor of the United States to produce pig iron from Carajás ore (*Business News Americas* 2002b; Flynn 2003b). CVRD signed a joint-venture agreement with JFE Steel of Japan to build an iron ore mine in Minas Gerais that would produce 15 million tons per year (*Nikkei Weekly* 2003) and signed a new contract with JFE for 70 million tons of iron ore between 2005 and 2014 (*Wall Street Journal* 2004). CVRD has contracts to supply a total of 275 million tons to Japan between 2003 and 2017 (*Lloyd's List* 2005a).

These strategies proved quite successful; CVRD earned US$1.3 billion in profits on sales of US$4.7 billion in 2001 (Kepp 2002). These profit levels continued in 2003 and 2004 (Welsh 2004) and profits reached US$4.8 billion on revenues of US$13.4 billion in 2005 (*PR Newswire Europe* 2006). CVRD reduced its production costs by 32 percent between the time of privatization in 1998 and 2002, making it the world's lowest-cost iron ore producer (*Business News Americas* 2003). The Brazilian government hopes to use CVRD's profitable relationship with China as the foundation for expanding Brazil's steel industry and exports and, more broadly, Brazil's economic relations with China in order to promote regional and national economic growth (Benson 2004), particularly in the Amazon (Watts 2005). As part of this broader relationship, Gerdau Steel of Brazil is buying steel-making equipment worth US$236.5 million from Chinese firms (Anderlini 2006).

CVRD's successful corporate strategies, however, do not necessarily contribute to local and national economic development goals. CVRD rejected several proposals to build a steel mill in the Amazon to process Carajás ore, despite pressures from Brazilian business leaders and from local and regional political leaders (*Business News Americas* 2002c). However, CVRD made efforts to attract foreign steelmakers to build steel mills in northern Brazil utilizing Carajás iron ore (Flynn 2003a) and signed an agreement with Baosteel of China for a US$8 billion investment in steel production in Brazil (*AFX-Asia* 2003), although this project is currently on hold.

The excess capacity and crises of the 1970s and early 1980s provoked an ongoing period of financial and operational restructuring by iron ore mining firms. BHP expanded its ownership shares of Goldsworthy Mining and the Mount Newman joint venture in Australia (USBM/USGS 1986b:526–27), as other firms decided that the industry did not offer good potential for future profitability. In 1986 several iron ore mining companies restructured ownership in efforts to deal with low prices and excess capacity, including MBR in Brazil, the Iron Ore Company of Canada, Cleveland Cliffs of the United States, and Robe River Iron Ore Associates, Mount Newman Mining, and the Yandicoogina project in Australia then under development by BHP and its partner, CRA (USBM/USGS 1987b:496).

An effort by the Robe River Iron Ore ownership to increase productivity and reduce labor costs confronted strong union resistance, and management locked out the workers for three weeks in 1986. This dispute cost Nippon Steel more than US$1 million in demurrage charges for two stranded ore carriers and "generated considerable misgivings among the integrated steelmakers in Japan.... placing it (Robe River) and other Australian producers at a serious disadvantage in their 1987 price negotiations, and has encouraged the Japanese to strengthen their relationships with Canadian, Indian, Swedish, and Venezuelan ore producers" (USBM/USGS 1987b:510–11). Operational restructuring efforts by other iron ore mining firms in Australia in order to reduce production costs encountered similar difficulties. However, RTZ and BHP transformed the Australian iron ore mining labor relationship in the late 1990s by moving from union representation to individual contracts. BHP induced 60 percent of its work force to move from union representation to individual contracts, allowing the firm to change work rules and increase productivity without negotiating with unions. BHP's workers on individual contracts received wage increases of 31 to 49 percent from 2000 through 2002, as well as other increased benefits, while unionized workers received no wage increases in 2000 or 2001. However, court challenges later forced BHP to equalize pay rates between individual contract and unionized employees (Way 2003:22), sharply constraining the benefits to these firms of these restructuring efforts.

As was the case in metallurgical coal, iron mining firms in Australia steadily expanded production despite these difficult market conditions and the negotiating power of the Japanese steel mills. BHP increased its ownership share in Australian iron ore as many other firms chose to exit the industry, opened new mines (USBM/USGS 1993b:179, 1994b:466, 1996b:423), and expanded production at others. BHP merged with Billiton, one of the world's largest mining firms, in 2001 (USBM/USGS 2002b: 41.6).

Hamersley, the other major Australian iron miner, opened the US$295 million, 12-million-ton Marandoo mine in 1994 (USBM/USGS 1995b:420), consolidating its position as one of the world's three largest iron ore exporters (USBM/USGS 1996b:424). In 1999 RTZ and BHP tried to negotiate a merger to create the world's largest iron ore exporter, but these negotiations failed (Gray 2000:2). In 2000 RTZ initiated and eventually won a bitter takeover battle for North Ltd. RTZ thus became a partner with three Japanese companies, Mitsui Iron Ore Development, Nippon Steel Australia, and Sumitomo Metal Australia, in Australia's third largest iron ore mining firm, Robe River Iron Associates, when it bought North Ltd. These Japanese partners strongly opposed RTZ's bid for Robe River and supported a competing bid by Anglo American, including agreeing to pay for half of the new West Angelas's mine rail infrastructure cost of US$350 million and offering to pay high prices for coal from Anglo American's recently acquired Australian coal mines (Armstrong 2000b). The Japanese steel mills feared that the acquisition of Robe River would give RTZ too much negotiating power (Armstrong 2000a, 2000b; USBM/USGS 2001b:3.7) as part of a three-firm oligopoly, particularly in light of the success of BHP and Fording Coal's successful collaboration in metallurgical coal prices negotiations in the mid-1990s. Analysts argued that the support offered by the Japanese steel mills for Anglo American's bid would "recoup every cent they spend on bankrolling Anglo by keeping iron ore prices down in future years. . . . part of the Japanese long-term strategy, designed to keep their iron ore costs down. They aim to do this by ensuring a production surplus and by preventing the big three Australian producers from becoming two" (O'Connor 2000:36).

The Japanese steel mills forced down prices for iron ore further in negotiations during the late 1980s (USBM/USGS 1987b:507). A new Japanese negotiating strategy emerged during 1987–88. Historically, European steel firms settled their annual contracts with Australian and Brazilian suppliers first, because the European steelmakers' contracts began on January 1, whereas the Japanese contracts began with the Australian fiscal year in April. Instead, the Japanese steel mills completed their negotiations first and, as a result, set global iron ore prices entirely on the basis of their own very strong negotiating position, a pattern repeated in about half of the years since. The Australian mining company that settled first, Hamersley Iron, had a very weak negotiating position because of a stockpile of 17 million tons of unsold ore. Hamersley agreed to a price cut of 4.01 percent, and other iron ore producers settled for price cuts between 4 and 5.9 percent as a result of this agreement (USBM/USGS 1989b:497). When market conditions improved in late 1988, the Japanese steel mills rewarded Hamersley with price increases of 13 percent for fines and 17.3 percent for lump ore, while negotiating several new long-term contracts (USBM/USGS 1989b:499).

The relationship with Hamersley and this pattern of competition to settle negotiations first between the Japanese and European buyers and between the Australian and Brazilian mining firms became a hallmark of the late 1980s and all of the 1990s in the global iron ore industry. This negotiating pattern was repeated in 1988, 1989, and 1990, with Hamersley's assistance in the 1989 negotiations helping to constrain efforts by CVRD to obtain higher prices (USBM/USGS 1990b:533). CVRD, the traditional price setter via its negotiations with the European steel firms, recaptured its role in the negotiations for 1990 and obtained a 15.96 percent price increase, with Japanese negotiations with Hamersley following this pattern quickly (USBM/USGS 1991b:586), a pattern repeated in 1991 (USBM/USGS 1992b:758). This competition continued throughout the 1990s and early 2000s.

Hamersley, Mount Newman, and Robe River signed new long-term contracts in

1989 for only seven years, in contrast to the initial contracts of 15 to 30 years that established the Australia-Japan iron ore relationship (USBM/USGS 1990b:535). Hamersley and the Japanese steel mills became increasingly tightly linked during the 1990s. In 1995 they renewed a seven-year contract for 11 million tons per year, and in 1996 they signed a new contract for 28.5 million tons per year between 1996 and 1999, with a total value of US$2.1 billion (USBM/USGS 1997b:7). Hamersley also built a new mine, Yandicoogina, that opened in 1999 with a capacity of 15 million tons per year at a cost of US$515 million (USBM/USGS 1998b:41.3).

By the end of 2000, Australian iron ore mining capacity totaled 211 million tons per year, with the vast majority owned by BHP and RTZ (USBM/USGS 2001b: table 2), and expansion continued in the early 2000s. Portman Mining, now Australia's third largest iron ore mining firm, expanded its Koolyanobbing mine to 8 million tons per year in 2001 (USBM/USGS 2001b:3.6). The RTZ–Japanese Robe River joint venture opened the West Angelas mine at a cost of A$880 million in 2002, with capacity expected to reach 20 million tons per year in 2006 (Haine 2001:651). Another 90 million tons per year of potential new mines were under evaluation by the end of 2001 (Haine 2001:659–70), which could bring Australian iron ore mining capacity to 329 million tons per year by the middle of this decade.

The battle to take over North disrupted the close relationship between RTZ and the Japanese steel mills because of the Japanese steel mills' fear of facing a three-firm iron ore oligopoly of CVRD, RTZ, and BHP. CVRD's 162 million tons of capacity owned or controlled, RTZ's 142 million tons, and BHP's 68 million tons represented approximately 60 to 80 percent of the world export market by the end of 2000 (*Financial Times* 2000:32; *Mining Journal* 2001:336; Wyatt 2000:30). Iron ore production by firm in 2002 was estimated at 163.6 million tons for CVRD, 93.8 million tons for RTZ, and 80.8 million tons for BHP, or a total of 30.1 percent of world production and 70 percent of seaborne exports (*Mining Journal* 2003:21). CVRD controlled 14.8 percent of world iron ore mining capacity in 2002, RTZ controlled 8.3 percent, and BHP Billiton controlled 7.2 percent (Minerals and Energy 2004:2:36). This concentration resulted from merger and acquisition expenditures in the global iron ore industry of US$1.56 billion in 2001, US$2.86 billion in 2002, and US$3.96 billion in 2003 (Lundmark and Nilsson 2003:111), historically unprecedented levels of merger and acquisition activity in what is usually considered an antiquated "old economy" industry that is once again booming because of rapid economic growth in China.

The creation of this near oligopoly made the negotiations between the Japanese and European steel mills and their iron ore suppliers more difficult in the early 2000s. The large iron ore firms sought to raise prices and increase profits using their increased bargaining power, resulting in a 9 percent price increase for 2003–4 after extended negotiations (*Mining Journal* 2003:21), and prices increased by 18.6 percent for 2004–5 (*Skillings* 2004b:27), by 71.5 percent in 2005–6 (*Lloyd's List* 2006a), and by another 19 percent for 2006–7 (Keenan 2006).

The Chinese steel mills and the Chinese state fought hard against this latest increase, arguing that iron ore and steel prices in China were too low to support yet another increase and that, due to the huge size of the Chinese market, Chinese steel firms should be the lead negotiators for setting prices. The Chinese state sought to intervene directly by trying to force Chinese firms not to accept large increases; measures included threatening to prevent Chinese steel companies that accepted price increases from importing any iron ore, holding a first-ever government-led conference between all Chinese steel firms to build a coordinated negotiating position (*Xinhua* 2006), and temporarily preventing two ships loaded with iron ore priced above a possible government-imposed price cap being unloaded (*Lloyd's List* 2006b). These Chinese government efforts to obtain lower prices drew strong negative reactions from Australia and Brazil, including efforts by Brazil's mining industry association to get the government of Brazil to appeal to the World Trade Organization for violations of free trade rules because of Chinese government intervention in the negotiations (*Skillings* 2006c; Wilson 2006b). The Chinese government even sought to work cooperatively with Nippon Steel to block efforts to increase iron ore prices (*AFX International Focus* 2006; Wilson 2006a, 2006b).

However, all of these efforts by the Chinese state failed (Cox 2006:7; *Sinocast* 2006b; *Skillings* 2006b:4, 2006d, June 2006:28; McGregor 2006:2). The Chinese steel firms and the Chinese state have sought to use the strategies developed by the Japanese steel firms and the Japanese state to control their iron ore costs, but China's own dramatic economic ascent based on heavy industrialization has so far undercut these strategies and left the Chinese steel firms in a situation of paying ever-increasing iron ore prices.

The major iron ore firms continue to expand production around the world, often in partnership with large iron ore consumers in Japan, South Korea, and China. Despite largely stagnant steel production since the early 1990s in Japan, the two major Japanese steel firms continue to negotiate joint ventures and long-term contracts in iron ore, just as they have done in coal. Australia continues to be Japan's most important iron ore supplier. RTZ and the Japanese steel mills restored their close ties after the battle over the North takeover, with Nippon Steel signing a new contract for 150 million tons of iron ore over twenty years in 2004 and increasing its ownership stake in two iron ore joint ventures with RTZ (*AFX News* 2004c; *Asia Pulse* 2004; *JCN Newswire* 2004b). JFE Steel signed a joint venture and iron ore supply contract with BHP Billiton in 2004 for 16 million tons per year of iron ore for sixteen years, BHP Billiton's first joint venture with a Japanese steel mill (*Skillings*, November 2004:5).

BHP formed a joint venture with POSCO Steel of Korea to develop a mine producing 15 million tons per year and a port for US$564 million (*Mining Journal* 2002a:241). Anglo American, the failed bidder for North, bought large shares of Kumba Resources and Avmin, two South African iron ore mining firms (McCarthy 2002:25), wants to build a new mine at Hope Downs in Australia with a capacity of 15 to 25 million tons, and is investigating new projects in Gabon and Senegal (Bain 2003:10).

Much of this expansion is being planned to export not to the relatively stagnant Japanese steel industry, but instead to the rapidly growing Chinese steel industry (Hextall 2002:67; *Mining Journal* 2002b). A Salomon Smith Barney report issued in 2003 argued that "in a relative sense, China is now more important to the metals and mining sector than, say, Japan in the 1960s and 1970s, since at that time Japan was growing against a backdrop of reasonable global growth whereas Chinese growth has occurred in relative isolation" (cited in Hextall 2003:63). Chinese steel firms imported 148 million tons of iron ore in 2003, surpassing Japanese iron ore imports for the first time and making China the world's leading iron ore importer (Buchanan 2004:23). Chinese iron ore imports rose to 208 million tons in 2004, with total global iron ore trade totaling 590 million tons; Australia and Brazil exported 205 and 203 million tons respectively (Zarocostas 2005:5).

The two major iron ore mining firms in Australia also formed new relationships with the Chinese steel mills. RTZ signed two long-term contracts with Baosteel totaling 70 million tons per year (*Skillings* 2005:4). RTZ is investing US$530 million to expand its Yandicoogina mine from 36 to 52 million tons per year and US$690 million to expand its port capacity from 116 to 140 million tons per year (*Skillings* 2005c:8) in order to supply the Chinese market. BHP Billiton signed a long-term contract with four Chinese steel firms under which the four Chinese partners would own 40 percent of the Jimblebar mine and would buy 12 million tons per year of iron ore for twenty-five years; this represents the first-ever Chinese equity investment in a foreign iron ore mine and includes two Japanese trading companies (Itochu and Mitsui) as partners to facilitate coordination and shipping (*AFX News* 2004b; Callick 2004; *Global Newswire* 2004b; Kirk 2004a:5; *Kyodo News* 2004; *Sinocast* 2004).

The Chinese steel firms typically pay US$3.50–4.00 more per ton for iron ore than do the Japanese steel firms, even though China is the world's largest iron ore importer, because the Chinese steel firms have not coordinated their purchases. However, in light of the recent long-term contracts and joint-venture investments, one industry analyst suggests that "in some ways the Chinese are beginning to do what the Japanese steel industry has already done to get pricing power" (*AFX News* 2004b). Chinese steel firms plan to invest A$10 billion in Australian mines in the next few years to guarantee iron ore supplies (*Skillings* 2005b:5). The coordinated strategy of the four Chinese partners in the joint venture with BHP Billiton clearly results from learning from the Japanese steel mills' model of forming joint ventures among themselves in order to increase bargaining power with the iron ore oligopoly, although these efforts to control costs have met with little success so far.

The Chinese steel firms' efforts to find new sources of iron ore even include trying to acquire iron ore in the United States, one of the world's highest-cost producers. Laiwu Steel formed a joint venture with Cleveland-Cliffs in 2003 to buy a bankrupt iron ore mine in Minnesota and ship iron ore pellets under a long-term contract to China (Minter 2004). Baosteel plans to buy 3 million tons per year of iron ore for fifteen years from iron ore mines in New Mexico and Arizona (*Skillings*, November 2004:10). Current high ore prices and demand make such arrangements viable, but these high prices are likely to decline over the medium term, threatening the long-term sustainability of these deals.

The China-driven boom in iron ore demand and prices is provoking a rush of new mining firms into the industry, just as is happening in metallurgical coal. This investment rush is particularly significant in Australia. New entrants in Australia include Cazaly Resources (*Skillings* 2005e:9), Midwest Corporation, Murchison Metals, Gindalbie Metals (*Skillings* 2006a:12), and Cape Lambert Iron Ore (*Skillings* 2006e: 10), all of which are planning or are already building mines that will produce 1 to 5 million tons per year each of iron ore. Sinosteel Corporation, a large Chinese iron ore trading firm, is seeking to buy a 70 percent ownership stake in yet another smaller Australian iron ore project, Grange Resources, combining a mine with a proposed 6.6 million tons per year and a pelletization project (*Global News Wire* 2006). Another midsize Australian iron ore producer, Fortescue, recently signed a contract to produce 7.5 million tons per year with four Chinese steel mills (*Skillings* 2005c:8). A closed mine on Koolan Island is also being reopened to supply iron ore to China (Holland 2004; Howarth 2003; *Skillings* 2006b:17). Clearly, the Chinese market is driving a boom in iron ore investment in and exports from Australia, Brazil, and other iron ore mining regions.

The Consequences for Iron Ore–Exporting Peripheries

These Japanese iron ore access strategies and iron ore mining firm restructurings reduced iron ore costs for the Japanese steel mills and progressively reduced the benefits of and increased the costs to Japan's iron ore peripheries. Australian analysts and state and national governments in the late 1950s and early 1960s viewed iron ore exports as a means to increase ore supplies and provide funds for the development of the domestic steel industry. Australian analyses at the time saw Japan as a competitor in the steel industry and sought strategies to increase Australian steel exports, based on their raw materials cost advantage over Japan. One study of the development of the Australian iron and steel industry from the 1840s through the early 1960s concluded that "during the 1950s Australia became a highly industrialized nation; by the end of the decade manufacturing provided a base for extensive building, construction and service industries, and, indeed, it was clear that in exports also manufactures ought soon to play a significant if not yet a key role" (Hughes 1963:151).

The steel industry played a major role in this development during the 1950s as the Broken Hill Proprietary (BHP) added new iron and steel capacity, with steel production totaling 4.06 million tons in 1962 (Hughes 1963:152–53), as table 5.5 shows. The efforts of the Australian government to preserve what were thought to be very limited national iron ore reserves, in the context of this growth and expected future development, appear quite understandable and prudent.

Moreover, in the early 1960s, analysts considered the Australian and Japanese steel industries as major competitors in Asia: "the Japanese steel industry which was becoming Australia's chief competitor adopted new techniques more rapidly than the Australian, and this was to be a decisive factor in bringing its prices below Australian

TABLE 5.5
Australian Pig Iron and Steel Production
(in millions of tons)

	Pig Iron	Steel
1907	.019	.006
1910	.04	.008
1915	.14	.11
1920	.35	.2
1925	.46	.4
1930	.31	.32
1935	.7	.7
1940	1.2	1.3
1945	1.1	1.4
1950	1.1	1.2
1955	1.9	2.2
1960	2.7	3.5
1965	4.8	6.02
1970	6.8	7.52
1975	8.2	8.65
1980	7.7	8.37
1985	6.2	7.25
1990	6.1	6.7
1995	7.5	8.5
2000	7.0	7.8

SOURCES: Hughes 1963:195–99 for 1907–60; USBM/USGS various years b for 1965–2000.

prices in spite of greatly inferior raw material resources. Japan's blast furnaces, like Australia's, were among the world's largest. . . . but Japanese firms were ahead of all other countries in developing self fluxing ores and sintering, and Japan led the world in the adoption of oxygen boosted steel smelting" (Hughes 1963:161). Hughes notes that Japanese steel production between 1939 and 1959 rose from 7 to 16 million tons, or at about the same rate as Australian production, and that, in comparison with other major steel-producing nations, "Australia had the best combination of natural resources for iron and steel production" (Hughes 1963:166).

As we have shown in this and the preceding chapter, Hughes's conclusion is clearly correct: the combination of immense, high-grade metallurgical coal and iron ore resources in Australia provided the essential ingredient for the world's most competitive steel industry. However, that steel industry was built in the MIDAs of Japan, not in Australia. Hughes places much of the blame for Australia's falling behind Japan during the 1950s on BHP's corporate strategies, particularly on its failure to achieve a position of global technological leadership, and its fear of building capacity in excess of local demand, rather than aggressively seeking export markets (Hughes 1963:166–82).

Hughes estimated that, in 1946, Australian pig iron had a cost advantage of 31 percent over U.S. pig iron production, 22 percent in bar steel, and 14 percent in structural steel (Hughes 1963:176), at a time when the U.S. steel industry led the world. Clearly, the potential existed for Australian steel and products manufactured in Australia with domestic steel to compete in global markets, despite the long shipping distances to most markets, a problem that confronted Japan as well. BHP, however, failed to make the investments made by the Japanese steel firms and lacked the government support that created the critical pattern of state-sector-firm coordination in Japan, supported by the U.S. government, that underlay the Japanese steel industry's transformation of the global steel industry and its creation of the global coal and iron ore industries that supported Japanese economic ascent.

As had been the case in metallurgical coal in Australia and Canada, the Australian government intended to use exports to Japan to support domestic industrialization via export earnings, rather than becoming the goal and main economic activity of the region. Japanese raw materials strategies effectively trapped these regions in the roles of quarries for Japan, choking off further domestic raw materials–based industrialization in favor of exports. For mining firms and states during the 1960s and early 1970s, the apparently extremely lucrative long-term contracts for exports to Japan provided a seemingly secure source of profits for mining firms and sources of employment, local development, export earnings, and tax revenues to regional and national governments.

As was the case in metallurgical coal, Japanese raw materials access strategies in iron ore imposed large costs on exporting regions. The tremendous bargaining advantage conferred by the combination of coordination between Japanese steel firms, the diversification of their supply sources, and their dominant position as a purchaser results in quite favorable terms of long-term contracts governing iron ore sales to Japan. In Australia competition between states, between state and federal governments, and between iron ore–producing firms for contracts with Japan exacerbated this problem. This produced severe downward pressure on iron ore prices, further benefiting the Japanese steel firms (Panda 1982:79–86). Similar inequalities in relative strengths of bargaining positions between the Japanese steel firms and other iron ore–exporting firms and nations, including Brazil, produced similarly favorable results for the Japanese steel firms.

Both Australian and Brazilian iron ore exports to Japan grew rapidly beginning in the mid-1960s, as table 5.6 shows. However, these two nations, the world's lowest-cost iron ore producers, sacrificed billions of dollars in rent from their naturally favorable mining conditions and their investments in mining and transport infrastructure over the past four decades. In comparison with the average cost of iron ore exports from the Philippines, a significant supplier to Japan but with much higher costs, Australian mining firms have forgone a total of US$16.2 billion in current terms and US$23.8 billion in constant 1998 dollars between 1976 and 2000, based on CIF prices in Japan. Similarly, Brazilian iron ore mining firms have forgone a total of US$5.8 billion in current dollars and US$8.5 billion in 1998 dollars between 1976 and 2000 (see table 5.6). This US$22 billion subsidy over twenty-five years explains a great deal of Japan's global competitiveness in steel production and steel-consuming industries, especially during the stagnation of the past decade in Japan. These massive subsidies from Japan's two largest iron ore peripheries, combined with the subsidies from Japan's coal peripheries, sustained Japan's steel and broader economic competitiveness for years by lowering steel production costs and thereby production costs for many other Japanese industries.

The origins and subsequent evolution of the Carajás project in Brazil demonstrate how core powers shape economies and politics in their raw materials peripheries and the consequences for these peripheries. Carajás began as an exploration and development project by U.S. Steel in the 1960s. Brazilian government efforts to promote Amazonian development and the need to increase export revenues led the Brazilian government to become a partner with U.S. Steel via state-owned CVRD in 1970 in a joint venture, Amazonia Mineracão, or AMZA. Spatial barriers dimmed public and legal concerns with questions of landownership and land. The iron ore deposits were located in a socially remote area with little social value in the early 1970s. The Brazilian government sought to use this social remoteness to its advantage to develop the mine

TABLE 5.6

Australian and Brazilian Iron Ore Production,
Total Export Volume and Value, and Value Forgone

	Australia						Brazil					
	Production[a]	Exports[a]	Total Value of Exports[b]	Volume of Exports to Japan[a]	Rent on Exports to Japan Forgone[b]	Rent on Exports to Japan Forgone[c]	Production[a]	Exports[a]	Total Value of Exports[b]	Volume of Exports to Japan[a]	Rent on Exports to Japan Forgone[b]	Rent on Exports to Japan Forgone[c]
1951	2.5	0		0			2.4	1.3		0		
1952	2.7	0		0			3	1.2		0		
1953												
1954	3.5	0		0			3	1.7		0		
1955	3.6	0		0			4.1	2.4		0.009		
1956	3.9	0		0			4	2.7		0.05		
1957												
1958	3.9	0		0			5.1	2.8		0.046		
1959	4.2	0		0			8.7	3.9		0.2		
1960	4.5	0		0			9.2	5.1		0.4		
1961	5.5	0		0			9.6	6.1		0.4		
1962	5.1	0		0			10.6	7.5		0.5		
1963	5.7	0		0			11	8.1		0.5		
1964	5.9	0.013		0			16.7	9.6		0.5		
1965	6.8	0.15		0.1			17.9	12.5		0.8		
1966	11.1	2		2						2		
1967	17.3	9.2		8						2		
1968	26.6	16.4		14						2		
1969	38.6	26.9		23						4		
1970	51.2	41.1		37						7		
1971	62.1	52.8		46								
1972	64.4	54.1		48						9		
1973	84.8	74.2		64						13		
1974	97	83.7		61.5								

Year												
1975	98	80.4	1,015	62.3	483	1,383	88.5	71.4	996	23.1	150	430
1976	93	81.2	1,056	56	591	1,590			908	24	154	414
1977	96	78.9	1,036	64	503	1,257			1,028	27	136	340
1978	83	75.3	1,127	53	545	1,224			1,338	21	219	492
1979	92	78.5	1,306	55	639	1,264			1,564	26	226	447
1980	96	80.4	1,348	57	714	1,280			1,651	23	280	502
1981	85	71.7	1,457	55	748	1,263			1,591	27	270	456
1982	88	72.6	1,420	54	661	1,082			1,427	27	214	350
1983	71	74.1	1,421	50	677	1,063	93.1	70	1,605	23.8	232	364
1984	94	85.5	1,400	59	604	915	92.1	88.6	1,658	29.1	300	455
1985	93	84.8	1,301	53	486	723	112.1	91.8	1,624	37.8	208	309
1986	94	79.5	1,182	43	503	722	128.2	92.3	1,615	26.8	194	278
1987	102	77.8	1,391	48	536	739	129.1	97.3	1,900	26.6	222	306
1988	96	94.9	1,620	53	605	796	134.1	105.3	2,176	27.9	259	341
1989	106	101.7	1,745	55	703	877	146	111.6	2,407	30.2	271	338
1990	111	95.9	2,259	56	793	949	154	114.3	2,612	29.2	305	365
1991	118	112	2,064	57	740	860	154	112	2,381	29.7	266	309
1992	112	104	1,965	54	654	738		105	2,257	26.7	255	288
1993	121	112	1,897	54	605	665		109	2,294	28	228	251
1994	129	119	1,897	55	594	635		124	2,548	28	242	259
1995	143	130	2,279	59	737	766		130	2,695	28	239	248
1996	152	128	2,645	60	807	820		129	2,846	26	258	262
1997	156	147	2,505	65	686	686		141	3,250	29	260	260
1998	161	136	2,303	54	755	739		143	2,746	26	207	203
1999	152	139	2,580	66	805	762		140	3,048	24	226	214
2000	172	157		71			209	160		27		
2001	181	164		70			239	156		25		
2002	187	176						170				

SOURCES: Tex Report 1994b; USBM/USGS various years a.

[a] In millions of tons.
[b] In millions of U.S. dollars.
[c] In millions of 1998 U.S. dollars.

and the area in ways that suited its own and its partner's interests, regardless of legal, political, and social considerations. In 1974 AMZA took the first steps in an unprecedented, and illegal, attempt to purchase from the state of Pará more than 400,000 hectares around the deposits, far more land than it needed to build the iron ore mine. AMZA treated the land as if it owned it as soon as it made the offer to buy the land, but there were very few claimants to the land in question, so AMZA's closing it off had little significant social effect. Eventually, the central state would remove Pará's authority over the area, but for more than two years after one of the largest illicit attempts to grab land in the Amazon, no public discussion occurred.

Only slowly did Carajás become included in the spatial and temporal systems governing the rest of the country, and then primarily in terms of the effects of Carajás on the surrounding, already more occupied space. In 1975 a highly politicized debate over the technical merits of alternative transport strategies began. An engineer from Belém published a three-part analysis in a local newspaper, criticizing AMZA's plans to construct a railroad to carry the ore to a deepwater port in the neighboring state of Maranhão and proposing that barging the ore down the Tocantins to be reloaded onto ships in Belém's river port would be more cost-effective and more beneficial to regional development. Having acceded to the state's loss of control over public lands, and feeling increasingly their own loss of political and economic autonomy, fractions of the regionally dominant classes looked for technical support to defend themselves against what threatened to be another loss, this one of control over the transshipment of ores and potential local linkages. These regionally dominant groups began to appreciate, still only dimly, how important mining would become in Pará's economy, and how much its impact would be mediated by spatial relationships, even if they still had little way of knowing how far its effects would penetrate the social, economic, and political organization of their state.

In 1977 conflict between the Brazilian government, CVRD, and U.S. Steel over plans for the Carajás mine erupted into fierce public debate because of the growing divergence between the interests, plans, and investment strategies of CVRD on the one hand and U.S. Steel on the other. The world market for iron ore weakened during the 1970s and U.S. Steel already owned iron mines in Venezuela. It wanted to maintain control over the Carajás deposits, but it did not want to open the mine until it recovered a significant share of its investments elsewhere or until world demand for iron ore increased significantly. U.S. Steel worried that a major addition to world supplies from Carajás would depress prices even further.

U.S. Steel aggravated the risk that now so worried it by pushing its Brazilian partner to greatly increase the projected annual rate of extraction from Carajás, from 12 million to 50 million tons a year. This higher rate of extraction made access to a deepwater port necessary, and thus rationalized the investments in the railroad, but it also raised the costs of that infrastructure. U.S. Steel proposed that the Brazilian government assume part of the cost of the railroad. When the Brazilian government refused, U.S. Steel started to delay its share of investments. By 1977, as the result of this conflict, CVRD bought out U.S. Steel interests for US$55 million in a deal negotiated by the Brazilian government.

Criticism of the large payment to U.S. Steel and the sudden prospect that Carajás might not be developed without some outside investors to take U.S. Steel's place pushed Carajás into public awareness and open political debate. Headline stories on front pages and lengthy technical reports in editorial sections of newspapers, not only in Belém but also in São Paulo, discussed each nuance and turn in the search for investors and about whether CVRD could develop the project on its own. Public awareness of Carajás increased even more when one of Pará's delegates to the national senate denounced Pará's governor for having proceeded with a sale of land to AMZA. As Carajás came more into public and political consciousness, questions about the space around it, particularly about control over it and rights to the value it represented, became more pertinent.

The debate revealed that in 1976, two years after AMZA started negotiations with Pará's Secretariat of Agriculture, the national government projected a road originally planned to end at the southern limits of the Amazon to extend all the way up the Transamazon Highway in the middle of the Amazon. The National Department of Roads and Highways had not actually determined the road's route and the areas in a 100-kilometer belt around the road that, under Brazilian law, became national government property because of the planned construction of the road. However, AMZA and the state and national governments presumed it would include Carajás, and AMZA paid the state of Pará 20 percent of the agreed price, equivalent to US$450 million, in apparent violation of national law.

The national government, however, had no real intention of building this road, because all road building in the area had been suspended in 1975. The planned road allowed the national government to take control over an area of great economic and political importance. AMZA's request and the state of Pará's processing of it violated federal law. No more than 3,000 hectares on any sale of land in the Amazon could be sold without Senate approval. No mining company could legally buy surface land in the way that AMZA intended to do. Furthermore, AMZA itself changed its justification for the request during this debate. AMZA said at first that it would need some of the land for transport and other support facilities, but that it planned to use more than half of the land requested for nonmineral economic activities. Subsequently, AMZA changed its rationale, pleading instead that it needed control over that land in order to guard its ecological integrity. The latter argument was reasonable but appears disingenuous in the light of the controversy provoked by AZMA's original, economically justified request. It seems more reasonable to conclude that AMZA devised a stratagem that became increasingly popular as environmental concerns about the Amazon gained national and international currency—the invocation of environmental safety to justify the private or corporate appropriation of large tracts of public land.

The scandal over the AMZA sale, and the controversy over the more general, but intimately related, constitutional and political issue of the central state's appropriation of control over public land, played into party politics directly, as Pará's senators and delegates used the issue either to attack or defend, in different cases, the governor of the state or the national administration. Despite this debate and violations of state and national law, CVRD eventually secured control over Carajás and developed the iron ore mine and a wide variety of other mines, mineral processing, agricultural, and other projects during the 1980s in response to Japanese and European demand for iron ore. The interests of core powers, CVRD, and the Brazilian national government eventually overcame local resistance and a variety of legal obstacles to restructure the Carajás region into part of Japan's raw materials periphery. This extended conflict illustrates the weakness of extractive governments and populations in the face of the strategies of core states and firms and of the extractive region's own national state in promoting raw materials exports to the core.

Despite these political battles over CVRD's role in the Amazon, CVRD's iron ore exports rose steadily from 1964 until their first peak in 1975, rising from 7.1 million tons to 47.3 million tons. From 1975 through the early 1980s, as the result of the crisis in the global steel industry and the negotiating strategies of the Japanese steel mills, CVRD's focus shifted from the stagnant export market to the internal market, with total sales of iron ore continuing their rise from 7.1 million tons in 1964 to 49.8 million tons in 1975 and to 61.3 million tons in 1981 (Raw 1987:16). The average price CVRD received for iron ore FOB between 1951 and 1959 averaged US$12.93 per ton, but this fell to US$7.99 per ton between 1960 and 1972, reaching a low point of US$6.87 per ton in 1969. However, the average price rose steadily throughout the 1970s, reaching US$17.79 per ton in 1980 (Raw 1985:299–301). Between 1964 and 1980, CVRD provided on average 65 percent of funding for its investments from its own funds from iron ore sales (Raw 1985:327–29). In other words, two-thirds of the funding for CVRD's rapidly increasing role as a global iron ore exporter came from its profits from selling Brazilian iron ore, rather than from domestic or foreign loans. CVRD could do this because its rate of profit (profits as a percentage of total sales revenues) averaged 25.4 percent per year between 1969 and 1980, with only one year of negative returns (Raw 1985:332), a rate of profit far in excess of core steel mills and of most core firms over this period. Iron ore exports were obviously a highly profitable business during this decade.

CVRD thus used its rents to pay for the very expansion that continued to exacerbate the global excess supply of iron ore that eventually forced down its prices severely. The contrasts between the consequences for CVRD as a firm and for regional and national development in Brazil are quite evident: what made sense as a corporate strategy, to reinvest profits derived in large part from the naturally produced quality of its iron ore in expanding its production capacity, resulted in a huge transfer of wealth from Brazil to Japan and the other nations that consume most of CVRD's iron ore.

Conclusion

These raw materials supply arrangements that reduced costs to the Japanese steel industry allowed Japan to become a leading producer and exporter of steel and to take advantage of the tremendous linkage opportunities presented by the development of a large-scale steel industry. Japanese access strategies restructured iron ore mining from an international system of captive mines (mines owned by the steel firms that consume the iron ore) to a largely unintegrated industry composed of a significant number of transnational and state-owned companies in Australia, Latin America, Africa, and Asia, all competing for markets in a condition of excess iron ore mining capacity. This excess capacity results from capacity additions fomented by Japanese steel firms, most notably the massive Carajás mine. The economies of scale resulting from these mining and infrastructure investments and Japanese involvement in large-scale shipping to reduce transport costs reduced the total cost of importing iron ore for use by Japanese steel mills, dramatically enhancing international competitiveness.

The cumulative effect of the Japanese-induced transformation of the world iron industry reshaped global iron ore reserves. A dramatic increase in world reserves took place between 1950 and the early 1990s; world reserves increased from 26.7 billion tons in 1950 (Manners 1971:228) to 64.6 billion tons in the early 1990s, despite the extraction of billions of tons of iron ore in the intervening years. In short, 79 percent of world reserves of iron ore are concentrated in only six countries. This high degree of concentration of remaining known reserves creates a significant potential for market power on the part of this limited number of countries. However, the relatively fragmented ownership of resources in most of these countries as a result of this Japan-driven restructuring largely negates this potential.

Japan's economic development drove a tremendous growth in world iron ore exports, world seaborne exports, and total ton-miles of seaborne exports since the 1950s,

TABLE 5.7
World Iron Ore Trade and Seaborne Trade
and Seaborne Ton-Miles

	Total World Exports[a]	Seaborne Exports[a]	Seaborne Ton-Miles[b]
1951	54		
1955	97		
1960	152		
1965	212		
1970	323		
1975	381		
1980	385		
1982	329	273	1,478
1985	376	321	1,702
1990	397	347	1,978
1995	446	402	2,287
2000	491	454	2,545
2002	512		

SOURCES: *Fearnleys World Bulk Trades* various years; USBM/USGS
various years b.
[a]in millions of tons
[b]in billions

as table 5.7 shows. Total world exports grew by a factor of 10 over the past fifty years, and seaborne exports and ton-miles also grew rapidly.

The world's three largest iron ore mining firms, CVRD, RTZ, and BHP, have finally learned from the Japanese-driven globalization and flexibility. These large firms are trying to take advantage of the collapse of state-owned enterprises, the need for foreign technology and capital, and the drive for privatization around the world to concentrate control over production and to try to increase iron ore prices. These large iron ore mining firms, however, face formidable opponents in the Japanese steel mills and the Chinese steel firms that are closely connected to the Japanese steel mills.

Transferring much of the cost and risk of restructuring world metallurgical coal and iron ore industries, capturing the benefits of large-scale transport in exporting regions and ocean shipping via the relocation of Japanese steel mills to Maritime Industrial Development Areas on the Japanese coast, and establishing linkages with shipbuilding and shipping industries all added up to the material foundations of Japan's economic ascent. In terms of our second question on how Japan globalized the world economy in support of its rapid economic growth, the Japanese steel mills and the Japanese state created global coal and iron ore industries from previously highly fragmented and often localized industries. These increasingly competitive global industries provided the building blocks of Japan's steel industry and the broader process of Japan's economic ascent at progressively lower costs. In terms of our third question on the consequences of the new forms of global inequality created by this globalization, it is equally clear that this Japan-driven globalization transferred the burdens of costs and risks to Japan's new coal and iron peripheries. Japanese raw materials strategies effectively trapped Australia, Brazil, and other iron ore– and coal-producing regions in the roles of quarries for Japan, choking off further domestic raw materials–based industrialization in favor of exports

Regarding our fifth research question on how China is utilizing and transforming the Japan-created global raw materials industries to support China's rapid development, it is clear that the emergence of the Chinese steel industry with the support of the Japanese steel mills may transform the global steel and iron ore industries, just as the development of the Japanese steel industry did after World War II. Japan's creation of a global iron ore industry opened the door for China's raw materials–based industrial deepening and potentially its sustained ascent by bringing into production new mines and firms in previously socially remote regions. These mining firms needed new markets, after the long stagnation of Japanese steel production in the 1990s. Chinese steel firms are using this opportunity and importing capital and technology from Japan to become the world's largest iron ore importer and steel producer.

CHAPTER SIX

Transporting Coal and Iron Ore

In the process of transporting raw materials to Japan, the Japanese shipping industry created economies of scale that lowered Japanese raw materials costs for the steel plants and their customers in the Maritime Industrial Development Areas (MIDAs). The growing scale of ships and ports as the outcome of the strategies of Japanese firms and the Japanese state dramatically reduced raw materials transport costs during the second half of the twentieth century and thus affected Japan's coal- and iron ore–exporting peripheries. Japan's success now serves as a model for China's rapid ascent and its role in raw materials transport and shipbuilding

In this chapter we bring together and integrate our answers to our first three research questions: What drove Japan's rapid economic ascent? How did Japan globalize the world economy in support of its rapid economic growth? What are the consequences of the new forms of global inequality created by this globalization? This integration manifests itself physically in the larger and larger ships hauling millions of tons of coal and iron ore from Japan's raw materials peripheries to the steel mills in the MIDAs. We also address our fifth research question: How is China utilizing and transforming the Japan-created global raw materials industries to support China's rapid development?

The tremendous increase in Japanese raw materials consumption and the resulting globalization of the coal and iron industries increased the volume of coal and iron ore trade dramatically (table 6.1). The increasing role of relatively remote raw materials–extracting regions, especially Australia, to supply Japanese, European, and U.S. raw materials needs significantly increased the average distance of seaborne raw materials trade (table 6.2). The combination of the increasing volume of international trade in raw materials and the increase in the average distance traveled by each ton of seaborne raw materials trade resulted in a major increase in the key metric of transport as part of the production process, the volume of ton-miles of raw materials transported (table 6.3). This chapter analyzes the completion of the "virtuous cycle" of steel, coal, iron, shipbuilding, and shipping as generative sectors that created Japan's global competitiveness.

TABLE 6.1
Global Seaborne Raw Materials Trade
(in thousands of metric tons)

	Petroleum	Coal	Iron Ore
1960	366,000 (1962)	46,000	101,000
1970	995,000	101,000	247,000
1980	1,320,000	188,000	314,000
1990	1,190,000	342,000	347,000
2000	1,608,000	523,000	454,000

SOURCES: Drewry 1972a:8, 1980:35; *Fearnleys Review* various years; *Fearnleys World Bulk Trades* various years; USBM, *Minerals Yearbooks* various years.

TABLE 6.2
Global Trade Average Distance Traveled
(in total ton-miles / tons transported)

	Petroleum	Coal	Iron Ore
1960	4,508 (1962)	3,152	2,614
1970	5,625	4,762	4,425
1980	6,227	5,090	5,258
1990	5,267	5,406	5,700
2000	5,087	4,797	5,606

SOURCES: *Fearnleys Review* various years; *Fearnleys World Bulk Trades* various years.

TABLE 6.3
Total Global Ton-Miles for Each Raw Material
(in billions of ton-miles)

	Petroleum		Coal	Iron Ore
	Crude	Products		
1960	1,650	145	264	34
1970	5,597	890	481	1,093
1980	8,219	1,020	957	1,651
1990	6,261	1,560	1,849	1,978
2000	8,180	2,085	2,509	2,545

SOURCES: *Fearnleys Review* various years; *Fearnleys World Bulk Trades* various years.

Coal and Iron Ore Ports in Japan and Its Raw Materials Peripheries

On the Japanese end of the ocean voyage, MIDAs restructured industrial location and topography, taking advantage of Japan's long deepwater coastline and the efficiencies of greenfield plants using the latest technologies and of having consumers of steel in close proximity to steel plants. Large ships using expanded or newly built ports financed by coordinated state and firm investments unload directly into stocking yards at plants in the port area, eliminating inland transport costs in Japan.

MIDAs change topography by reclaiming land, digging new ocean and river channels, and other modifications in port areas to provide both location and transport facilities for industrial plants. MIDAs represent a very high degree of manipulation of nature, not simply a means of overcoming the natural bulkiness and resulting high cost of moving raw materials to inland plants. They restructure both nature and the national economy through state policies and investment, in combination with private firms, in order to manipulate nature, space, topography, and existing economic and social structures in search of private profits.

MIDAs represent state-sector-firm organization of unprecedented scope and cost in response to the increasing scale, geographical scope of sources and markets, and technical complexity of the bulk raw materials industry as Japanese firms and the Japanese state sought to resolve the contradiction between economies of scale and diseconomies of space in the 1950s and 1960s. Japan could only compete against the regionally based comparative advantages of a U.S.-dominated world market by using the ocean to become global.

This next step of global sourcing needed new institutions for the tight coupling of firms, sectors, and states. The Japanese government and MITI's successful response to this challenge and resolution of the internal conflicts over the steel industry's future restructured both domestic and global social and economic organization. MIDAs epitomize the tightly coupled internal and external restructuring and reorganization to support Japan's industrial transformation. They efficiently articulate with a network of far-flung sources of precisely distinguished types of coal and iron that became economically viable to import only with the scale of transport MIDAs made possible. MIDAs also provided the basis for the tightly coupled internal system of very large-scale, very efficient downstream distribution, and the quality control that the basic oxygen furnace and continuous casting machines operating at full capacity required. MIDAs looked inward to the domestic economy, sustaining economies of scale and distribution, and outward to global sources, making possible very large cargoes and also providing the capacity for efficient storage and movement needed for precise blending of coal and iron ores.

The MIDA illustrates how Japanese strategy and organization link the domestic and the international. The strategy for raw materials access is so tightly coupled with the organization of production in Japan that the internal and the external become continuous in their organized relationship of the flows of raw materials, while at the same time strong incentives for state-sector-firm collaboration within Japan draw the internal-external distinction very clearly in terms of the distribution of cost savings and profits. The tightly coupled flow of raw materials from mine to market obliterates the internal-external line. At the same time, the conjunction of interests in promoting national economic growth heightens the internal-external division by systematically favoring Japanese domestic interests at the level of the firm, the sector, the national economy, and the society.

Steel firms, dependent on huge volumes of imported iron ore and coal, built large greenfield mills in the MIDAs. By 1982 MIDAs included twelve iron and ten coal ports capable of unloading ships exceeding 100,000 deadweight tons (dwt) in Japan (CSR 1982:37–38). All of the major Japanese steel firms had their own dedicated large-scale iron ore ports. Nippon Steel had one port capable of unloading 300,000-dwt ships, four capable of unloading 160,000- to 200,000-dwt ships, and four capable of unloading 70,000- to 80,000-dwt ships. Nippon Kokan Steel, Kawasaki Steel, and Sumitomo Metal each had two ports for 160,000- to 200,000-dwt ships, and Kobe Steel and Nisshin Steel each had one port for 155,000-dwt ships; only Nakayama Steel had a port limited to 63,000-dwt ships (Penfold 1984:29). By 2000 thirteen Japanese ports could unload ships exceeding 250,000 dwt (IEA 2002:III.66–68).

Chapters 4 and 5 described the creation of a model of exporting state and/or firm provision of infrastructure in Australian coal and iron ore that then served as a template for expanding Japan's raw materials supply systems into a global sourcing network. The size of ports and the efficiency of loading and unloading processes became increasingly important as ship size increased, because larger ships tie up larger amounts of capital, raising the cost of each day in port.

The scale of port and inland railroad transport also depend on the scale of extraction at the mine. The increasing scale of extraction at new mines meant that ports and inland transport systems must increase in scale as well. Ports reduced the labor required through the introduction of relatively simple but costly mechanical equipment in order to speed up the turnaround time of large bulk carriers.

The high cost of terminal facilities makes it crucial to match demand for the terminal's services with the terminal's capacity in order to minimize inefficiencies and costs to exporters and shippers. Because buyers of raw materials typically ship ore FOB from the exporting port (which means the purchaser of the cargo pays for ocean transport), the responsibility for and cost of building and operating a terminal falls to the exporting firm, while the risk of wasted ships' time falls on the consumer of the raw material. The very costly construction of terminals to accommodate large bulk carriers required large investments by exporting firms and/or governments. Suppliers produce the equipment used in port terminals in limited quantities and therefore at a high unit cost for design and engineering, because suppliers must custom-design equipment to meet the needs of a particular terminal. The fundamental physical-economic relationship that characterizes port equipment is that "typically a machine's weight—and cost—varies with the square of its size and the first power of the supported weights" (Frankel et al. 1985:133). Put simply, the cost of the increased equipment size necessary to load and unload larger ships increases geometrically rather than linearly, meaning that the costs of terminal equipment rose dramatically as bulk carriers became larger, with this burden borne by exporting states and firms.

However, the benefits of these terminals accrue to the importers who can use lower-cost, large-scale ocean transport. The cases of metallurgical coal in western Canada and iron ore in Brazil followed the model developed in the Australian coal industry, with a combination of extractive state and firm provision of the infrastructure necessary to match the increasing scale of extraction, ocean shipping, and processing. The Japanese steel mills in the MIDAs could then utilize the lowest-cost ocean transport technology available, thanks to these huge subsidies from their raw materials suppliers.

Japanese raw materials access strategies dramatically expanded the scale of coal- and iron ore–exporting ports. In 1982 twenty-one iron ore–exporting ports could load ships exceeding 100,000 dwt (CSR 1982:37), including five in Australia and four in Brazil. In 1982 seven coal ports capable of handling more than 100,000 dwt existed (CSR 1982:48), including three in Australia, one in South Africa, and one in western Canada, all built specifically to serve the Japanese market. By 2001 eighteen coal-exporting ports could load ships exceeding 175,000 dwt, including seven in Australia, three in western Canada, four in the United States, and one in South Africa (IEA 2002:III.53). Extractive state and firm investment in expensive port infrastructure costing several hundred million dollars each thus subsidized the Japanese-driven globalization of the coal and iron ore industries with billions of dollars of infrastructural investment. An important gap remains in the story: the ships that linked Australia, Brazil, Canada, and other raw materials peripheries to the Japanese steel plants.

The Role of Shipping in the Japanese Steel Industry

The Japanese shipping industry evolved very differently in the years after World War II, in comparison with the steel and shipbuilding industries. Japanese shipping firms, after the brief boom from the Korean War, endured a long period of low profitability throughout the rest of the 1950s and through the mid-1960s (Chida and Davies 1990:99–101). Japanese government policy during the 1950s and early 1960s focused on the expansion of Japanese-owned liner shipping (regularly scheduled ships that carried a wide variety of cargoes along an established route). Liner ships transported Japanese exports of light manufactures and reduced the burden on the balance of payments because shipping did not have to be purchased from foreign firms in foreign currencies. The government also focused its concessionary financing for the construction and purchase of ships by Japanese firms on a small number of larger firms, forcing the small firms to link themselves with larger firms, reducing competition and increasing cooperation in the industry (Chida and Davies 1990:104–5).

This government-directed reorganization of the Japanese shipping industry created an even more concentrated structure through the Two Laws for the Reconstruction of the Shipping Industry, passed by the Diet in June 1963. The government forced this reorganization by limiting subsidies to firms that participated in the reorganization. This reorganization into six groups—NYK, Yamashita-Shin Nihon Kisen Kaisha, Showa Kaiun, Japan Line, Kawasaki Kisen, and Mitsui-OSK Line—made the shipping industry very profitable between 1964 and 1973 by eliminating "excessive" competition between the previously very numerous shipping lines.

The reorganization also made capital available for the massive investments in larger bulk carriers and in container ships essential for international competitiveness during the period (Chida and Davies 1990:140–47). The rise of general freight rates and bulk shipping rates during the closure of the Suez Canal resulted in the share of ocean freight costs rising to more than half of the CIF price of iron ore imported to Japan. This supplied a tremendous incentive for the creation of a large fleet of Japanese ore carriers in the late 1950s and 1960s. Although the Japanese steel firms initially intended to build their own fleets of ore carriers, Japanese government control over concessionary financing and its refusal to supply financing to firms other than the major shipping lines forced the Japanese steel firms to invest in shipping firms in order to secure partial ownership of bulk shipping (Chida and Davies 1990:119). State-sector-firm coordination controlled potential competition in a capital intensive and cyclical industry, balancing the interests of steel, shipbuilding, and shipping firms with broader societal interests in conserving scarce capital and ensuring low-cost supplies of raw materials. As the result of these government policies, Japanese firms developed large bulk shipping fleets by the 1970s that linked coal- and iron ore–exporting regions to Japanese MIDAs.

The Japanese shipbuilding industry led the world in building and the Japanese shipping industry led the world in buying and operating larger-scale bulk ships. As a result, the average and maximum sizes of dry bulk carriers increased dramatically over the past four decades (table 6.4). The average size of dry bulk carriers increased by 182 percent since 1961, but data on average size conceal an even greater increase in the maximum size of bulk carriers. In 1957, for example, the world's largest bulk carriers were three ships in the 60,000- to 64,000-dwt range. Less than ten years later, the world's first 100,000-dwt bulker was launched. By the mid-1980s a Japanese shipyard

TABLE 6.4
*Average Size of Dry Bulk Carriers
in the Global Fleet*
(in deadweight tons)

	Number of Ships	Total Tonnage	Average
1961	471	8,700,000	18,471
1970	1,964	55,100,000	28,055
1980	4,020	137,700,000	34,254
1990	4,730	202,700,000	42,854
2000	5,391	269,200,000	49,935
2002	5,554	289,800,000	52,179

SOURCES: *Fearnleys Review* various years; *Fearnleys World Bulk Fleet* various years; UNCTAD 1969.

TABLE 6.5
*Average Newbuilding Prices for Bulk Carriers
of Various Deadweight Ton*
(in millions of current U.S. dollars)

	30,000 dwt	120,000 dwt
1969		13.5
1970		17.2
1972	7.5	22.0
1975	13.5	32.0
1980	20.0	44.0
1985	10.0	20.5
1990	21.5	46.0
2000	20.0	40.0
2001	18.0	36.5

SOURCE: *Fearnleys Review* various years.

launched the world's first bulk carrier exceeding 300,000 dwt (Nagatsuka 1991:2). These large bulk carriers and the ore-bulk-oil combined carriers allowed the shipment of iron ore from the giant Carajás mine in Brazil to Japan at competitive costs, permitting the Japanese steel mills to diversify away from often unstable Australian sources.

The tremendous increase in ship sizes since the 1960s, coupled with the dramatic increases in the production costs of necessary inputs, resulted in a significant upward trend in the cost of ships. As table 6.5 shows, new-building prices for bulk carriers peaked in 1980, declined sharply, recovered to new record levels in 1990, and then fell again in nominal terms. Overall, between 1972 and 2001, nominal new-building prices increased by 140 percent for 30,000-dwt bulkers and by 170 percent for 120,000-dwt bulkers between 1969 and 2001. In constant 1992 dollars, however, real ship prices fell sharply. Between 1972 and 2001, the cost of 30,000-dwt bulkers fell by 39 percent; between 1969 and 2001 the real price of 120,000-dwt bulkers fell by 39 percent as well. Tremendous economies of scale in new-building prices provide powerful incentives for utilizing newer, larger-scale ships in bulk transport. For 30,000- versus 120,000-dwt bulkers, the quadrupling in size resulted in a 27 percent cost saving on a dwt basis in 1972, while in 2001 the differential reached 49 percent. These data indicate the dramatic economies of scale in terms of the investment cost of ships created by the development of larger ships.

The increased amount of capital invested in a ship dedicated to traffic in one or a few commodities places a tremendous importance on the rate of turnaround on this invested capital. This leads to an emphasis both on increasing speed at sea of new ships (or at least ensuring that newer, larger ships do not travel more slowly than their predecessors) and of reducing the turnaround time in port at both ends of the voyage in order to allow the ship to make more trips and therefore earn more revenues in a particular time period.

These larger ships also produce significant economies of scale in operating costs, with larger ships costing far less to operate on a per ton basis than smaller ships (table 6.6). An important part of these operating economies of scale result from technological advances that reduced the amount of labor needed per ton transported on newer, larger ships. Bulk carrier crew requirements fell from forty-five per ship in 1950 to twenty-eight in 1980 (Stopford 1988:104).

These economies of scale increase with ship size and distance of voyage (table 6.7). The trend toward larger and larger ships that so greatly benefited Japanese shipbuilders, however, presented a serious problem for the Japanese shipping industry, as it did for established shipping firms in other nations. The tremendous cost reductions presented by the economies of scale of larger ships made existing ships obsolete and forced down freight rates. This required Japanese shipowners to replace older ships

TABLE 6.6
Operating Cost per Deadweight Ton
(*in dollars / year*)

Ship Size (dwt)	Cost
40,000	80
65,000	59
120,000	40
170,000	35

SOURCE: Stopford 1988:103 based on Drewry Shipping Consultants data.

TABLE 6.7.
*Relative Economies of Scale
by Ship Size and Voyage Length*
(in percent of cost / ton-mile)

Voyage in Miles	Ship Size (dwt)		
	15,170	65,500	120,380
1,000	100	47	37
6,000	56	27	20
22,000	52	24	17

SOURCE: Stopford 1988:277.

with new, larger ones in order to survive in the low freight rate markets (Chida and Davies 1990:133). Japanese shipbuilders and importers of raw materials greatly benefited from these investments in new ships, but Japanese shipping firms bore the high cost and risk of these investments. Concessionary government funding only partially offset these costs (Chida and Davies 1990:137–38).

The decline in world trade, especially in petroleum, after the first oil crisis left Japanese shippers with a great deal of excess capacity (too much tonnage) and Japanese shipyards with excess capacity (the ability to build too many ships per year) in the context of lower demand for shipping services and ships (Chida and Davies 1990:152–54). This situation benefited Japanese steel firms and the Japanese economy by further reducing raw materials transport costs, but Japanese shipping and shipbuilding firms faced a very difficult financial situation. A new form of state-sector-firm cooperation, however, emerged in Japan to deal with this problem.

This situation led to the shifting of the registry of Japanese-owned ships from registry in Japan to registry in flag-of-convenience nations (Chida and Davies 1990:152–54). Under a flag-of-convenience registry, a firm based in a core nation with higher labor costs, strong maritime union organization, and strict government regulations on ship maintenance and crew working conditions registers a ship in a peripheral nation (Panama and Liberia are by far the leaders in this practice) with much less stringent and costly government and union oversight, greatly reducing operating costs. Japanese shipping firms took advantage of the lower costs resulting from registration under flags of convenience through two mechanisms:

"Tie-in" ships . . . [refer to] tonnage which is built for foreign owners in the berths of Japanese shipyards, arranged by Japanese shipping firms who intend to charter the vessels constructed in this way for long periods. . . . (and) ships which had previously been Japanese-owned and had been sold to foreign firms before being chartered back. They were usually manned with crews from the developing countries so that operating costs could be reduced. . . . It is via these legal technicalities that many ships which are truly Japanese in everything except their flag are operated by Japanese firms carrying largely Japanese cargoes on Japanese routes and yet are able to take full advantage of the economies offered by flag of convenience registry. (Chida and Davies 1990:177)

The use of flag-of-convenience tie-in ships resulted in

the slowing down in the growth of the Japanese fleet since 1970 (which) is attributable to a planned policy on the part of Japanese operators of bare-boat chartering foreign-flag vessels under the "shikumisen" or "tie-in" system. Under this arrangement, a Japanese shipping company will sell a contracted newbuilding to a foreign buyer-either a foreign shipowner or an overseas subsidiary of the original company, which may exist only "on paper"—and in return secure a long-term charter on the vessel at delivery. This has the advantage of turning the order into an export sale, and therefore making it eligible for Export-Import Bank of Japan finance, as well as permitting the use of a foreign crew. (Drewry 1978a:41)

Government financing subsidies and the lower cost of flag-of-convenience operation thus led Japanese firms to "export" ships to themselves. This strategic adaptation to the shipping and shipbuilding crises helped to improve the financial condition of Japanese shipping and shipbuilding firms.

Flag-of-convenience registry originated in Panama and Liberia during the late 1940s as the result of efforts by U.S. transnational raw materials firms to reduce the cost of importing raw materials. U.S. raw materials firms lobbied the U.S. government to support the creation of open registries for flag-of-convenience registries in the two nations to escape their dependence on high-cost European-controlled shipping firms and on high-labor-cost U.S. shipping (Cafruny 1987:91–97). This mechanism created by U.S. transnational raw materials firms and the U.S. government later served Japanese steel and shipping firms quite well as they similarly sought to reduce transport costs. The existing hegemon opened the door for a new Japanese shipping strategy, just as it did in the late 1940s for Australian coal access.

These innovations in large-scale shipping led to dramatic reductions in Japanese raw materials import costs. In metallurgical coal, on a per ton basis it costs less to import metallurgical coal from Australia and the United States today than it did in 1980. Shipping costs from Australia to Japan fell by 32 percent in nominal terms and by 65 percent in real terms between 1980 and 2000. Shipping costs of imports from the United States fell by 40 percent in nominal terms and by 70 percent in real terms over this period. Shipping costs for imports from Canada increased in nominal terms between 1983 and 2000 by 46 percent, but fell by 11 percent in real terms (table 6.8). This

TABLE 6.8
*Estimated Transport Cost of Japan's Metallurgical Coal Imports
Calculated from CIF-FOB Average Unit Values*
(in US$ / metric ton)

	Australia	United States	Canada
1980	10.77	17.95	
1981	11.07	18.62	
1982	11.17	17.38	
1983	7.60	15.93	7.78
1984	8.79	11.93	8.42
1985	8.40	12.15	11.20
1986	8.00	10.12	16.49
1987	8.09	12.74	16.36
1988	8.26	12.58	13.60
1989	8.33	15.03	13.32
1990	6.85	16.18	12.04
1991	9.55	15.98	14.48
1992	11.40	14.10	13.90
1993	7.62	13.83	14.39
1994	7.65	14.62	16.59
1995	7.78	16.02	15.73
1996	7.96	14.54	12.92
1997	7.21	15.30	14.80
1998	7.00	12.91	13.58
1999	7.23	11.33	12.86
2000	7.37	10.70	11.37

SOURCES: Calculated from IEA 1992:21 for 1981–91; IEA 1998:I72 and I77 for 1992–98; IEA 2002:I.69 for 1999–2000.

transport pattern allowed Japanese steel mills and shipping firms to take advantage of the tremendous economies of scale available in bulk shipping to dramatically reduce production costs of steel and to capture all of these benefits for themselves, rather than sharing them with coal producers and coal-producing regions.

The success of Japanese shipping and shipbuilding industries in lowering the cost of importing raw materials often raised suspicions on the part of their competitors, as Drewry (1972b:21) notes:

Japan has to import the majority of her raw materials and therefore it is to her advantage that bulk commodities should be carried in the cheapest possible way. This has led to many Europeans being of the opinion that over-capacity in world shipbuilding is to the advantage of the Japanese economy as it will continue to depress freight rates and therefore newbuilding prices. It is argued that in Japan shipbuilders, shipowners, steelmakers, banks and the Government are all dedicated in working together to ensure continuing Japanese domination in the shipping and shipbuilding field.

Our analysis of Japanese state and firm strategies in the steel and transport industries makes it clear that this suspicion was well grounded during the 1950s, 1960s, and 1970s as the scale of the Japanese steel industry and its raw material needs expanded rapidly. The Japanese state and Japanese firms created and implemented technological innovations, adapted organizational innovations, and fomented the creation of huge amounts of new capacity across the coal, iron ore, shipbuilding, and shipping industries.

As was discussed in chapter 3, the Japanese shipbuilding industry repeatedly restructured over the past three decades. However, the industry declined only relative to Japan's almost total dominance of the world shipbuilding industry in the 1960s and early 1970s. In 2002, for example, Japanese shipyards completed 401 ships totaling 12.2 million gross tons, South Korean shipyards completed 208 ships totaling 12.8 million gross tons, and Chinese shipyards completed 613 ships totaling 2.8 million gross tons (OECD 2003). Further, Japanese shipyards remain global technological and organizational leaders, with one analysis arguing that Japan's shipyards implement lean production more effectively and extensively than even Toyota, the paragon of manufacturing efficiency (Koenig, Narita, and Baba 2002).

The Consequences of Japanese Shipbuilding and Shipping for Extractive Regions

Transport innovations and the construction of new transport systems affect different regions of the world in distinct ways. Extractive economies differ from industrial economies, and environmental and physical conditions far more directly constrain the former than they do the latter. Therefore, the indiscriminate application of industrial models to extractive processes and economies leads to serious distortions (Bunker 1985, 1992). Put simply, states and firms in extractive regions cannot manipulate nature in the ways that firms and states in industrial economies can (see Bunker and Ciccantell 2005 for an extended discussion of these issues).

As a result, transport systems constructed to link raw materials sites with foreign markets typically fail to simultaneously serve existing population centers in the extractive region. This occurs both because of the increasing social remoteness of naturally produced raw materials sites and because exporting firms design transport systems to move the raw materials as cheaply as possible to a port site for export. Unless the most economical transport route between the mine and the ocean happens to pass through an existing population center, the transport system will not serve any use but that of raw materials export (Bunker and Ciccantell 2005).

In some cases, however, established population centers successfully press to influence the location of ports and rail lines. These campaigns usually involve processing plants and so reflect the intersection of domestic firm and state interests with international access strategies. The naturally determined location of raw materials similarly constrains government policies to promote raw materials–based development. In order to use raw materials in existing industrial centers within the extractive nation, states must construct new, expensive, and typically small-scale (and therefore inefficient) transport systems to link the remote extractive region to the existing industrial center. If a government wishes to process the raw materials near the extractive site, the movement of the necessary population and equipment into the remote region similarly requires investment in transport and high costs to establish and maintain. These and other difficulties imposed by the natural constraints on extractive economies combine with the economic and political strength of core states and firms to ensure that minerals extraction, processing, transport, and consumption contribute to their further development. Overall, efforts by extractive region states and firms to capture benefits face great difficulties (Bunker and Ciccantell 2005).

Transport infrastructure often proves to be the most formidable obstacle to capturing benefits in the extractive region. Tremendous economies of scale in the cost of building ships resulted from the increasing size of ships, making it far cheaper on a per ton basis to purchase a larger ship versus a smaller ship. Despite the lower cost per ton, however, the tremendous size of larger ships requires a much larger total capital investment. This places a premium on efficient operation and quick turnaround times in port in order to maximize the revenue earned by the ship so that the ship's owner can repay the huge investments and loans required to buy the ship. This high capital cost makes it imperative for shipowners to employ their ships in tightly integrated transport systems to maximize revenues, but these integrated transport systems leave little opportunity for smaller-scale, regionally focused developmental uses of this infrastructure that could impede efficient operations.

The depth of harbors at the importing and exporting ends of a voyage limits the ability to take advantage of economies of scale in ocean shipping. Stopford (1988:278) illustrates this limitation (table 6.9). Taking advantage of the economies of scale resulting from the technological development of ocean shipping in the period following World War II thus requires either a great deal of naturally produced luck (the coincidence of large deposits of raw materials with existing or potential port sites with deepwater drafts) or, far more commonly, a high degree of social manipulation of water depth on coastlines relatively near to important raw materials deposits. The vast majority of the 19 percent of world ports accessible to 123,000-dwt bulk carriers by the late 1980s became accessible only because exporting states and firms spent hundreds of millions of dollars to dredge channels and/or construct artificial islands for

TABLE 6.9
Bulk Carrier Size and Port Accessibility

Ship Draft in		Average Ship	Percentage of World
Feet	Meters	Size (dwt)	Ports Accessible
25–30	7.6–9.1	16,150	73
30–35	9.2–10.7	23,600	55
36–38	10.8–11.6	38,700	43
39–44	11.7–13.4	61,000	27
45–50	13.5–15.2	89,200	22
51–55	15.3–16.7	123,000	19

SOURCE: Stopford 1988:278.

port facilities. Governments in extractive regions assumed huge debt burdens to make possible the appropriation of nature by private raw materials firms for sale to core consumers, mainly in Japan.

Taking advantage of the increasing economies of scale in shipping required the careful matching of all the stages of the transport system in order to minimize the total cost of transport (Garrod and Miklius 1985; Jansson and Shneerson 1982; Kendall 1972). Tailoring transport systems from the mine to the consumer to take advantage of these economies of scale dramatically reduces the cost to the importer of the raw materials of each ton.

However, this careful matching of the various components of raw materials transport systems carries important risks for the sellers of raw materials. By tailoring their mines, inland transport systems, and port facilities to those of their customers' ships, importing ports, and processing plants, the number of potential buyers of an exporter's raw materials declines sharply, placing raw materials producers in a disadvantaged position in bargaining with buyers. Selling to other potential customers whose shipping and importing facilities do not match the characteristics of the exporter may result in increased storage costs, underutilization of inland transport systems and ports (with resulting higher per ton operating costs), and lower prices because these potential customers require lower prices to offset higher ocean transport costs per ton. The careful tailoring of mines and export transport infrastructure in many raw materials industries in Australia, Brazil, Canada, and other nations to the shipping and import infrastructure of Japanese firms gave Japanese firms important advantages in bargaining over the prices of raw materials purchased from these nations.

Japan, China, and Ocean Transport Today

As in steel, coal, and iron ore, the Japanese model of development and the relationship between Japan and China shape in critical ways China's economic ascent and the restructuring of the world economy since the early 1980s. An attempt by China to follow Japan's model of coastal heavy industrialization to supply export industries and domestic-market-oriented industries drove the huge increase in China's imports of coal and iron ore. This created an equally huge and rapidly growing demand for ocean transport of raw materials from Australia, Brazil, Canada, and other nations to China.

The Japanese shipping and shipbuilding firms that became global leaders during Japan's economic ascent seized the tremendous opportunities now available in transporting raw materials to China. During the early 2000s, Chinese demand for raw materials has driven a booming demand for shipping space and a dramatic increase in freight rates. Extremely depressed shipping market conditions in 2000–2001 ended abruptly as freight rates soared. Daily charter rates to ship iron ore from Brazil to China rose from US$15,000 per day in 2002 to US$46,000 per day in 2003 (Bradsher 2003), although rates stabilized at high levels during 2005. Shipping firms in Japan and around the world earned high profits, sparking a boom in merger and acquisition activity in the industry (Bradsher 2003; Chambers 2003).

Japanese shipping firms, the leaders of this global industry, benefit most from this China-driven boom. In March 2004 Mitsui OSK signed a twenty-year contract with Baosteel to transport iron ore from Brazil to China in a dedicated 300,000-dwt ship to be built just for this route, building on an agreement between the two firms in late 2003 for Mitsui to build and operate three 200,000-dwt bulk carriers to ship iron ore from Australia to Baosteel under long-term contracts. Two other Japanese shipping firms, Nippon Yusen KK and Kawasaki Kisen Kaisha, are buying a total of more than 200 new ships, mainly to serve the Chinese market (*Financial Times*, April 27, 2004). Mitsui OSK also signed long-term contracts for iron ore transport with Maanshan Iron and Steel from Brazil to China (*JCN Newswire* 2004a). Kawasaki and government-owned China Shipping Group formed a joint venture to import cars into China because of its rapidly growing demand for automobiles (Barling 2003).

High demand for bulk shipping also creates high demand for the construction of new ships, with Japanese shipbuilders capturing a large share of this demand. Orders for new ships won by Japanese shipyards increased by 300 percent between 2002 and 2003, reaching the highest level (13.4 million gross tons) since 1973 because of the China-driven boom (*AFX News* 2004a). Shipyards in Korea and China also benefit tremendously from this boom in ship construction. In 2003 new orders for Japanese shipyards totaled 16.1 million gross tons valued at US$11.7 billion, while Korean shipyards had orders for 27.8 million gross tons valued at US$23.9 billion and Chinese shipyards had orders for 11.5 million gross tons valued at US$8.1 billion (OECD Working Party on Shipbuilding 2004).

However, as the Japanese government recognized during the late 1800s and after World War II, reliance on foreign shipping and shipbuilding is expensive and risky, while promoting domestic shipping and shipbuilding can create powerful generative sectors that can drive economic ascent. The Chinese government today clearly recognizes both these risks and opportunities as it seeks to reduce its 90 percent dependence on foreign shipping for Chinese oil imports (*AFX-Asia* 2004). The National Development and Reform Commission of the central government drafted a plan in 2004 to make China the world's leading shipbuilder by 2015 by establishing three large shipbuilding centers. State policies to support shipbuilding include large tax incentives for investing in shipyards, the encouragement of joint ventures with foreign firms, state financing for ship construction and export, supporting the formation of business alliances between steel and shipbuilding firms to guarantee domestic supplies of high-quality steel for shipbuilding, and export tax rebates on exported ships (*Global News Wire-Asia Africa Intelligence Wire*, December 31, 2003).

China is already the world's third largest shipbuilding nation, has labor costs only 20 to 30 percent of those in Japanese shipyards, and is rapidly improving its technological capabilities and productivity, including building large bulk carriers for Japanese shipping firms (Freeth 2004; Lague 2003; Marine Log 2004; *Xinhua* 2004). One state-owned shipbuilding firm, China State Shipbuilding Corporation (CSSC), is now the world's third largest shipbuilding firm (*Sinocast Transportation Watch* 2006b) and is building a US$3.6 billion shipyard near Shanghai that it claims will be the largest in the world (Lague 2003:32). One report noted that for CSSC "the new shipyard would also help to boost relevant industries like steel and engine manufacture, as well as to create job opportunities for more than 700,000 people" (*Sinocast Transportation Watch* 2006b). Another of the world's largest shipbuilding firms, Samsung Heavy Industries of South Korea, is investing US$500 million in a new shipyard in China because of China's lower production and labor costs (*Sinocast Transportation Watch* 2006a).

More generally, one analysis of Chinese shipbuilding policy argues that "the Chinese leadership, with an eye on history, has identified advanced shipbuilding along with vibrant foreign trade, a big merchant fleet and a powerful blue-water navy as the formula to expand China's global reach" (Lague 2003:30). As we have shown in our analysis of Japan's economic ascent and of earlier cases of the most rapid and transformative economic ascent, for those nations that rose to dominate world trade, ship-building served as a critical generative sector (Bunker and Ciccantell 2005).

China's dramatic growth in industry, trade, and transport also requires a massive expansion of port facilities. In 2004 Shanghai surpassed Rotterdam to become the world's busiest port, with 380 million tons of imports and exports (Asia Pacific Foundation of Canada 2005). One recent analysis reported that "unlike almost all other ports in the world, China's port authorities anticipated this massive increase in trade volume. . . . they have surpassed others in building infrastructure capacity to keep apace with growth" (Asia Pacific Foundation of Canada 2005).

Port investments include a new US$12 billion port in the Shanghai region, a total investment of US$3.6 billion by the central government just during 2004, private investment just in the port of Dalian of US$3.4 billion in 2004 (Asia Pacific Foundation of Canada 2005), and the investment of US$3.3 billion by the Tianjin Port Authority to expand its port and deepen its harbor to accommodate 200,000-dwt ships (*Schiff & Hafen* 2003). China's Tenth Five Year Plan calls for an increase in port capacity of 2.6 billion tons per year (Asia Pacific Foundation of Canada 2005). Chinese government regulations, especially after the regulatory changes implemented as part of World Trade Organization (WTO) accession, call for decentralized local control of ports, competition between ports to lower costs, and permitting foreign firms to own joint ventures in or even full ownership of ports (Asia Pacific Foundation of Canada 2005; Wang, Ng, and Olivier 2004). These strategies closely parallel the Japanese MIDA-based development strategy.

In short, the relationship between Japan and China and the example of Japan's development model are clearly shaping China's economic ascent in a variety of ways.

Conclusion

These Japanese transport strategies for raw materials access successfully guaranteed long-term access at low cost to huge volumes of imported raw materials. Just during the 1960s, Sasaki (1976) estimated that Japanese government efforts to reduce the 20 to 30 percent share of freight charges in the total cost of imported raw materials through transport subsidies had a significant impact: "during the ten years beginning in 1961, the freight costs for both crude oil and iron ore were reduced by 40 per cent. . . . The effects of this reduction were significant and the consequent reductions in the price of electricity, petrol, iron and steel and many other products have made an immeasurable contribution to the national economy" (Sasaki 1976:7). Ocean transport closes the "virtuous circle" of generative sectors in steel, shipbuilding, and shipping. Japanese strategies restructured and globalized these industries and turned remote ecosystems in Australia, the Brazilian Amazon, and western Canada into raw materials peripheries that provided the material ingredients for Japan's economic ascent.

Equally important, the processes of technological, organizational, and institutional innovation and learning inseparably linked these international relations with Japanese internal development. Economic ascent resulted from the complex coordination between firms and nature, between firms in Japan and in its emerging raw materials peripheries, between the Japanese state and states in these raw materials peripheries and the United States, and between the Japanese state, sectors, and firms. In overcoming complex challenges presented by material, economic and political processes across multiple ecosystems and multiple political boundaries in the shadow of a powerful existing hegemon, the Japanese state and Japanese firms learned and innovated repeatedly to construct the world's third largest economy by making itself the global competitive leader in a wide range of industries. The "virtuous circle" analyzed in these four chapters provided the material and social foundation for this process of economic ascent and simultaneously globalized previously localized raw materials industries and transferred much of the burden of the costs and risks of these globalized industries onto exporting states and firms.

Japan's globalization of raw materials transport systems also opened the door for the economic ascent of China, the most rapid case of economic ascent in recent decades. Chinese development strategies have focused on deepening industrialization in recent years via raw materials and transport industries. These Chinese strategies build on Japan's restructuring of the world economy that created transport technologies, fostered the development of large-scale port infrastructures in raw materials–exporting regions, brought new large-scale producing mines and firms into the iron ore and coal industries, and made available Japanese technology and capital to develop China's ports, steel, and other raw materials industries. The Japanese-driven globalization of the capitalist world-economy over the past five decades opened the door for potential new ascendants.

CHAPTER SEVEN

The Restructuring of Global Markets and the Future of the Capitalist World-Economy

We first summarize our analysis of Japan's economic ascent and then compare this case to earlier cases of dramatic economic ascent that have transformed global industries and environments. We also analyze Japan's economic stagnation, as well as the relationship between Japan's and China's dramatic rise. We then use our analysis of Japanese and Chinese economic ascent to assess the emerging parameters of the capitalist world-economy in the twenty-first century.

Conclusions from Our Analysis of Japan

The pattern of state-sector-firm relations that funded and assisted the steel and shipbuilding industries and the MIDAs drove Japan's internal development in a wide range of industries linked directly and indirectly to these generative sectors. This pattern of state-sector-firm relations provided the foundation for Japan's rapid economic growth from the 1950s through the 1980s. The Japanese development model of the post–World War II era embodied a dynamic tension between the material processes underlying economic ascent, processes of global economic and political competition, and a constellation of social groups seeking to shape this development model and capture the benefits that resulted.

MIDAs, the linchpin and physical manifestation of the Japanese model of capital accumulation, restructured nature, the Japanese economy, and the capitalist world-economy. State policies and investments combined with private firms' strategies and investments to enable the smooth and efficient movement of massive volumes of raw materials to Japan for transformation into industrial products. This coordination manipulated nature, space, topography, and existing economic and social structures in search of private profits. MIDAs represent a clear case of state-sector-firm organization of unprecedented scope and cost in response to the increasing scale, geographical scope of sources and markets, and technical complexity of bulk raw materials industries. The cumulatively sequential punctuated evolution of the world economy by the end of the twentieth century made development on this scale imperative in order to resolve the contradiction between economies of scale and diseconomies of space on a truly global scale.

In the international arena, the experience gained from accessing coal and iron ore in Australia via long-term contracts with minimal Japanese capital investment laid the foundation for the tremendously successful program for diversifying sources, with capital expenses largely met by exporting states and firms. The Japanese steel firms and the Japanese government, with initial and ongoing support by the existing hegemon, the United States, successfully restructured the world coal and iron ore industries to supply low-cost coal and iron ore to Japan. These strategies transferred the vast bulk of costs and risk to mining firms and state and national governments in Australia and, later, in Canada, Brazil, South Africa, Indonesia, and even in the United States itself.

The new combination of large-scale mines and large-scale transport facilities, while reducing the cost per ton of production and transport, greatly restricted the markets available for these mines' production. The coordination of Japanese steel firms in negotiating prices for coal and iron ore, the high capital costs of these mines that make sales even at a loss essential in order to service high debt loads, and the construction of dedicated infrastructure by extractive states and firms all combined to give Japanese steel firms tremendous advantages in bargaining over purchase terms. This restructuring and globalization of the world coal and iron ore industries became a fundamental material and economic pillar of Japan's rise as an industrial power and challenger to U.S. economic hegemony.

At the same time that this model of capital accumulation had such salutary effects in Japan, equally dramatic but far more negative consequences for raw materials–exporting regions emerged. Japan's success in stimulating excess capacity in the now global coal and iron ore industries and the cheap long-distance transport its shipping technology made possible enabled Japanese firms to choose between multiple suppliers of coal and iron. They used their strengthened bargaining position to push down prices, to reduce their equity participation, and in some cases, particularly in Canada and Australia, to reduce the volume of imports to which their long-term contracts had committed them. The cumulative costs and losses to exporting regions and firms totaled many billions of dollars as the price of becoming part of Japan's raw materials periphery.

Real prices of coal and iron ore exports to Japan declined dramatically over the past fifty years as the result of Japanese raw materials access strategies. Japan's rapid ascent relied on this globalization of raw materials industries and the resultant transfer of costs and risks just as much as it did on the inseparably linked technological and organizational innovations to create and take advantage of increasing economies of scale and other domestic innovations.

Japan's rapid rise to trade dominance in the late twentieth century globalized raw materials markets and bulk transport of extremely-low-value-to-volume cargos more dramatically than any previous national economic ascent had done. Its rise, though, was far more conditioned by geopolitical forces beyond its control than any previous rise had been, so whatever dominance it achieved was extremely precarious. Japan's challenge to world-system hegemony appears to have ended in economic crisis, but the globalizing effects of its economic strategies, and the inequalities they exacerbated, endure.

The growing power and legitimacy of state control over business, though, together with Japan's continued subordination to U.S. military and geopolitical goals and needs and continued dependence on U.S. product and financial markets, left it more vulnerable to economic crisis and policy change in the established hegemon than other rising national economies had ever been. We have seen how Britain benefited from Dutch investment and from Dutch markets during its rise to trade dominance, and how the United States similarly drew on British finance while profiting from British demand for raw materials. Neither of the earlier ascendant economies, though, were as directly subordinate to, nor as integrally entwined with, the established hegemon's geopolitical agenda. Indeed, both fought wars against the established hegemon during their rise.

Under the aegis of U.S. diplomatic, military, and financial support, the Japanese thus culminated historical processes of globalization by globalizing two of the lowest-value-to-volume industrial inputs. The increases in the scale and scope of raw materials transport and procurement under three decades of unequal partnership between Japan and the United States were vastly greater than either could have achieved alone, and greater than those achieved in any three-decade period of the far more equal interdependence of Britain and the United States. Their extreme speed, and their evident precariousness, may well be due to the fact that their roots were geopolitical rather than spatiomaterial. To compensate for the absence of particular spatiomaterial advantages, the Japanese had to institute extremely large increases in economies of scale. To overcome the financial and organizational barriers the necessary technical scale imposed, they had to create more tightly coupled relations between state and capital than any nation had previously developed. The Japanese state devised extraordinarily close and effective ways to collaborate with national financial and industrial capital, not just to overcome these obstacles, but to use the technological, organizational, political, and financial innovations that the state-capital partnership developed to radically restructure world raw material, product, and money markets in Japan's favor and against the interests of peripheral raw materials suppliers.

U.S. geopolitical campaigns to restrain China, North Korea, North Vietnam, and insurgent movements in Laos and Cambodia as well as the Soviet Union engendered continued tactical support, military protection, and huge demand for military equipment and supplies. These effects of U.S. foreign policy made available additional finance for implementing technologies of scale in smelting and in downstream industry and easy, expansive markets in which to sell the increased volume of products they generated. These innovations, combined with the material and spatial conditions for which they were developed, catalyzed the globalization of investment and trade in even the bulkiest, lowest-value-to-volume industrial inputs, in the process imposing extremely low rents and extremely high debt loads on extractive economies. In other words, the globalization that resulted from the geopolitical interdependence of Japan and the United States rested on an unsustainably precarious and overextended financial system in the core and on impossible levels of debt and excess extractive capacity in the periphery.

The same closely coupled coordination with firms, sectors, and finance that enabled the Japanese state to organize economic expansion enabled the United States to pressure it to adopt financial policies that favored the United States rather than Japan. The resulting crisis in the Japanese economy shows that its earlier success was very much conditioned by U.S. support in pursuit of U.S. geopolitical goals. That support enabled Japan to globalize markets for low-value-to-volume raw materials, to catalyze the transport systems that led to this culminating stage of globalization, and in the process to devolve much of the cost of globalization to its raw materials peripheries.

Parallels between Japan and Earlier Ascendant Economies

Successful raw materials access strategies in each of the five cases of most rapid and transformative economic ascent (Japan, Portugal, Holland, Great Britain, and the United States) included effective institutions that expanded, strengthened, and coordinated states, firms, sectors, and financial institutions. By cheapening and stabilizing supplies, they simultaneously supported rapid capital accumulation and provided a critical condition for allowing increased wages without losing competitive position in world trade. The strategies of raw materials procurement in the external arena created these effects in the domestic economy.

The successful solutions to the challenge of cheapening raw materials access created institutions of enduring impact for the national society and for the capitalist world-economy because they were so critical to national economic ascent; because they required and rewarded coordinated and costly activity by firms, sectors, and the state, because their degree of success shaped the economic activity and social welfare of the nation as a whole; and because the solutions transformed production, exchange, financial, diplomatic, and infrastructural relations with other nations sufficiently to reorganize the capitalist world-economy. All of these effects occurred during the early period of economic ascent, when both national institutions and world-systemic organization constituted "greenfields" for both technical and institutional innovations. Greenfield conditions allowed the implementation of innovative economic forms at optimal scale without opposition from vested interests in earlier, smaller scales of investment and operation.

Dutch ascent created the shipping dominance that underlay the expansion of European control over world trade long before European colonialism spread around the world in the 1800s, as well as a model of state-firm relations adopted by Holland's European competitors. British ascent created banks, a colonial administration, and large firms capable of operating in multiple nations. U.S. ascent created banks, a stock market, interlocking directorates, and vertically integrated firms that dominated the world economy for decades. Japanese ascent created interlocked industrial groups, state and private banks providing highly subsidized credit, and state-sector-firm coordination (Bunker and Ciccantell 2003a, 2003b, 2005; Ciccantell and Bunker 2002).

All of these effects expanded and intensified in and through time. Each national economy rising toward preeminence competed with earlier ascendants (Holland with Portugal, Great Britain with Holland, the United States with Great Britain, and Japan with the United States). Each nation adapted to and changed to its own advantage product and financial markets, dominant technologies, and the political ideologies and organizations that govern the capitalist world-economy. The Dutch utilized shipbuilding and shipping dominance to greatly expand European influence around the world via entrepôt trade. The British state created a model of global free trade in the context and in support of a long era of sustained British hegemony. The U.S. state and transnational corporations based in the United States after World War II promoted the end of colonialism in order to open new markets for their products and acquire raw materials sources previously controlled by European imperial powers (Bunker and O'Hearn 1992). The Japanese steel firms and the Japanese state appeared to support resource nationalist efforts by raw materials peripheries' states and firms to capture more of the benefits of their raw materials exports via the use of long-term contracts and joint ventures that apparently gave peripheral states and firms greater power over their raw materials industries (Ciccantell and Bunker 2002).

Its continued dependence on U.S. hegemony created various anomalies in Japan's rapid rise and changing role in the world-system. There is no question that Japan ascended extraordinarily quickly toward trade dominance, and in the process radically transformed and extended world raw materials markets and transport. Unlike other ascendant nations, it did not figure first as a major supplier of raw material to an already established hegemon. Unlike any other successfully ascendant nation, Japan provoked and lost a devastating war in an earlier attempt to dominate world trade. With the support of the nation that won that war, though, Japan quickly followed military failure with economic success. Finally, Japan alone of all of the nations that rose to trade dominance did not increase military power and activity in support of financial, productive, and commercial growth. Rather, it continued to rely on U.S. supremacy both for its military security and for a great share of its financial and product markets. The Japanese economy could respond to the opportunities that international tensions created without incurring the costs of military protection against foreign threats. The state was thus able to focus all of its efforts and resources on promoting technological innovations, regulating coordination and competition in critical sectors of the economy, and assuring that firms in those sectors had access to voluminous, cheap raw materials abroad and to ports large enough to unload them efficiently at home. These circumstances combined to support a very rapid rise of the national economy, and a deep and extensive increase in the globalization of the capitalist world-economy.

Japan's trade dominance was uniquely rooted in subordination to geopolitical dynamics rather than in control over spatiomaterial advantages. Even though it radically transformed world markets for bulk goods and expanded them across the entire globe, Japan's trade dominance was conditional, limited only to some sectors, and ultimately vulnerable to the fiscal needs and deficiencies of the overextended, economically troubled, and fiscally irresponsible U.S. hegemon. Japan's financial and economic crises, and the crises of excess capacity, falling rents, and state weakness of its extractive suppliers underscore the need to explain these anomalies.

These effects also expanded across space. As the world economy grew in both spatial scale and in the total volume of production, as technical advances diversified the materials used in production and sharpened the specification of their chemical properties, as the most easily accessible raw materials depleted, and as nationalist goals of industrial development and self-determining sovereignty spread around the world, the complexity of solutions to the raw material challenge increased in each of these cases.

The success of each of these nations in resolving the contradiction of increasing economies of scale and diseconomies of space drove the material intensification and spatial expansion of trade in the capitalist world-economy. Each of these five nations ascended rapidly in the global economic and political system of its time, becoming the dominant player in the leading industries and overall world trade. To accomplish this ascent, coordinated state-sector-firm strategies simultaneously transformed its domestic economy and created its raw materials peripheries that supplied increasing quantities of raw materials at lower costs than those of its major competitors. The success of the strategies employed by each of these five ascendant economies brought each of them to the highest levels of the system of global stratification of its era, while simultaneously incorporating new regions and/or restructuring already incorporated regions into raw materials peripheries with low returns on their raw materials exports and resulting low positions for these regions in the system of global stratification.

These five cases of spectacular economic ascent must, however, be considered within the wider context of a far greater number of partially successful and failed efforts to ascend within the system of global stratification. In Europe, France and Germany repeatedly sought to emulate the strategies that brought Holland and Great Britain to global preeminence. These efforts to create the raw materials supply and transport systems to increase their competitiveness in the world economy made both nations powerful members of the core, but their efforts to challenge existing hegemons and other rising economies to become hegemonic have not been successful, despite employing quite similar strategies. Material obstacles attenuated these strategies, we would argue, such as inadequate supplies of timber for shipbuilding in France and shortages of petroleum in Germany during the first half of the twentieth century.

In other regions, nations ranging from Argentina, Brazil, and Mexico in Latin America to India, Indonesia, and South Korea in Asia followed strategies intended to develop domestic steel, railroads, shipbuilding, shipping, and other industries, the generative sectors in the five cases of spectacular ascent. However, all succeeded only partially, ascending from the periphery to the semiperiphery of the capitalist world-economy and remaining subject to severe financial instability and crisis. In these cases, we would argue, the inability to achieve the economies of scale of more successful ascendant economies (e.g., length and density of rail networks in these Latin American nations versus the United States during the second half of the nineteenth century, smaller scale of steel production facilities in these Asian nations compared to Japan during most of the second half of the twentieth century) critically limits the potential of these aspiring ascendant economies to successfully reach core status. Our long-term research agenda includes an extended comparative analysis of these and other cases of partial and failed ascent. We will utilize the same theoretical framework in order to explain how the success of the five most dramatic cases of economic ascent effectively outpaced the efforts of other ascendant economies to achieve higher positions in a competitive capitalist world-economy.

Our methodology begins with the most basic raw materials. Generative sectors emerge only when they take into account natural characteristics of raw materials' quality, location, and usage characteristics. This analysis of generative sectors highlights the role of the state: generative sectors do not arise and cannot be maintained without certain types of state-sector-firm coordination and cooperation. This model has important implications for development policy: not just any industry can be a generative sector. State development policies throughout the capitalist world-economy that assumed that any industry could become a generative sector typically failed miserably. All ascendant economies that achieved core status and challenged for hegemonic status successfully met the social and material challenges we analyzed in this book. Even the Japanese economy, often viewed as knowledge intensive, rests on the foundation of successfully resolving the issue of raw materials access to provide the built environment and material building blocks of a technologically advanced economy.

Equally important, the strategies of the existing hegemon and of other ascendant economies to resolve the contradiction between the potential for increasing economies of scale and the increasing diseconomies of space provide the social and material context within which any economy seeking to ascend must operate. Successful ascendant economies, and especially our five cases of spectacular ascent, raised the material, spatial, economic, organizational, and political bar by orders of magnitude that made it extremely difficult for other potential ascendants. Our analysis demonstrates that there have been a few spectacularly successful policy initiatives that focused on the right sector at the right historical moment and under the right natural, technological, political, and economic conditions, but emulating these successes is extremely difficult.

Explaining Economic Stagnation in Japan since 1990

In this section, we address our fourth research question, why did such a successful model in Japan come to such a sudden halt? The Japanese political economic system drove Japan's rapid growth through several business cycles between the mid-1950s and 1973 on a trajectory of sustained, rapid growth led by generative sectors in steel, shipbuilding, and automobiles. The disruption of cheap energy supplies in 1973–74 by the first oil shock, in combination with Nixon's shock of the ending of gold-standard fixed exchange rates and increasing trade conflicts with the United States and other buyers

of Japanese manufactured goods, severely disrupted this system. Japanese firms, industry sectors, and the state reacted comparatively quickly (relative to the United
States and Western Europe) to this new global context and suffered only relatively
mild disruption from the second oil price shock of 1979–80, supported particularly
by an automobile industry that led the world in fuel efficiency by using progressively
lighter and stronger steels and incorporating growing quantities of other, lighter materials. Rapid growth continued during the 1980s, with steel and automobiles continuing their leading roles and now joined by other sectors such as electronics and computers; however, the shipbuilding industry entered an ongoing period of decline in
the 1970s, as we showed in chapter 3.

After the collapse of the bubble economy in 1990, a long-term crisis of stagnation
developed in Japan. Many industries began a long-term decline, with many firms
shifting investment abroad (Katz 1998; Pempel 1998).

A variety of analysts have suggested reasons for Japan's decline: speculative investment in and bank lending for incredibly overvalued property in Japan and to uncompetitive firms that created a bad-debt crisis for Japanese banks (Bernier 2000; de
Bruin and de Bruin 2002; Fukao 2003; Ikeda 2004; Kerr 2002; Sawabe 2002; Suzuki
2000); too much state intervention in the economy (Katz 1998; Porter, Takeuchi, and
Sakakibara 2000; Suzuki 2000); the decline of state directive power and the rise of civil
society groups (Pekkanen 2004); widespread political corruption (Calder 1993; Johnson 1982:295–96; Katz 1998; Pempel 1998); the rise of new, low-cost competitors (e.g.,
POSCO Steel, which led Korea's economic ascent [Woo 1991]) that induced the hollowing out of the Japanese economy as Japanese companies moved production
abroad and, more generally, moved from a position of protecting the domestic market to one of investing internationally (Bernier 2000; Calder 1993; Ikeda 2004; Katz
1998; Pempel 1998; Yoshimatsu 2002); the increasing value of the yen that began in 1971
with Nixon's abandonment of the gold standard (Ikeda 2004; Katz 1998:213; Murphy
1996; Nakamura 1981:218–26); the loss of LDP hegemony (Pempel 1998); the ascendance of the interests of noncompetitive, protectionist sectors such as textiles and
agriculture over the earlier focus on global competitiveness, with recession cartels organized by trade associations and assisted by MITI and supported by the LDP in return for political support (Calder 1993; Ikeda 2004; Katz 1998; Tilton 1996; Yoshimatsu
2002;); declining competitiveness in previously highly competitive sectors, including
shipbuilding and steel (Katz 1998; Tilton 1996); recognition of the environmental
problems created by heavy industrialization in port areas (Broadbent 1998); increased
politicization of the regulatory process (Johnson 1982; Pempel 1998); atrophied embeddedness that reduced competitiveness and constrained continued economic
growth (de Bruin and de Bruin 2002); the retention of economic institutions that were

no longer effective or beneficial (Katz 1998; Porter and Sakakibara 2004); and inadequate domestic consumption (Katz 1998:197–234).

Calder's (1993:229) discussion of the role of liberalization in the financial sector, ending the ability of the state to channel the flow of credit, raises another possibility: did financial liberalization, brought about at least in part by international pressure, particularly from the United States (Calder 1993:243), itself create the current crisis by ending the existing pattern of credit allocation (an argument also advanced by Werner 2004), rather than intrinsic flaws in the earlier model of development, as many analysts (e.g., Katz 1998; Porter, Takeuchi, and Sakakibara 2000) claim? Gao (2001), Grimes (2001), Murphy (1996), Goyal and McKinnon (2003), Peek and Rosengren (2003), Ikeda (2004), and Fukao (2003) present strong cases in various ways that highlight the close relationship between the structural rigidities created in the period of rapid growth and the problems of adjusting to the changing international environment over the past two decades, emphasizing the difficulties resulting from Japan's increasing integration into global financial markets and the decline of the earlier model of state-financial sector relations that had supported rapid growth. This recognition of the tightly linked relationship between the production and financial sectors provides the analytic foundation for our explanation of the long period of stagnation.

We argue that Japan's economic stagnation of the past fifteen years derived directly from the successes of the developmental model that evolved in the years following World War II. The works just discussed all highlight various dimensions of the causes of Japan's stagnation; our analysis focuses on the role of generative sectors in creating these problems. Just as steel, shipbuilding, and shipping as generative sectors led Japan's economic ascent, these sectors and the broader developmental model based on these sectors, including the pattern of state-financial sector relations, played critical roles in Japan's stagnation. In the external arena, low-cost raw materials underlay and fed Japan's growth, and the disruptions of the two oil price shocks badly damaged Japan's economic competitiveness in these generative sectors. The steel industry adjusted relatively well by taking advantage of the opportunity to foment excess capacity by projecting unrealistic long-term raw materials prices based on the price spikes of the mid-1970s and early 1980s, particularly in Australia, Canada, and Brazil. This strategy renewed the long-term decline in real raw materials prices and helped maintain Japan's competitiveness in steel. However, shipping and then shipbuilding entered the long-term secular declines discussed in chapters 3 and 6, as did other raw materials-based heavy industries, most notably the aluminum industry.

Successful management of the iron-coal-steel-based generative sector rested on and intensified both external dependence on and vulnerability to the United States (as Chalmers Johnson emphasized in a recent interview [Nascimento Rodrigues

2005]) and the internal authority of the central state in Japan. These two conditions combined to leave the Japanese state highly vulnerable to direct U.S. intervention in commercial and fiscal policy. During the 1980s, the fiscal imbalances created by Reagan's transformation of the United States from global creditor to global debtor, and subsequent pressure from the U.S. government for Japan to strengthen the yen against the dollar (Murphy 1996) and to open Japanese capital markets to U.S. participation (Gao 2001), destabilized and devalued the financial and productive systems that drove Japan's rapid economic growth. The Japanese government and its tightly controlled banks used their moral authority and legitimacy with private financial institutions to support the valorization of the yen under the 1985 Plaza Accords. The resulting strength of the yen against the dollar encouraged Japanese firms and banks to invest massively in U.S. real estate, but the U.S. economic crisis of the late 1980s and early 1990s devalued these holdings dramatically. U.S. leverage over Japan's fiscal policies, combined with the control over finance that the Japanese state achieved during its active coordination and subsidization of the rapidly expanding steel and shipping sectors, thus contributed importantly to the Japanese crisis and stagnation.

By the mid-1990s, the broader slowdown in the Japanese economy began to severely reduce the global competitiveness of steel as well, particularly due to the hollowing out of Japanese manufacturing as Japanese companies moved industrial production abroad (Bailey 2003). This relocation of production, motivated by a combination of environmental concerns about heavy industry in the MIDAs, increasing labor and other costs, and the rising value of the yen on the part of large Japanese firms with a high degree of power over investment decisions (Bailey 2003), disrupted the steady growth of the Japanese market and of Japanese export production that these generative sectors fed and depended upon for further growth. These decisions to relocate benefited firms but greatly damaged the Japanese economy (Bailey 2003).

At the broader level of the developmental model pioneered by the generative sectors, the banking system developed to fund the generative sectors with a high degree of state intervention and subsidization was increasingly rechanneled for political and speculative purposes by industries and groups with strong connections to the LDP, often via corruption, but also with declining or even nonexistent global competitiveness. This often means that banks continue to loan money long after a firm is bankrupt, keeping "zombie" firms operating and decreasing national efficiency and competitiveness (Hoshi and Kashyap 2004).

This refocusing of the financial pillar of Japan's post–World War II political economy fueled the stock market and real estate speculation that culminated in the collapse of the bubble economy in 1990. The collapse of the financial pillar triggered the broader collapse of Japan's political economy that existing patterns of state-sector-firm cooperation and government economic regulation could not resolve because they had been developed to support rapid growth and not to deal with stagnation and decline. Efforts to promote domestic consumption, liberalize financial markets, and reduce other forms of state intervention during the crisis only deepened the problems confronting the system (Werner 2004). By the mid-1990s, MITI sought to use deregulation and liberalization as tools of a new strategy of economic nationalism (Hall 2004), but MITI's skills and tools could not function effectively in the new global context confronting Japan. Resolving the crisis requires a new model of development, not just simplistic ideas about open markets and the withdrawal of the state from the economy.

The Koizumi government's plan to privatize the postal savings system and its US$3 trillion in assets that had long been used to finance government spending (Onishi 2005b) and had provided a critical pillar of the financial system that funded Japan's economic growth since World War II will do little to resolve the fundamental challenges confronting the Japanese economy today. The postwar development model has reached its limits because the underlying dynamic tension has collapsed. Privatizing the postal savings system will severely constrain the Japanese government's spending ability, making it even more difficult for the Japanese state to carry out its basic functions, let alone helping to create a new development model. This privatization will not create a new form of dynamic tension but only ensure that the old model is dismantled. This dismantling will make Japan even more vulnerable to changes in the capitalist world-economy, including the continued ascent of China and the increasingly desperate attempts of the United States to maintain its declining hegemonic position.

The Japanese development model of the postwar era embodied a dynamic tension between the material processes underlying economic ascent, processes of global economic and political competition, and a constellation of social groups seeking to shape this development model and capture the benefits that resulted. Domestically, these social groups included firms and industry associations in the generative sectors; labor in the generative sectors; managers and other professionals in the generative sectors; government agencies charged with national development, led by MITI; other government agencies, including the Ministry of Finance, the Ministry of Transport, and the Bank of Japan; banks and other financial institutions; firms and industry associations in often less-favored and less-competitive sectors; labor, managers, and professionals in these less-favored, less-competitive sectors; and particular spatial and sectoral interests, represented by political leaders and various levels of government whose support is critical for legitimacy. At the global level, key factors included the economic and political alliances and rivalries with the existing hegemon and other rivals that shape national development strategies and competitiveness, embodied in the efforts of the Allied Occupation Forces and the U.S. State Department to secure access to coal from Australia to resolve the coal crisis of the late 1940s (discussed in chapter 4) and the modeling of Japanese corporate accounting law on U.S. standards (Chiba 2001); global political competition, including the Cold War and efforts to set the rules of the global economy, that similarly shape the success or failure of any strategy of national economic ascent; global market forces and relative competitiveness that shape the nature and relative success of any nation's development strategy, particularly evident in the crisis in Japan because of efforts to ignore global competitiveness that led to growing state subsidies, increased burdens on various social groups (Katz 1998), and ultimately halted the pattern of state-sector-firm relations and the economic ascent of the nation; and, finally, the relationship between the ascendant economy and its extractive peripheries that supply the ascendant economy and subsidize its global competitiveness.

If any component of this constellation of social forces and processes becomes too powerful and overwhelms the interests of others, this dynamic tension collapses and economic ascent ends. These patterns are both long-lasting (even staying in place long after ascent ends) and very difficult to maintain in dynamic tension, helping explain why dramatic ascent and the resulting restructuring of the world economy occurs so infrequently, despite the efforts of states and firms to accomplish this in support of their own interests over the past five centuries. The creation and maintenance of these patterns of dynamic tension result from the efforts of states and firms to resolve the fundamental material challenge for rapidly ascendant economies, acquiring, transporting, processing, and utilizing the rapidly growing amounts of raw materials essential for economic growth.

In Japan, the loss of dynamic tension as political payoffs, financial and land speculation by fractions of capital focused on making money without investing in the productive process, misdirection of state subsidies to industries that cannot compete globally, and competition from the existing hegemon and other rising economies, including China, in the context of the global economy that Japan's ascent helped create exposed the limitations of Japan's postwar development model and the opportunities that the increased economies of scale developed in steel, shipbuilding, shipping, and other industries created for other rising nations. Modest but sustained economic growth in Japan during 2004 and 2005, based on a combination of domestic demand and the burgeoning export and investment relationship with China, offers some analysts reason to hope that Japan's long-term stagnation may now be ending (Associated Press 2006; Fackler 2006; *FT.com* 2006). Japanese firms have been able to take advantage of China's economic ascent in a variety of ways, as has often happened in the past with core powers investing in and trading with much faster-growing ascendant economies.

New Historical Materialism: Learning from Japan and the Economic Ascent of China

We return to our fifth research question in this book, how is China utilizing and transforming the Japan-created global raw materials industries to support China's rapid development? The data for the generative sectors emerging in China are quite striking. In the steel industry, Chinese steel production increased from 158,000 tons in 1949 to 40 million tons in 1980 and to 349 million tons in 2005; steel exports totaled 27 million tons in 2005 (Brizendine and Oliver 2001; Gale Group 2003; Hogan 1999a, 1999b; ISSB 2006; OECD 2005; Serchuk 2001;); and steel employment now totals approximately 3 million workers (Brizendine and Oliver 2001:22). The Chinese government closed some small, globally uncompetitive steel mills and now emphasizes building new coastal steel mills using the latest technology and the least costly globally available coal and iron ore, rather than relying on lower-quality, higher-cost domestic resources, as was formerly done under state policies of domestic economic self-sufficiency (Hogan 1999a). China now leads the world in steel production, surpassing Japan, the United States, and Europe (Serchuk 2001:32). China also became the world's largest importer of iron ore (275 million tons of a world total of 715 million tons in 2005 [ISSB 2006]), utilizing a global system of raw materials supply created by Japan during its economic ascent via a variety of innovations in technology and social organization of steel production, ocean shipping, and raw materials supply agreements.

China is following the Japanese model of heavy industrialization in coastal greenfields to supply other industries at low cost (Ciccantell and Bunker 2004; Hogan 1999a; Todd 1996), as state policies focus on deepening industrialization in steel, shipbuilding, and other heavy industries. However, following the models of earlier ascendant economies, even in terms of fomenting what have historically been key generative sectors in the most successful cases of ascent, does not guarantee success, in part because older models may be surpassed by new technological and organizational innovations by other competitors and in part because successful sustained ascent is a relational process of competition with the existing hegemon and other ascendant economies. Historically, for example, Germany surpassed both Great Britain and the United States in terms of steel production in the early twentieth century as part of its devel-

opmental drive, but German ascent eventually encountered both raw materials difficulties and direct conflict with the existing hegemon and other emerging rivals, with
the conflict eventually resolved in favor of the United States

China's efforts to follow Japan's model of ascent confront similar challenges from
the existing hegemon, the United States, and other competitors, including the European Union, Japan, and Russia. The economic and social consequences of closing
and/or ending state support for inland industry, especially in the Northeast (a long-
standing policy of autarky and domestic security under the Communist Party), are
also a potential internal limitation of China's ascent.

Analyses of China's dramatic growth focus on changes in government control of
the Chinese economy (see, e.g., Lardy 1992; Morris, Hassard, and Sheehan 2002); the
availability of tremendous numbers of low-cost workers for export production by
Japanese, European, U.S., and other transnational corporations that led to foreign direct investment inflows totaling US$387 billion between 1979 and 2002 (Andersen and
Rand 2003:11); and the historical characteristics of the Chinese economy and society,
including China's historical role as the center of the world economy (Frank 1998) and
the role of family business networks in organizing production and trade (Arrighi et
al. 2002; Hui 1995; Irwan 1995; Wang 1991; Yeung and Olds 2000). All of these analyses
identify key components of China's economic ascent as China's role in the world economy changed and expanded dramatically in recent decades.

An important recent advance in our understanding of the Chinese development
model is the recognition that, despite very different state policies and roles in global
geopolitics since World War II, the Chinese state since 1978 closely resembles the
model of the East Asian developmental state (So 2003). The Chinese state from 1949
through 1978 created a legacy of a strong state developed in the context of the Cold
War, encouraged a strong nationalist sentiment with the goal of creating a wealthy nation, created rural infrastructure and local institutions, and did all of this without creating a large foreign debt, all of which laid the foundation for the creation of a developmental state since 1978. The transition to a developmental state resulted from a
combination of the ending of the Cold War, the collapse of the socialist development
model, the search for lower-cost production sites by China's neighbors as their costs
of production increased, the increasing investment of Chinese diaspora capitalists in
China (Gao 2003; Smart and Hsu 2004), and the transition from revolutionary leadership to younger, more innovative leadership in China. Beginning in 1978, the Chinese state implemented reforms from above, taking advantage of the state autonomy
and capacity created in the earlier era to carefully control and adjust the process of
change in order to achieve high economic growth and to avoid many of the problems
of the former socialist nations of Eastern Europe (So 2003).

All of these approaches highlight key parts of China's economic ascent in recent decades, identifying and explaining many of the components of this process. However, none addresses what we argue has been the central driving force underlying sustained economic ascent in earlier cases of economies that have risen to challenge the existing hegemonic power of their era: the role of raw materials and transport industries as generative sectors. If China is to create a sustained trajectory of growth for the future, these generative sectors, which are already key strategic sectors for the Chinese state, will have to play roles in China similar to those they played in earlier cases of dramatic and transformative economic ascent. These generative sectors in the most successful historical cases of economic ascent articulate domestic economic development with the creation of new systems of international economic and political relations, ultimately restructuring the capitalist world-economy in support of a nation's economic ascent to core status and its ability to challenge the existing hegemon and other ascendant economies for hegemony. From our theoretical and methodological perspective, we focus analytically on a critical set of industries and indicators and on the often highly conflictual process of developing a system of state-sector-firm relations that supports these generative sectors and, via a range of material, economic, and sociopolitical mechanisms, the broader process of economic ascent.

The steel, transport, and other linked industries in the generative sectors of China began to develop during the first half of the twentieth century under the aegis of invading imperial powers, most importantly the Japanese, who built China's first steel mill at Anshan (Hogan 1999a; Serchuk 2001). Under the Communist Party from 1949 through the late 1970s, government policy focused on domestic self-sufficiency in key economic sectors, including steel (Dorian 1999). During the 1950s, the Soviet Union provided technical support and technology, including building steel mills in China, such as the Wuhan mill (Hogan 1999a). The Chinese government supported the development of a large steel industry, with production of 40 million tons in 1980 (Serchuk 2001). These steel mills were relatively small scale and often located far inland for security purposes. Rural areas of China supplied coal and iron ore, and the coal industry became one of the most important employers in rural China, producing 871 million tons of coal in 1985 and employing millions of people. A limited and antiquated railroad transport system linked mines and steel mills, severely limiting interregional trade and raising costs of production; this transport system also made imports and exports of resources extremely difficult.

Chinese government policies for steel, coal, and linked industries began to change in 1978. The Chinese government planned to make minerals and metals industries key components of efforts to expand China's role in the global economy (Dorian 1999; Schneider et al. 2000). The pace of change accelerated in the 1980s as part of the broader process of economic reform instituted by the Communist Party (Dorian 1999). For the steel industry, this meant a dramatic increase in steel capacity and production, often from new steel mills located in coastal regions (Ruiyu 1999). Steel production increased by almost a factor of nine in China between 1980 and 2005, rising from 40 million to 349 million tons (OECD 2005), and steel firms improved their technology both through imports and domestic research and development, including raising the continuous casting rate dramatically and slowly replacing antiquated equipment (Hogan 1999a, 1999b; Liu and Jin 1994; Ruiyu 1999). China's Metallurgical Council announced that Chinese steel production capacity totaled 310 million tons per year at the end of 2004, and another 150 million tons per year of capacity would be completed by the end of 2006 (AME 2004c:11).

The Chinese government fears "overheating" of the steel sector because of this rapid growth and seeks to prevent it (Bogler 2004; Cockerill 2003; *Global News Wire* 2004c). Overheating would result in a huge excess of investment that leads to excess capacity, wasted capital, bank loans that cannot be repaid, and potentially stock market and banking crises as companies and banks fail. This type of investment, banking, and stock market "bubble" closely parallels the crises that initiated Japan's stagnation and the Asian crisis of the late 1990s (Cockerill 2003). Government policies now seek to restrict new investments to avoid overheating and encourage consolidation in the steel sector to help control investment (*Global News Wire-Asia Africa Intelligence Wire* 2006), but these policies are difficult to enforce and so far only partially successful. Excess capacity in China has led to low prices for steel, with one senior Chinese government official reporting that steel prices have fallen below production costs for 95 percent of steel products (*AFX International Focus* 2005).

The parallels between Japan's property and financial bubble that brought on the prolonged period of stagnation and the potential for such a broader property and financial bubble in China are quite strong as well. The Chinese government has taken a variety of measures to try to control the rapid escalation of property prices and investment, but many firms and government agencies benefit from increasing property prices (Barboza 2005a, 2005b), making it very difficult to control. Increasing property prices and the ability to earn profits and borrow money based on increasing property prices can contribute to capital accumulation, but, as happened in Japan, this process can come to a quick and highly destructive end.

To supply China's coastal steel mills, imports of far-higher-quality Australian, Brazilian, and other imported iron ore increased from only 10 million tons in 1985 and 14 million tons in 1990 to 41 million tons by 1995 and 92 million tons in 2001 (*International Bulk Journal* 2002:28). Several ports serving coastal steel mills, including Dalian, Tangshan, Tianjin, and Majishan increased or are increasing their capacity to accommodate ships of 100,000 to 200,000 deadweight tons bringing ore from Australia and Brazil (Hogan 1999a, 1999b; *International Bulk Journal* 2002:27–28), and Shougang Group Corporation is building a greenfield steel mill in a new MIDA in Tangshan of Hebei province that will be able to unload 250,000-dwt ships (*Sinocast* 2006a). Plans are being made for even larger-scale ports: a contract was recently signed with the world's largest iron ore–exporting firm, CVRD of Brazil, for the construction of a bulk ship of 450,000 deadweight tons. This will be the world's largest bulk carrier and will take Chinese coal to Brazil and Brazilian iron ore to China.

Raw materials supply concerns state-owned and private steel firms in China, as well as the Chinese government. A report by China's State Administration for the Metallurgical Industry called for an expansion of iron ore imports from Chinese joint-venture mines overseas from 12 percent in 2003 to 50 percent in order to supply the growing quantities and specific qualities of iron ore needed for the rapidly growing steel industry. Such joint ventures and long-term contracts in Australia, Brazil, Peru, and India already form key elements of Chinese iron ore supply, and Chinese steel firms and the Chinese state seek similar arrangements in Russia and other nations (Kirk 2003).

For the coal industry, the emphasis on steel and electric power as generative sectors to supply the broader economy entailed increases in domestic capacity and production, as well as an emphasis on exports of coal. China now rivals Australia as the world's largest coal exporter (*International Bulk Journal* 2002:54; Schneider et al. 2000; Tse 2000). The Chinese government promoted the consolidation of the coal industry in order to create a smaller number of larger, more globally competitive firms to supply domestic and export markets more efficiently (Nolan and Rui 2004; Rui 2005).

Steel production in China also depends on large-scale imports of scrap steel, a situation very similar to that in Japan from the late 1940s through the 1970s. China imported more than 3 million tons of scrap from the United States in 2003, more than 30 percent of U.S. steel scrap exports, at a cost of more than US$1 billion (Minter 2004; Pollack and Bradsher 2004). Mongolia, Russia, and other neighboring nations also export millions of tons of scrap to China (Brooke 2004a).

In 1995 China became the world's largest steel producer. This dramatic increase in capacity and production, however, encountered three major problems. First, in terms of supplying the growing demand for steel from China's manufacturing industries, important limitations on the quality and product lines of the Chinese steel mills required significant volumes of imports of products such as steel sheet for appliance and automotive production (Hogan 1999a, 1999b; Serchuk 2001:32). Second, aging and often antiquated technologies at many steel mills contributed to these quality problems and to management difficulties and environmental problems (Brizendine and Oliver 2001; Hogan 1999a, 1999b; Serchuk 2001). Third, extremely low levels of productivity per worker made Chinese steel uncompetitive globally without extremely low-cost labor. Chinese steel mills produce 37 tons of steel per year per employee, while in Japan, Europe, and the United States output per employee is closer to 400 tons (Brizendine and Oliver 2001:22).

The Chinese government instituted a series of new policies in the past decade in order to address these problems in the steel and coal industries in particular and more generally to prepare the broader economy for joining the World Trade Organization and to increase global competitiveness. In both steel and coal, government policies called for restructuring steel mills and firms to improve productivity and reduce employment, including closing many small steel mills and coal mines and encouraging concentration into a smaller number of more competitive and potentially more profitable firms (Brizendine and Oliver 2001; Gale Group 2003; Hogan 1999a, 1999b; Mehta 1998). Investment in steel has been refocused from building new capacity, with three new coastal steel mills with a capacity of 10 million tons per year each postponed indefinitely (Serchuk 2001), to improving steel quality and broadening Chinese production into high-end product lines to replace imported steel, including lighter, stronger steel and ultrafine grained steel (Brizendine and Oliver 2001; *Global News Wire* 2004b; Hogan 1999a, 1999b; Serchuk 2001).

In order to accomplish this technological upgrading, Chinese steel firms sought to attract foreign firms as joint-venture partners and technology suppliers, a strategy that proved very effective. Most of the world's leading steel mills and firms supplying technology to steel mills are now involved in dozens of projects in China, as are Japanese trading firms and banks, including Nisshin Steel, Nippon Steel, Sumitomo Metal Industries, Mitsui and Company, Mitsubishi Corporation, Mitsubishi Heavy Industries, the Industrial Bank of Japan, Sakura Bank, Dai-Ichi Kangyo Bank, Sanwa Bank, Marubeni Company, and Itochu International Corporation of Japan, the Asian Development Bank, Posco of South Korea, Thyssen-Krupp of Germany, and Mittal Steel (Brizendine and Oliver 2001; Dorian 1999; *Financial Times* 2005; Gale Group 2003; Hogan 1999a, 1999b; Huskonen 2001).

Efforts to increase the global competitiveness of China's steel industry and other raw materials–processing industries also include another form of cooperation with foreign firms: Chinese joint ventures in iron ore, copper, aluminum, oil, and other types of minerals and processing facilities in Australia, Brazil, Canada, Papua New Guinea, Chile, Peru, the Philippines, Jamaica, Zambia, Vietnam, Venezuela, and New Zealand (Dorian 1999; Tse 2000), in most cases following the lead of Japanese firms in creating joint ventures and long-term contracts with firms and states in these mineral-producing regions. These overseas investments by Chinese firms as minority joint-venture partners and buyers of output under long-term contracts are explicitly modeled on the raw materials access strategies of Japanese steel firms, reducing the costs and risks to the importing firms while transferring the vast majority of the costs and risks of large investments in mines and infrastructure to firms and states in the exporting region (Bunker and Ciccantell 1995a, 2003a, 2003b, 2005). Since China became the world's largest iron ore importer, the China Iron and Steel Association wants its members to take the lead in annual iron ore price negotiations, with the goal of negotiating lower prices (Paxton 2003), taking over the leading role of Japanese and European steel firms. Baosteel and CURD settled the first 2007 contract for a 9.5 percent price increase, helping to control China's iron ore import costs.

The Chinese and Russian governments are developing close economic and political relationships, motivated both by goals of creating a counterweight to U.S. hegemony and by efforts to promote domestic economic development. Russian raw materials feed a growing share of Chinese industry. Petroleum exports to China receive the greatest attention, most notably Chinese government support for Russian government renationalization of Yukos via a long-term contract and US$6 billion credit arrangement between state-owned China National Petroleum Corporation and Russian state-owned Rosneft (Arvedlund 2005; Arvedlund and Romero 2004; N. Buckley 2005; Reuters 2005a; Watson 2005).

China's rapidly growing petroleum imports motivate an intense search for supplies of oil from many parts of the world. In addition to Russia, Chinese oil firms and the Chinese state pursued rapidly growing supply relationships that concern other major oil importers, most notably the United States, Japan, and India. The Chinese government arranged oil and natural gas supply deals in Cameroon, Nigeria, Gabon, Angola, the Sudan, Brazil, Peru, Venezuela, Kazakhstan, Azerbaijan, Iran, Saudi Arabia, and even in Canada's oil sands region of Alberta (*Alberta Oil* 2005; Cheng 2006; Ebner 2004; EIA 2004; Engdahl 2005; Fattah 2006; Luciw 2005; Reuters 2005c; York 2004), creating a great deal of concern for the U.S. and Japanese governments about future access to oil supplies for their own nations.

The proposed acquisition of Unocal by China National Offshore Oil Corporation (CNOOC) because of Unocal's extensive Asian oil reserves marked a new escalation of this rivalry between major oil importers. Members of the U.S. Congress called for hearings on the proposed takeover as a potential national security threat (King, Hitt, and Ball 2005; Lohr 2005; Wayne and Barboza 2005), highlighting the intense economic and political rivalry over raw materials supplies between China and the existing hegemon.

China's leading role in the world economy, most notably as a purchaser of raw materials, also discouraged other global oil firms from bidding against CNOOC for Unocal, because these oil firms feared it would damage their potential future sales to China (*Financial Times* 2005b). Unocal accepted a bid from Chevron after CNOOC withdrew its bid because of political opposition in the United States (Sorkin and Mouawad 2005), but this will not end China's efforts to acquire oil around the world.

This takeover battle signifies a major change in China's role in the global economy, as one international banker notes: "it is a wake up call for the global financial community. China is no longer a hunting ground for foreign investors. It has become a source of takeover activity" (*Financial Times* 2005c). The Chinese government's development strategy now emphasizes both acquiring raw materials around the world and creating globally competitive enterprises. One adviser to the Chinese government reported that the effort to buy Unocal was not just about oil fields but also about promoting foreign investment by Chinese firms, with the National Development and Reform Commission, the leading economic planning agency in China, guiding CNOOC's bid for Unocal (*Financial Times* 2005d). Rapid economic growth depends on rapidly growing supplies of raw materials, and the Chinese state now focuses a great deal of effort on establishing raw materials supply relationships around the world (Watts 2005). These efforts often come into conflict with efforts by the United States, Japan, and the European Union to gain access to these same resources, particularly energy resources. These economic conflicts, particularly in conjunction with what some analysts argue is the impending peak in global oil production (see, e.g., Simmons 2005), threaten to create political and even military conflicts over scarce resources in the coming years (Zweig and Jianhai 2005).

However, China and the existing hegemon, the United States, are not simply rivals over raw materials imports; the relationship between the existing hegemon and rapidly ascending China is far more complex. The Chinese government buys tens of billions of dollars per year of U.S. government Treasury bonds and held US$243 billion at the end of 2005 (El Akkad 2005). The Chinese government also holds foreign currency reserves (mainly of U.S. dollars) of more than US$850 billion as of February 2006 (Bradsher 2006), all of which support U.S. government operations and the value of the U.S. dollar. Chinese firms supply huge and growing volumes of manufactured goods to the United States (often in competition with U.S.-based manufacturing and leading to large job losses in the United States). Chinese firms buy billions of dollars of imports from the United States, such as the US$5 billion purchase of nuclear reactors from Westinghouse supported by loans from the U.S. Export-Import Bank (Wald 2005). As one recent analysis argues, "the result is a historically unusual relationship in which the rising power, developing China, provides both exports (second-leading supplier) and loans (second-leading holder of government debt) to the superpower, the industrialized United States" (Deng and Moore 2004:132). This parallels Japan's relationship with the United States since the 1970s after more than two decades of rapid industrial development in Japan; China plays this same role for the United States after two decades of rapid economic ascent in China. However, no similar relationship developed during the earlier processes of economic ascent that we have studied (Bunker and Ciccantell 2005).

Rivalry between the United States and China extends to potential military conflict. As one Chinese general recently stated, "if the Americans draw their missiles and position-guided ammunition on to the target zone on China's territory, I think we will have to respond with nuclear weapons" (Kahn 2005b), referring to the ongoing conflict over the status of Taiwan. Many conservative political leaders in the United States continue to view China through the lens of Cold War rivalry and oppose close political and economic relations between the United States and China more than three decades after Nixon's rapprochement with China. The U.S. Department of Defense produces an annual assessment of China's military power (U.S. Secretary of Defense 2005) as the result of this view of China as a geopolitical rival. The Chinese vice minister of foreign affairs responded quickly to the publication of the most recent issue of this report, arguing that "this report ignores the facts and tries its utmost to spread the notion of a China threat. It's a crude meddling in Chinese internal affairs, and it tries to sow discord between China and other countries" (C. Buckley 2005). This type of political and military rivalry with the existing hegemon characterized all of the earlier cases of transformative ascent we have studied, except for Japan after World War II after the defeat of Japan's imperial strategy for ascent by the United States and Great Britain (Bunker and Ciccantell 2005).

However, the emphasis on current and potential rivalry obscures the close cooperative relationship between the United States and China that is largely responsible for China's economic ascent over the past three decades. Shared opposition to the Soviet Union led the United States and China to form what Henry Kissinger referred to as a "tacit alliance" by 1973 during which "Washington proceeded to support, arm, share intelligence with and nurture the economy of a Chinese government it had previously attempted to overthrow" (Mann 1999:8, cited in Nayar 2004:31). The U.S. government supported China's military modernization and, via granting most-favored-nation trading status to China, supported the origins and development of China's export-led development strategy (Mahbubani 2005; Nayar 2004).

Another analyst argued that "the training of People's Republic of China (PRC) students and scholars in the West, most importantly in the United States, by itself constitutes the most significant transfer of technology to one country in a short period of time ever. Without doubt, over the past twenty years, China has obtained what it needed for its economic modernization from abroad (capital, technology, and access to markets) in greater amounts and at less cost than any country previously" (Van Ness 2002:133). This tacit alliance played a critical role in helping the United States in its geopolitical rivalry with its most formidable political rival of the mid-twentieth century, the Soviet Union, but, just as was the case of Japan-U.S. relations after World War II, it led to the dramatic rise of a new economic and political ally and rival that transformed the world economy. As in the earlier cases of rapid and systemically transformative economic ascent that we have analyzed (Bunker and Ciccantell 2005), the existing hegemon unintentionally created a major new rival.

Many analysts argue that, from the Chinese perspective, the relationship with the United States is multifaceted: "many Chinese still view the United States as a major threat to their nation's security and domestic stability. . . . in the long term, the decline of U.S. primacy and the subsequent transition to a multipolar world are inevitable; but in the short term, Washington's power is unlikely to decline, and its position in world affairs is unlikely to change" (Jisi 2005:39). However, China's economic health still depends to a great extent on the continued health of the U.S. economy as well (Jisi 2005).

The Chinese government has developed a variety of strategies in order to strengthen China's position in the economic and political rivalries with the United States. One of the most important is the creation and expansion of the Shanghai Cooperation Organization. Founded in 2001, the organization formally links China, Russia, Kazakhstan, Kyrgystan, Tajikistan, Uzbekistan, Mongolia, Iran, India, and Pakistan and, by promoting regional integration through economic, security, and political ties between members, provides a counterweight to U.S. hegemony in the region (Bhadrakumar 2006; Chung 2005). Chinese and Russian cooperation includes their first joint military exercises in 2005 (Herman 2005). The Chinese government has also strengthened its economic and political ties with the members of the Association of Southeast Asian Nations, including providing economic support to help resolve the Asian financial crisis of 1998–99 (De Santis 2005). The Chinese and Indian governments, longtime political and military rivals and, due to rapid economic growth in both countries, now rivals for securing energy supplies, formed a strategic partnership in 2005 aimed at promoting peaceful economic and political cooperation between the two nations (Associated Press 2005; Sengupta and French 2005). All of these strategies are intended to strengthen China's economic and political power on the world stage in the face of U.S. hegemony.

For the Chinese coal industry, a major effort to increase exports during the 1980s and early 1990s now takes a subordinate position to providing coal to steel mills and especially to the rapidly growing cities of the southeast coast, where it is used for electricity generation (Todd 1996:52). Several coal ports were previously targeted for upgrading for export sales and as locations for the new coastal steelworks, including the new industrial development area at the natural deepwater harbor at Rizhao (Todd 1996). However, many of these ports now focus on transshipping coal railed from internal coal mines, loading the coal onto small bulk carriers for shipment to the southeast coast cities. Rail network upgrading is underway as well to improve interregional flows of coal and other cargoes, but coastal shipping remains the key link for getting coal to the industrial southeast (Schneider et al. 2000; Todd 1996).

Efforts to promote foreign investment in coal production continue, including in the relatively undeveloped but geologically rich coal regions of Inner Mongolia, such as a joint venture to upgrade China's major coal mines with an Australian firm that included a US$200 million investment, as well as a joint venture for the construction of an underground coal pipeline, coal washery, and port facilities between a Chinese government firm and U.S. and Australian partners for an investment of US$888.6 million (Dorian 1999; Tse 2000). Restructuring of the coal industry closed more than 40,000 small, uncompetitive coal mines, reducing capacity by 320 million tons per year and contributing to a decline in coal production from 1.38 billion tons in 1996 to 880 million tons in 2000 (*International Bulk Journal* 1999:23; Tse 2000).

The most fundamental obstacle to these strategies for increasing the competitiveness of the Chinese steel and coal industries derives from the social costs of closing high-cost mills and mines and ending the jobs of millions of workers. In many of China's industrial regions developed between 1949 and the early 1980s, particularly in the northeast, unemployment rates already reach levels estimated at 30 to 70 percent in many cities (Brizendine and Oliver 2001:22). High unemployment levels create tremendous social unrest and put a great deal of budgetary strain on local and regional governments. These governmental units have pressured the central government to slow the restructuring in steel and coal in order to protect jobs and tax revenues in these already declining regions, with at least some success. The emerging class conflict between the unemployed and state officials, many of whom use their government positions to transform themselves into capitalists, in combination with growing financial crises because of nonperforming loans, financial losses by state-owned firms, and the growing government budget deficit, creates tremendous challenges for the Chinese state and for the sustainability of the Chinese development model (A. Chen 2002; F. Chen 2003; Gordon 2003; Kahn 2004; So 2003; Wolf 2004; Xiaoguang 2003).

These social costs and problems underscore the challenges involved in a problem of scale that may be unique to China among the world's rapidly ascendant economies: the challenge of the scale of the population to be employed, provided with goods and services, and persuaded to support the legitimacy of the state and its model of economic development, political relations, and their socioeconomic and environmental consequences. For Holland, Great Britain, and the United States, issues related to population focused much more on potential shortages of labor and the need to create political, economic, and organizational strategies to guarantee adequate supplies of labor at reasonable costs. In the United States and Holland in particular, labor shortage and technological innovation created a win-win situation for labor and capital because it made labor more productive and capital more profitable. However, this is not the case in China today. Only in Japan after World War II was the issue of how to employ millions of unemployed soldiers and workers displaced from wartime factories and agricultural production a salient concern for an economy that later constructed a sustained pattern of economic ascent. This challenge facing China, common to many nations of the periphery and semiperiphery during the twentieth century but on a much greater scale in China, presents a fundamental challenge to sustained ascent, because the shift from the earlier model of autarky to greater openness and global competitiveness creates immense numbers of job losses and growing political unrest.

This scale of population, however, also presents an important opportunity, as the multitude of foreign firms investing in China well know: a market of almost one-quarter of the world's population under one political unit with a common language and culture that simplifies marketing efforts and offers the potential for huge revenues and profits. While even the most productive of these efforts have met with only limited success and many others have yet to prove profitable, the potential offered by the scale of China's population remains an important economic factor and lever for the Chinese government to use with potential foreign investors.

Another key strategy for the Chinese government in the early twenty-first century is massive deficit spending on infrastructure as a form of "New Deal" to resolve infrastructural problems and simultaneously to employ huge numbers of workers and stimulate continued rapid economic growth. Government investment plans include spending US$200 billion to turn the city of Chongqing in southwestern China into a transportation and industrial hub near what had been (until these and other government development plans were announced) the world's single largest infrastructural investment, the US$30 billion Three Gorges Dam (Kahn 2003). The Chinese government invested US$60 billion in new road construction during the end of the 1990s and early 2000s, US$30 billion on railroad construction during the same period (*33 Metalproducing* 1998:42; Nogales and Smith 2004), and billions more on port construction (*International Bulk Journal,* May 2002:54). These infrastructural investments derive from efforts by the central government to ensure support from city and regional governments by attempting to reduce unemployment and to further economic development, but this program and the resulting deficit spending create potential government fiscal and financial sector problems (Kahn 2003).

Closely linked to these infrastructural investments are efforts to attract foreign investment into the interior regions of China in order to reduce interregional disparities. World Trade Organization accession and a series of new government regulations regarding foreign investment (Tse 2000) opened the door to additional foreign investment, and the government launched a "Go West" campaign (Tse 2000) to lure foreign companies to invest in the interior via a new series of tax and other incentives (Gelb and Chen 2004; Todd 1996; Tse 2000). This strategy includes efforts to link ports with coal-producing areas to spread growth from the coast inland via coal-mining-based development (Todd 1996).

Based on our earlier research on the process of hegemonic succession (Bunker and Ciccantell 2005) and the work of Arrighi (1994), one of the most interesting questions about the long-term sustainability of China's economic ascent is the role played by Japan, the most recent case of sustained economic ascent. In each earlier case of rapid ascent, the existing hegemon played a key role as the supplier of capital and technology to the rising economy as part of what Arrighi (1994) analyzed as the period of financialization and decline in the existing hegemon and the efforts of financial capital in the hegemon to find new opportunities for investment in rapidly growing economies (Bunker and Ciccantell 2005).

At least to some extent, Japanese firms play this role in the ascent of China, both in the manufacturing growth in southeastern China, the focus of most analyses of Chinese economic growth, and in the steel, transport, and other raw materials industries on which we focus. The largest and most modern steel mill in China, Baoshan, opened in 1985 on the southeastern coast near Shanghai and was built with technical assistance from Nippon Steel and other Japanese companies (Hogan 1999a), an explicit replication of the Japanese steel-based MIDAs program. Japanese steel firms are currently joint-venture partners in several steel mills and steel-processing plants (Tse 2000), supplying capital and technology to their Chinese partners. In other raw materials industries, a wide variety of Japanese raw materials–processing firms, trading companies, and banks play similar roles (Tse 2000). Japanese firms supplied 5 to 16 percent of total annual inflows of foreign direct investment in China from 1986 to 2002, with 7 to 9 percent the usual range (Invest in China, www.fd.gov.cn), making Japan the fourth largest foreign investor. However, because the single largest investor according to available data has been Hong Kong throughout the period and much of this investment is in fact from other nations, including Japan, it is difficult to state with certainty the exact total share of Japanese investment in China.

Another important example of this direct transfer of the Japanese model, Japanese technology, and Japanese investment is the industrial development built on the natural deepwater port of Rizhao. The development plan includes a large-capacity rail connection to the interior coal fields; a port completed in 1986 that can load and unload capesize ships with the goal of importing iron ore and exporting coal to Japan; an integrated steel mill and industrial complex that has been at least postponed; and all the other components of a growth pole. This particular coastal growth pole, however, confronted serious problems by the mid-1990s, and many of the planned facilities have not been built, and the city remains only a minor part of China's coal transport network and industrial base (Todd 1996).

More generally, Chinese economic ascent relies on and critically supports Japanese firms and the Japanese economy. Much of the hollowing out of the Japanese economy was blamed on China during the 1990s, but trade with and investment in China by Japanese firms, including exports of steel, capital goods, and other products from Japan to China, now drive Japan's economic growth (Bremner, Tashiro, and Roberts 2004; Coleman 2004; Moffett and Dvorak 2004; Mukoyama 2003–4; Sanchanta 2004;).

Analysts often characterize relations between China and Japan as schizophrenic, with very close, extensive, and positive economic relations and interdependence, but with very negative and conflictual political relations. Controversies such as Japan's political portrayal of Japanese actions during World War II, the intrusion of a Chinese submarine into Japanese waters, Japan's recent emphasis on increasing ties with Taiwan (including calling for the defense of Taiwan against a potential Chinese attack), China's efforts to block Japan's bid for a seat on the United Nations Security Council, and frequent anti-Japanese public protests in China all illustrate the severe political conflicts that threaten to disrupt close economic relations (Brooke 2004b, 2005c; Kahn 2005a; Onishi 2005a). Such political rivalry despite close economic relations between an economically ascendant economy and an established core power is historically quite common. The United States and Great Britain, the partners in the longest such relationship historically, fought two wars over this relationship, along with a proxy war (extensive British support for the Confederacy during the U.S. Civil War). Holland had a similar relationship with Portugal (Bunker and Ciccantell 2005).

Just as in the case of China's relationship with the United States, significant conflicts and rivalries also mark the relationship between China and Japan. Energy supplies are one major arena of conflict, most notably over supplies of oil and gas from Russia (Engdahl 2005; Kenny 2004). Japan's government won one recent battle by promising billions of dollars to build a US$15.5 billion oil pipeline to move Russian oil to a port for export to Japan, but the Chinese and Japanese governments both seek to buy natural gas from a major development at Sakhalin Island (Brooke 2004b, 2005a). The Chinese government is exploring a potential natural gas field in an area of the East China Sea that both China and Japan claim, and the Chinese government refuses to halt exploration despite repeated Japanese requests (Reuters 2005b).

China's rapid development creates a tremendous incentive for Japan and Russia to form closer ties in order to protect their economic and political interests. Trade, investment, and military cooperation are all growing rapidly in response to the perceived threat from China (Brooke 2005b). This highlights the impacts that successful ascent on the part of one nation has on other nations with whom they compete economically and politically. Success leads to strategic responses that change the regional and global economic and political environments and, unless the successful ascendant economy can adjust and refine its strategies to accommodate these new environments, ascent may soon halt.

Chinese efforts to explicitly follow the Japanese postwar model of development, and especially the cases of Baoshan and Rizhao, illustrate both the potential benefits and risks of following this model and creating an integrated set of generative sectors in steel and transport. Growth poles based on the steel and other heavy industries following this model can be found on the coasts of a number of nations in Europe, Asia, Latin America, and Africa. However, most, despite billions of dollars of investment by states, international financial institutions, and domestic and foreign firms, remain at best poorly integrated enclaves that have failed to generate sustained economic growth. State policies and the availability of funding are only parts of the broader process of international competition that shapes the developmental trajectories of particular growth poles, regions, and states within the world economy.

The strategies, successes, and failures of other ascendant economies and the existing hegemon shape the technological, organizational, socioeconomic, and political parameters that determine global competitiveness, and more successful rivals can effectively circumscribe the best policy choices and largest investments of other competitors. In the steel industry since World War II, dozens of nations invested billions of dollars in what has been in some cases this driving force of economic development. However, the steel mills built by Japanese firms with the support of the Japanese state and those built following the Japanese model in South Korea have been far more successful in terms of international competitiveness than similar complexes in Europe, Latin America, and other nations in Asia. The outcomes of these developmental efforts are highly contingent on the strategies of other competing economies, and the long-term sustainability of China's efforts to sustain its economic ascent by following the Japanese model is far from assured.

Japan, China, and the Future of the Capitalist World-Economy

The Chinese government and Chinese and foreign firms are clearly moving to deepen industrialization by investing in and promoting what have historically been the key generative sectors of steel, transport, and other linked industries, recognizing both the fundamental challenges of resolving the material input needs of a rapidly growing economy and the opportunities these challenges create for generative sectors to drive economic ascent. The example of Japanese coastal industrialization since World War II has been an important model for China, and Japanese firms, the Japanese state, and Japanese banks play leading roles in the transfer of this model technologically, organizationally, and financially to China. This model and the efforts underway to restructure the Chinese steel, coal, and other industries offer a potential avenue for a sustained process of economic ascent to core status and perhaps even to challenging for hegemonic status in the future. Our series of comparative historical cases that analyze how generative sectors form around raw materials and transport provide us with lessons that inform our analysis of this case of still uncertain outcomes in China.

Successfully following the Japanese model is only one potential future scenario for Chinese development. A second possible scenario is the formation of a Japanese-Chinese economic and political alliance similar to that between Great Britain and the United States in the 1700s and 1800s. Japanese financing and technology already combine with Chinese firms in many industries to create some of the world's most competitive firms that dominate many industries and global export markets. In combination with China's conventional and nuclear military capabilities, this potential geopolitical and economic alliance could challenge U.S. hegemony.

Another possible future scenario for Chinese development is quite different. China faces both internal and external obstacles to this potential sustained economic ascent. Domestically, the huge social and political costs of moving from the model of autarky and guaranteed employment to global competitiveness create economic and political problems that will be difficult to resolve. Rising unemployment, growing rural-urban and geographic inequality, corruption, and decreasing political legitimacy of the Communist Party all threaten to create social disorder and even to cause the breakdown of the Chinese political system.

More generally, it is not clear that China's ascent is supported by the kind of dynamic tension we have identified in our analysis of Japan's economic ascent. We have identified a similar list of domestic and international groups and relationships that have driven China's economic ascent since the early 1980s. Internationally, conflict and cooperation with the United States, Japan, and Russia, the construction of a network of raw materials suppliers following the Japanese model of long-term contracts and joint ventures, and highly globally competitive export industries that are outcompeting industries in existing core countries mark China's ascent, just as they did for Japan. Domestically, conflict and cooperation between the growing capitalist class, the working class and managers in globally competitive industries, workers and managers in globally uncompetitive industries, government agencies, and political leaders (similar to that identified in Japan) are further complicated by immense regional inequalities, challenges to the political legitimacy of Communist Party rule, and internal political divisions and conflicts with minority groups.

Long-term sustained ascent requires a difficult-to-maintain dynamic tension between these groups and their often divergent interests. The decision to allow millionaires to join the Communist Party, for example, marks one such effort to balance competing interests. Perhaps the most compelling evidence for the potential development of dynamic tension is offered by Zhu (2004:424), who argues that "the forces of decentralization, marketization, and political legitimization have transformed China's local governments into local states with a strong interest in development. . . . China's local state is a developmental state of its own kind. . . . Local governments are empowered to carry out development by means of a realignment of revenue distribution between the central coffers and localities, leading to autonomous local governments that are highly motivated to maximize revenues in order to support local growth." These processes mark a significant transfer of power from a highly centralized national state that severely constrained the development and maintenance of any dynamic tension, opening the potential for dynamic tension that could support sustained ascent. Mahbubani (2005:51) argues that "after more than a century of misrule, China is now run by the best governing class in generations. . . . (providing) incredibly deft economic management." Again, this offers the potential for the creation of a dynamic tension between increasingly skilled government agencies and state-owned and private firms in generative sectors that could eventually parallel those created in Japan after World War II.

However, other evidence indicates a lack of such a dynamic tension in China. The uncertainty of private property rights (exemplified in the struggle over oil rights in Shaanxi [French 2005]) makes private investors very vulnerable to confiscation by the state or other politically powerful groups, leaving private investors with limited power to protect and advance their own interests. State-mandated coal industry restructuring, intended to increase the global competitiveness of Chinese coal firms (*AFX News* 2003), reveals the weakness of state-owned and private firms in the face of state power. The opposition of state-owned firms, some state agencies, some sectors of the Communist Party, and a variety of other groups to the financial reforms required by China's accession to the World Trade Organization (Breslin 2003) constitutes a major obstacle to China's continued economic ascent.

Overall, in the context of competition in the global economy, replicating a highly successful model created during the 1950s and 1960s by Japanese firms and the Japanese state may not be sufficient to overcome existing and potential future challengers for economic ascent and hegemony. The next decade may bring a fundamental restructuring of the capitalist world-economy in support of sustained Chinese economic ascent, but China's economic ascent could also prove to be sharply constrained by economic and political competition, including the emergence of new organizational, technological, socioeconomic, or political innovations that increase scale and competitiveness in a rival economy and render China's immense investments in steel mills, coal mines, shipyards, and other industries as relics of an earlier era of the capitalist world-economy.

More broadly, Japan's economic ascent profoundly globalized the world economy, creating a very new political economy that the existing hegemon and any potentially ascendant state will need to take into account in their efforts to promote economic ascent in a highly competitive global economy.

AAP Newsfeed. 2003. "Rio Tinto Subsidiary Pacific Coal Opens New Qld. Mine." November 5.
———. 2006. "Macarthur Coal to Develop Five New Mines." February 15.
Abe, Etsuo. 1999. "Japanese Business Culture: The Government, Mainstream Enterprises and Mavericks in the Steel Industry." *Asia Pacific Business Review* 6(2):21–28.
Abegglen, J., and G. Stalk. 1985. *Kaisha: The Japanese Corporation.* New York: Basic Books.
Abbott, Andrew. 1997. "Of Time and Space: The Contemporary Relevance of the Chicago School." *Social Forces* 75(4):1149–82.
Ackerman, E. 1953. *Japan's Natural Resources and Their Relation to Japan's Economic Future.* Chicago: University of Chicago Press.
AFX-Asia. 2003. "Shanghai Baosteel to Set up US$8 Billion Steel JV in Brazil." June 23.
———. 2004. "China Urged to Spend 10 Bln. USD on Shipping to Boost Energy Security." January 7.
AFX-European Focus. 2000. "BHP/CVRD in JV to Rationalise Alegria Complex in Brazil." May 31.
AFX International Focus. 2005. "China NDRC Official Says Government to Have Its Say in Iron Ore Price Talks." November 25.
———. 2006. "China, Japan Reach 'Understanding' Prior to Next Iron Ore Talks." March 1.
AFX News. 2003. "China to Restructure Coal Industry, Forming 8–10 Large Firms." December 21.
———. 2004a. "Japan Major Shipbuilders Saw Three-Fold Surge in Orders Last Year." January 25.
———. 2004b. "BHP Wins 9 Bln. USD, 25-Year Iron Ore Supply Deal with 4 China Steel Cos." March 1.
———. 2004c. "Rio Tinto Strikes Iron Ore Deal with Nippon Steel, Eyes Coking Coal Expansion." April 7.
———. 2006. "Australia Coal Producers Resist Calls for Price Cuts." January 10.
Agnew, John A. 1987. *The United States in the World-Economy: A Regional Geography.* Cambridge: Cambridge University Press.
Akao, Nobutoshi. 1983. "Resources and Japan's Security." Pp. 15–44 in Nobutoshi Akao (ed.), *Japan's Economic Security: Resources as a Factor in Foreign Policy.* Aldershot: Gower Publishing.
Alberta Oil. 2005. "Fueling the Dragon." 1(2):28–29.
Albion, R. 1926. *Forests and Sea Power: The Timber Problem of the Royal Navy, 1652–1862.* Cambridge, Mass.: Harvard University Press.

Amin, Samir. 1996. "The Challenge of Globalisation." *Review of International Political Economy* 3:216–59.

Anderlini, Jamil. 2006. "Mainland Metal Firms Tap Banks in Brazil Deal." *South China Morning Post*, January 10:2.

Andersen, Thomas Worm, and John Rand. 2003. *Foreign Direct Investment (FDI) in Five Developing Economies in East Asia and Southeast Asia.* Copenhagen: University of Copenhagen.

Anderson, D. 1987. "Japan's Coking Coal Procurement System: An Evaluation." *Materials and Society* 11(1):23–36.

Aoki, Masahiro, and Serdar Dinc. 2000. "Relational Financing as an Institution and Its Viability under Competition." Pp. 19–42 in Masahiro Aoki and Gary Saxonhouse (eds.), *Finance, Governance, and Competitiveness in Japan.* Oxford: Oxford University Press.

Aoyama, Yuko, and Manuel Castells. 2002. "An Empirical Assessment of the Informational Society: Employment and Occupational Structures of G-7 Countries, 1920–2000." *International Labour Review* 141(1–2):123–59.

Armstrong, Paul. 2000a. "Rio Tinto Makes Pounds 1.1 Billion Hostile Bid for Rival North." *Times of London*, June 24.

———. 2000b. "Rio Tinto Poised to Counter Anglo's Pounds 1.2 Billion Bid for North." *Times of London*, July 22.

Arrighi, Giovanni. 1994. *The Long Twentieth Century: Money, Power, and the Origins of Our Times.* London: Verso.

———. 1998. "Globalisation and the Rise of East Asia: Lessons from the Past, Prospects for the Future." *International Sociology* 13:59–77.

Arrighi, Giovanni, Po-Keung Hui, Ho-Fung Hung, and Mark Selden. 2002. "Historical Capitalism, East and West." Paper presented at the American Sociological Association annual meetings.

Arvedlund, Erin. 2005. "China Denies It Had a Role in Sale of Yukos Gas Unit." *New York Times,* February 4.

Arvedlund, Erin, and Simon Romero. 2004. "Kremlin Reasserts Hold on Russia's Oil and Gas." *New York Times,* December 17.

Asia Pacific Foundation of Canada. 2005. "Is Vancouver Prepared for China's Return to the High Seas?" *Asia Pacific Bulletin:* 217.

Asia Pulse. 2004. "Rio Tinto Signs New Iron Ore Deals with Japanese Partners." April 7.

Associated Press. 2005. "China, India Agree to 'Strategic Partnership.'" *Globe and Mail,* April 11.

———. 2006. "Japan in 2nd-Longest Economic Expansion." *New York Times,* April 15.

Australian Bureau of Mineral Resources. Various years. *Australian Mineral Industry.* Canberra: Commonwealth of Australia.

Australian Mineral Economics (AME). 2004a. *AME Mineral Economics Focus, May 2004.* Sydney: AME.

———. 2004b. *AME Mineral Economics Focus, June 2004.* Sydney: AME.

———. 2004c. *AME Mineral Economics Focus, December 2004.* Sydney: AME.

Bailey, David. 2003. "Explaining Japan's Kudoka Hollowing Out: A Case of Government and Strategic Failure?" *Asia Pacific Business Review* 10(1):1–20.

Bain, Julie. 2003. "Kumba Aims to Raise A$1.5 Billion for Hope Downs." *Business Day* (South Africa), July 1:10.

Ball, D. 1976. "Exploring Canada's Steeply Pitching Coal Resources." *World Coal* 2(4):34–37.

Ball, W. 1949. *Japan-Enemy or Ally?* New York: John Day Company.

Barbour, Violet. 1950. *Capitalism in Amsterdam in the Seventeenth Century.* Baltimore: Johns Hopkins University Press.

Barboza, David. 2005a. "China Acts to Curtail Property Speculation." *New York Times,* May 13.

———. 2005b. "China Builds Its Dreams, and Some Fear a Bubble." *New York Times,* October 18.

Barham, B., S. Bunker, and D. O'Hearn. 1994. "Raw Materials Industries in Resource-Rich Regions." Pp. 3–38 in B. Barham, S. Bunker, and D. O'Hearn (eds.), *States, Firms, and Raw Materials: The World Economy and Ecology of Aluminum.* Madison: University of Wisconsin Press.

Barham, B., and O. Coomes. 1994a. "Wild Rubber: Industrial Organization and Microeconomics of Extraction during the Amazon Rubber Boom (1860–1920)." *Journal of Latin American Studies* 26:1.

———. 1994b. "Reinterpreting the Amazon Rubber Boom: Investment and the Role of the State." *Latin American Research Review* 29:2.

Barling, Russell. 2003. "China Shipping and K-Line Join Forces." *South China Morning Post,* November 27:3.

Barnet, Richard J., and Ronald E. Müller. 1974. *Global Reach: The Power of the Multinational Corporations.* New York: Simon and Schuster.

Barnett, Donald. 1985. "The Australian Export Coal Industry in the Mid-1980s: An Overview." *Materials and Society* 9(4):443–60.

Barnhart, Michael. 1987. *Japan Prepares for Total War: The Search for Economic Security, 1919–1941.* Ithaca, N.Y.: Cornell University Press.

Bayly, Christopher. 1989. *Atlas of the British Empire: The Rise and Fall of the Greatest Empire the World Has Ever Known.* New York: Facts on File.

Benson, Todd. 2004. "China Fuels Brazil's Dream of Being a Steel Power." *New York Times,* May 21.

Bernier, Bernard. 2000. "Flexibility, Rigidity and Reactions to Globalization of the Japanese Labour Regime." *Labour, Capital and Society* 33(1):8–45.

Bhadrakumar, M. K. 2006. "China and Russia Welcome Iran, India, Pakistan and Mongolia into Shanghai Cooperation Organization." *JapanFocus.org,* April 18.

Biersteker, Thomas. 1998. "Globalisation and the Modes of Operation of Major Institutional Actors." *Oxford Development Studies* 26:15–31.

Bisson, T. 1949. *Prospects for Democracy in Japan.* New York: Macmillan.

———. 1954. *Zaibatsu Dissolution in Japan.* Berkeley: University of California Press.

Blainey, Geoffrey. 1969. *The Rush That Never Ended: A History of Australian Mining.* 2nd ed. Melbourne: Melbourne University Press.

Bolis, J., and J. Bekkala. 1987. *Iron Ore Availability—Market Economy Countries: A Minerals Availability Appraisal.* Washington, D.C.: United States Bureau of Mines.

Borden, W. 1984. *The Pacific Alliance: United States Foreign Economic Policy and Japanese Trade Recovery, 1947–1955.* Madison: University of Wisconsin Press.

Boswell, T. 1987. "Accumulation Innovations in the American Economy: The Affinity for Japanese Solutions to the Current Crisis." Pp. 95–126 in T. Boswell and A. Bergeson (eds.), *America's Changing Role in the World-System.* New York: Praeger.

Botsman, Peter, Brett Evans, and Roger Millis. 1994. *Respect and Maturity in the Australia-Japan Coal Trade.* Sydney: Evatt Foundation.

Bowden, Bradley. 2001. "Heroic Failure? Unionism and Queensland's Coal Communities, 1954–67." *Labour and Industry* 11(3):73–88.

Boxer, Charles. 1965. *The Dutch Seaborne Empire: 1600–1800.* New York: Alfred A. Knopf.

Boxill, Ian. 1994. "Globalisation, Sustainable Development, and Post-Modernism: The New Ideology of Imperialism." *Humanity and Society* 13:3–18.

Bradsher, Keith. 2003. "China's Growth Creates a Boom for Cargo Ships." *New York Times,* August 28.

———. 2006. "China Passes Japan in Foreign Exchange Reserves." *New York Times,* March 29.

Bremner, Brian, Hiroko Tashiro, and Dexter Roberts. 2004. "Japan's Joyride on China's Coattails." *Business Week* 3872:20.

Breslin, Shaun. 2003. "Paradigm Shifts and Time-lags? The Politics of Financial Reform in the People's Republic of China." *Asian Business & Management* 2:143–66.

Brizendine, Thomas, and Charles Oliver. 2001. "China's Steel Sector in Transition." *China Business Review,* January–February:22–26.

Broadbent, Jeffrey. 1998. *Environmental Politics in Japan: Networks of Power and Protest.* Cambridge: Cambridge University Press.

Brooke, James. 2001. "Accelerating Decline in Japan Evokes Rust Belt Comparisons." *New York Times,* August 31.

———. 2002a. "Japan's Export Power Drifts across the China Sea." *New York Times,* April 7.

———. 2002b. "Japan Braces for a 'Designed in China' World." *New York Times,* April 21.

———. 2002c. "Japan Looks to Eastern Russia for Oil." *New York Times,* October 3.

———. 2003. "Koizumi Visits Energy-Rich Russian Region, Seeking Oil." *New York Times,* January 13.

———. 2004a. "Asian Scavengers Feed China's Hunger for Steel." *New York Times,* June 11.

———. 2004b. "China and Japan Jockey for Share of Russian Gas." *New York Times,* November 3.

———. 2004c. "Japan's New Military Focus: China and North Korea Threats." *New York Times,* December 11.

———. 2005a. "Disputes at Every Turn of Siberia Pipeline." *New York Times,* January 21.

———. 2005b. "Japan and Russia, With an Eye on China, Bury the Sword." *New York Times,* February 13.

———. 2005c. "Japan's Ties to China: Strong Trade, Shaky Politics." *New York Times,* February 22.

Brubaker, Sterling. 1967. *Trends in the World Aluminum Industry.* Baltimore: Johns Hopkins University Press for Resources for the Future.

Buchanan, Sandra. 2004. "Iron Ore Throws Its Weight About." *Metal Bulletin Monthly* 401:22–25.

Buckley, Chris. 2005. "Calling in Envoy, Beijing Assails Pentagon Report." *New York Times,* July 21.

Buckley, Neil. 2005. "Banks Call in $540m Yukos Loan." *Financial Times,* February 2.

Bunge, Mario. 1997. "Mechanism and Explanation." *Philosophy of the Social Sciences* 27(4):410–65.

Bunker, S. 1985. *Underdeveloping the Amazon*. Chicago: University of Chicago Press.

———. 1992. "Natural Resource Extraction and Regional Power Differentials in a Global Economy." Pp. 61–84 in S. Ortiz and S. Lees (eds.), *Understanding Economic Process*. Lanham, Md.: University Press of America.

Bunker, S., and P. Ciccantell. 1995a. "A Rising Hegemon and Raw Materials Access: Japan in the Post–World War II Era." *Journal of World-Systems Research* 1(10):1–31.

———. 1995b. "Restructuring Space, Time, and Competitive Advantage in the World-Economy: Japan and Raw Materials Transport after World War II." In D. Smith and J. Borocz (eds.), *A New World Order? Global Transformations in the Late Twentieth Century*. Westport, Conn.: Greenwood Press.

———. 2003a. "Transporting Raw Materials and Shaping the World-System: Creating Hegemony via Raw Materials Access Strategies in Holland and Japan." *Review of the Fernand Braudel Center* 26(4):339–80.

———. 2003b. "Generative Sectors and the New Historical Materialism: Economic Ascent and the Cumulatively Sequential Restructuring of the World Economy." *Studies in Comparative International Development* 37(4):3–30.

———. 2005. *Globalization and the Race for Resources*. Baltimore: Johns Hopkins University Press.

Bunker, S., and D. O'Hearn. 1992. "Strategies of Economic Ascendants for Access to Raw Materials: A Comparison of the U.S. and Japan." Pp. 83–102 in R. Palat (ed.), *Pacific Asia and the Future of the World System*. Westport, Conn.: Greenwood Press.

Business News Americas. 2002a. "CVRD and Baosteel Discuss Stronger Links." April 17.

———. 2002b. "CVRD Outlines Steel Sector Strategy." July 5.

———. 2002c. "Analyst: Carajas Steel Mill 'Unsound.'" July 12.

———. 2002d. "CVRD to Construct Ship for Iron Ore Exports." December 6.

———. 2003. "Study: CVRD Enjoys Lowest Iron Ore Costs." February 4.

Cafruny, A. 1987. *Ruling the Waves: The Political Economy of International Shipping*. Berkeley: University of California Press.

Calder, Kent. 1993. *Strategic Capitalism: Private Business and Public Purpose in Japanese Industrial Finance*. Princeton: Princeton University Press.

Callick, Rowan. 2004. "Beijing's First-Stop Shop for Resources." *Australian Financial Review*, March 2:16.

Canada NewsWire. 2003. "CVRD Acquires Mitsui Stake in Caemi." March 31.

Canadian Corporate Newswire. 2006a. "Cline Mining Corporation: Feasibility Study Completed on Lodgepole Coal Project." January 24.

———. 2006b. "Hillsborough Resources Announces Finalization of Definitive Agreement with Anglo Coal." February 6.

———. 2006c. "Grande Cache Coal Corporation Announces Third Quarter 2006 Financial Results." February 13.

———. 2006d. "Pine Valley Announces Third Quarter Results." February 13.

Canadian Mines Handbook / Canadian Mining Handbook. Various years. Toronto: Northern Miner Press.

Canadian Press Newswire. 2006a. "West Hawk Development Teams with Anglo Pacific on B.C. Coal Project." January 11.

————. 2006b. "Fording Canadian Coal's Q4 Profit More Than Doubles to $218M from Year-Ago $85M." February 1.

————. 2006c. "NEMI Ships 1st Coal to Ridley Terminal at Prince Rupert, B.C." February 7.

Cargo Systems Research Consultants (CSR). 1982. *Large Bulk Carrier Employment in the Eighties (50,000 DWT+)*. Surrey: Cargo Systems Research Consultants.

Castells, Manuel. 2000a. *The Information Age: Economy, Society and Culture.* 2nd ed. Vol. 1. Oxford: Blackwell.

————. 2000b. "Materials for an Exploratory Theory of the Network Society." *British Journal of Sociology* 51(1):5–24.

————. 2000c. "Information Technology and Global Capitalism." In W. Hutton and A. Giddens (eds.), *On the Edge: Living Global Capitalism.* London: Jonathan Cape.

Chadwick, John. 2002. "World Coal Report." *Mining Magazine,* September:102–12.

Chambers, Sam. 2003. "China: Blockbuster Beijing Turns World Trade on Its Head." *Lloyd's List,* November 27:12.

Chandler, A. (ed.). 1965. *The Railroads: The Nation's First Big Business.* New York: Harcourt, Brace and World.

————. 1977. *The Visible Hand: The Managerial Revolution in American Business.* Cambridge, Mass.: Belknap Press of Harvard University Press.

Chase-Dunn, C. 1989. *Global Formation: Structures of the World-Economy.* Cambridge: Basil Blackwell.

Chase-Dunn, C., and Thomas Hall. 1997. *Rise and Demise: Comparing World-Systems.* Boulder, Colo.: Westview Press.

Chen, An. 2002. "Socio-economic Polarization and Political Corruption in China." *Journal of Communist Studies and Transition Politics* 18(2):53–74.

Chen, Feng. 2003. "Industrial Restructuring and Workers' Resistance in China." *Modern China* 29(2):237–62.

Cheng, Wing-Gar. 2006. "CNOOC to Buy Nigerian Oil Field State for $2.27 Bln." *Bloomberg.com,* January 9.

Chiba, Junichi. 2001. "The Designing of Corporate Accounting Law in Japan after the Second World War." *Accounting, Business and Financial History* 11(3):311–30.

Chicago Tribune. 1991. "Sir John Kerr, 76; Fired Australian Government." March 27.

Chida, T., and P. Davies. 1990. *The Japanese Shipping and Shipbuilding Industries.* London: Athlone Press.

Chung, Chien-peng. 2005. "The Shanghai Cooperation Organization: Institutionalization, Cooperation and Rivalry." *JapanFocus.org,* October 14.

Ciccantell, Paul S. 2000. "Globalisation and Raw Materials-Based Development: The Case of the Aluminum Industry." *Competition and Change* 4:273–323.

————. 2001. "NAFTA and the Reconstruction of U.S. Hegemony: The Raw Materials Foundations of Economic Competitiveness." *Canadian Journal of Sociology* 26(1):57–87.

Ciccantell, Paul, and Stephen G. Bunker. 1999. "Economic Ascent and the Global Environment: World-Systems Theory and the New Historical Materialism." Pp. 107–22 in W. Goldfrank et al. (eds.), *Ecology and World-Systems Theory.* Westport, Conn.: Greenwood Press.

————. 2002. "International Inequality in the Age of Globalization: Japanese Economic Ascent and the Restructuring of the Capitalist World-Economy." *Journal of World-Systems Research* 8(1):62–98.

————. 2004. "The Economic Ascent of China and the Potential for Restructuring the Capitalist World-Economy." *Journal of World-Systems Research* 10(3):565–89.

Coal Age. 2004. "Australian Miners to Pay Higher Coal Royalties." 109(June):7.

————. 2005. "Canada's Elk Valley Secures Long-Term Supply Agreement with JFE Steel." 110(November):6, 14.

Coal Association of Canada. 1993. *Canadian Coal, 1993.* Vancouver: Naylor Communications.

Coal Task Force. 1976. *Coal in British Columbia.* Victoria: Coal Task Force.

CoalTrans. 2005. "Steelmakers Buying into Canadian Mines." January–February:8.

Coatsworth, J. 1981. *Growth against Development: The Economic Impact of Railroads in Porfirian Mexico.* DeKalb: Northern Illinois University Press.

Cockerill, Chris. 2003. "A Lot of Steel to Build Steel Plants." *Euromoney,* September:254–59.

Coleman, Joseph. 2004. "Japanese Business Ties with China Explode." *Associated Press,* February 8.

Commonwealth of Australia. 2001. *Australia's Export Coal Industry.* Brisbane: Commonwealth of Australia.

Coronil, Fernando. 1997. *The Magical State: Nature, Money, and Modernity in Venezuela.* Chicago: University of Chicago Press.

Cox, Benjamin. 2006. "Steel Companies Should Fight for New Price-Setting System." *Skillings Mining Review* 95(4):7.

Curtotti, Robert, and Andrew Maurer. 2001. "Australian Coal Supply: Investing in Additional Capacity." *Australian Commodities* 8(4):635–46.

De Bruin, Anne, and Jan de Bruin. 2002. "Atrophied Embeddedness: Towards Extending Explanation of Japan's Growth Slowdown." *Journal of Interdisciplinary Economics* 13:401–27.

De Santis, Hugh. 2005. "The Dragon and the Tigers: China and Asian Regionalism." *World Policy Journal* 22(2):23–36.

De Vries, Jan, and Ad van der Woude. 1997. *The First Modern Economy: Success, Failure, and Perseverance of the Dutch Economy, 1500–1815.* Cambridge: Cambridge University Press.

Deng, Yong, and Thomas Moore. 2004. "China Views Globalization: Toward a New Great-Power Politics?" *Washington Quarterly* 27(3):117–36.

Dorian, J. 1994. *Minerals, Energy, and Economic Development in China.* Oxford: Clarendon Press.

————. 1999. "Mining in China: An Update." *Mining Engineering* 51(2):35–34.

Douglas, G. 1992. *All Aboard! The Railroad in American Life.* New York: Paragon House.

Dower, John. 1999. *Embracing Defeat: Japan in the Wake of World War II.* New York: W. W. Norton / New Press.

Downing, Donald. 2002. "Dynamics of Canadian Coal Supply." *CIM Bulletin* 95(1061):63–66.

Drewry Shipping Consultants. 1972a. *The Prospects for Bulk Carriers of "Panamax" Size Plus.* London: Drewry Shipping Consultants.

————. 1972b. *The Cost of Ships.* London: Drewry Shipping Consultants.

————. 1976. *Ports and Terminals for Large Bulk Carriers.* London: Drewry Shipping Consultants.

————. 1978a. *Organization and Structure of the Dry Bulk Shipping Industry.* London: Drewry Shipping Consultants.

————. 1978b. *Trends in Japanese Dry Bulk Shipping and Trade.* London: Drewry Shipping Consultants.

————. 1980. *Changing Ship Type/Size Preferences in the Dry Bulk Market.* London: Drewry Shipping Consultants.

Duncan, J. 1932. *Public and Private Operation of Railways in Brazil.* New York: Columbia University Press.

Durie, John. 2003. "China: It's All the Go for Our Miners." *Australian Financial Review,* July 25:84.

Dyster, Barrie, and David Meredith. 1990. *Australia in the International Economy in the Twentieth Century.* Cambridge: Cambridge University Press.

Ebner, Dave. 2004. "China's Oil Sands Role Tests U.S." *Globe and Mail,* December 30.

Eckes, Alfred E., Jr. 1979. *The United States and the Global Struggle for Minerals.* Austin: University of Texas Press.

Economist. 2004a. "Chinese Shipping: Full Steam Ahead?" February 21:60.

————. 2004b. "China's Material Needs: The Hungry Dragon." February 21:59–60.

Ednie, Heather. 2002. "Canada's Black Gold-Mountains of Coal Mean Profits for Fording." *CIMM Bulletin* 1064:10–18.

El Akkad, Omar. 2005. "China Loosens Dollar Peg." *Globe and Mail,* July 21.

Elsham, Robin. 2004. "Japan Steelmakers to Use Low-Iron Ore, Offset China-Driven Price Rise." *AFX-Asia,* January 13.

Energy Information Agency (EIA). 2004. "Country Analysis Briefs: China." July. Washington, D.C.: United States Department of Energy.

Engdahl, F. William. 2005. "China Lays Down Gauntlet in Energy War: The Geopolitics of Oil, Central Asia and the United States." *JapanFocus.org,* December 22.

Evans, Peter. 1995. *Embedded Autonomy: States and Industrial Transformation.* Princeton: Princeton University Press.

Fackler, Martin. 2005. "New Optimism about the Japanese Economy after a Bleak Decade." *New York Times,* December 7.

————. 2006. "Japan's Economy Surged 5.5% in 4th Quarter." *New York Times,* February 17.

Fattah, Hassan. 2006. "Chinese Leader Increases Trade Ties with Saudi Arabia." *New York Times,* April 23.

Fearnleys. Various years a. *Fearnleys Review.* Oslo: Fearnleys.

————. Various years b. *World Bulk Trades.* Oslo: Fearnleys.

————. Various years c. *World Bulk Fleet.* Oslo: Fearnleys.

Financial Times. 2000. "Commodities & Agriculture: Three groups 'to Control 80%.'" August 22:32.

————. 2004. "Shipping Companies Bolster Fleets." April 27.

————. 2005a. "Mittal Steel Buys Stake in China's Hunan Valin." January 14.

————. 2005b. "Oil Groups Fear Upsetting China." *New York Times,* March 3.

————. 2005c. "CNOOC Offer May Be a First Salvo." *New York Times,* June 22.

————. 2005d. "Beijing Policy Steers CNOOC Ambitions." *New York Times,* June 23.

Fisher, Chris. 1987. *Coal and the State.* Melbourne: Methuen.

Fishlow, Albert. 1965. *American Railroads and the Transformation of the Antebellum Economy.* Cambridge, Mass.: Harvard University Press.

Flynn, Matthew. 2003a. "CVRD Seeking More Steel Partners." *Business News Americas,* March 24.

———. 2003b. "CVRD, Arcelor to Pay US$162 Million for 14% of CST." *Business News Americas,* March 31.

———. 2003c. "CVRD, Mitsui Reach Equity Agreements." *Business News Americas,* April 1.

Fording Coal. 1993. *1992 Annual Review.* Calgary: Fording Coal.

Frank, Andre Gunder. 1998. *ReOrient: Global Economy in the Asian Age.* Berkeley: University of California Press.

Frank, Robert, and Mark Heinzl. 2002. "Sherritt Coal Bids about $1 Billion for Fording Inc." *Wall Street Journal,* October 23:B4.

Frankel, E., et al. 1985. *Bulk Shipping and Terminal Logistics.* World Bank Technical Paper Number 38. Washington, D.C.: World Bank.

Freeth, Margaret. 2004. "China Has Staked Its Claim to be the Number One Shipbuilder by 2015." *Shipping World and Shipbuilder* 4200:32–37.

French, Howard. 2005. "Whose Oil Is It? Property Rights at Issue in China." *New York Times,* July 18.

Frost, D. 1984. "The Revitalisation of Queensland Railways through Export Coal Shipments." *Journal of Transport History* 5(2):47–56.

FT.Com. 2006. "Growth Puts Japan Back with the Leaders." February 17.

Fujimori, T. 1980. "Setouchi and Northern Kyushu Region." Pp. 93–103 in Kiyoji Murata and Isamu Ota, *An Industrial Geography of Japan.* New York: St. Martin's Press.

Fukao, Mitsuhiro. 2003. "Japan's Lost Decade and Its Financial System." *World Economy* 26(3): 365–84.

Gale Group. 2003. "Chinese Markets for Steel and Steel Products." Asia Market Information & Development Company.

Gao, Bai. 2001. *Japan's Economic Dilemma: The Institutional Origins of Prosperity and Stagnation.* Cambridge: Cambridge University Press.

Gao, Ting. 2003. "Ethnic Chinese Networks and International Investment: Evidence from Inward FDI in China." *Journal of Asian Economics* 14(4):611–29.

Garrett, G. 1998. "Shrinking States? Globalisation and National Autonomy in the OECD." *Oxford Development Studies* 26:71–97.

Garrod, P., and W. Miklius. 1985. "The Optimal Ship Size: A Comment." *Journal of Transport Economics and Policy* 19(1):83–89.

Gelb, Catherine, and Dennis Chen. 2004. "Going West: A Progress Report." *China Business Review* 31(2):8–10, 12, 19–23.

George, Jeff. 1991. "36 Hours to Tidewater." *Kootenay Business Journal,* March:16–21.

Gereffi, Gary, and Miguel Korzeniewicz (eds.). 1994. *Commodity Chains and Global Capitalism.* Westport, Conn.: Greenwood Press.

Girvan, N. 1976. *Corporate Imperialism: Conflict and Expropriation.* New York: Monthly Review Press.

Global News Wire. 2003. "China Aims at World's Largest Shipbuilding by 2015." December 31.

———. 2004a. "Steel Companies Seek Steady Ore Supply from Australia." April 20.

————. 2004b. "Steel Firms to Develop High-Grade Products." April 20.

————. 2004c. "Steel Sector Surge Shows No Sign of Cooling Down." April 27.

————. 2005. "Coal Exports Fall by 15% This Year." December 12.

————. 2006. "Sinosteel Seeks Iron Project Stake." March 6.

Global News Wire-Asia Africa Intelligence Wire. 2006. "Baosteel Signs Strategic Tie-Up with Maanshan's Parent." January 20.

Goldsmith, Tim. 2004. "Moving Times." *World Coal* 13(6):19–23.

Gordon, M. J. 2003. "Is China's Financial System Threatened by Its Policy Loans Debt?" *Journal of Asian Economics* 14:181–88.

Gordon, Richard. 1987. *World Coal.* Cambridge: Cambridge University Press.

Goss, R. 1967. "The Turnaround of Cargo Liners and Its Effect upon Sea Transport Costs." *Journal of Transport Economics and Policy* 1(1):75–89.

Goss, R., and M. Mann. 1977. "The Cost of Ships' Time." Pp. 138–77 in R. Goss (ed.), *Advances in Maritime Economics.* Cambridge: Cambridge University Press.

Goto, S. 1984. *Japan's Shipping Policy.* Tokyo: Japan Maritime Research Institute.

Goyal, Rishi, and Ronald McKinnon. 2003. "Japan's Negative Risk Premium in Interest Rates: The Liquidity Trap and the Fall in Bank Lending." *World Economy* 26(3):339–64.

Graham, Paul, Sally Thorpe, and Lindsay Hogan. 1999. "Non-competitive Market Behaviour in the International Coking Coal Market." *Energy Economics* 21(3):195–212.

Gray, Tony. 2000. "Rio Tinto in Dollars 1.6 Billion Bid for North." *Lloyd's List,* June 24:2.

Grimes, William. 2001. *Unmaking the Japanese Miracle: Macroeconomic Politics, 1985–2000.* Ithaca, N.Y.: Cornell University Press.

Grundy, Jim. 2001. "Queensland Case Study: Bowen Basin Coal." *Queensland Government Mining Journal,* October:35–38.

Hadley, E. 1970. *Antitrust in Japan.* Princeton: Princeton University Press.

Haine, Ian. 2001. "Minerals and Energy: Major Development Projects." *Australian Commodities* 8(4):647–66.

Hall, Derek. 2004. "Japanese Spirit, Western Economics: The Continuing Salience of Economic Nationalism in Japan." *New Political Economy* 9(1):79–99.

Hamada, Koichi. 2000. "Explaining the Low Litigation Rate in Japan." Pp. 179–94 in Masahiro Aoki and Gary Saxonhouse (eds.), *Finance, Governance, and Competitiveness in Japan.* Oxford: Oxford University Press.

Hanappe, P., and M. Savy. 1981. "Industrial Port Areas and the Kondratieff Cycle." Pp. 11–22 in B. Hoyle and D. Pinder (eds.), *Cityport Industrialization and Regional Development.* Oxford: Pergamon Press.

Hanmyo, Masayuki. 2002. "Production and Technology of Iron and Steel in Japan during 2001." *ISIJ International* 42(6):567–80.

Harris, J. R. 1988. *The British Iron Industry, 1700–1850.* Houndsmills: Macmillan Education.

Harvey, D. 1982. *The Limits to Capital.* Chicago: University of Chicago Press.

————. 1990. *The Condition of Post-Modernity.* Oxford: Blackwell.

————. 1995. "Globalization in Question." *Rethinking Marxism,* Winter:1–17.

Hayes, Jason. 2004. "Canadian Metallurgical Coal Market Expanding." *CIM Bulletin* 97(1082): 15–16.

Heathcote, Andrew. 2002. "Coking Coal Gives Off a Warming Glow." *Business Review Weekly* 24(18):41.

Hein, L. 1990. *Fueling Growth: The Energy Revolution and Economic Policy in Postwar Japan.* Cambridge, Mass.: Harvard University Press.

Heinzl, Mark. 2002. "Fording to Become Income Trust in Deal with Teck, Westshore." *Wall Street Journal,* December 5.

Herman, Burt. 2005. "China, Russia Kick Off First Joint Military Exercises." *Globe and Mail,* August 18.

Herman, R., et al. 1989. "Dematerialization." Pp. 50–69 in J. Ausubel and H. Sladovich (eds.), *Technology and Environment.* Washington, D.C.: National Academy Press.

Hextall, Bruce. 2002. "Miners in Ore over Pilbara's Key to China." *Australian Financial Review,* May 24:67.

———. 2003. "Chinese Remedy for Miner Pains." *Australian Financial Review,* January 17:63.

———. 2004. "BHP Billiton Following Peers in Locking Up Chinese Iron Ore Contracts." *AFX-Asia,* March 1.

Hirschman, Albert. 1958. *The Strategy of Economic Development.* New Haven: Yale University Press.

Hobsbawm, Eric. 1968. *The Age of Industry.* New York: Charles Scribner's Sons.

Hogan, Lindsay, and Kim Donaldson. 2000. "Mineral Royalties: Net Economic Benefits of Mining in Australia." *Australian Commodities* 7(3):519–31.

Hogan, William. 1999a. *The Steel Industry of China: Its Present Status and Future Potential.* Lanham, Md.: Lexington Books.

———. 1999b. "The Changing Shape of the Chinese Industry." *New Steel* 15(11):28–29.

Holland, Tom. 2004. "Feeding China's Giant Appetite." *Far Eastern Economic Review* 167(22):44–48.

Hopkins, Terence, and Immanuel Wallerstein. 1986. "Commodity Chains in the World-Economy Prior to 1800." *Review* 10(1):157–70.

Hoshi, Takeo. 1994. "The Economic Role of Corporate Grouping and the Main Bank System." Pp. 285–309 in M. Aoki and R. Dore (eds.), *The Japanese Firm: Sources of Competitive Strength.* Oxford: Oxford University Press.

Hoshi, Takeo, and Anil Kashyap. 2004. "Japan's Financial Crisis and Economic Stagnation." *Journal of Economic Perspectives* 18(1):3–26.

Hotta, Kenji. 2002. "Offshore Construction and Ocean Space Utilization in Japan." Pp. 103–19 in J. Chen et al. (eds.), *Engineered Coasts.* Amsterdam: Kluwer Academic Publishers.

Howarth, Ian. 2003. "China Iron-Ore Imports Drive WA Boom." *Australian Financial Review,* June 4:21.

Hughes, Helen. 1963. *The Australian Iron and Steel Industry, 1848–1962.* Melbourne: Melbourne University Press.

Hugill, Peter. 1994. *World Trade since 1431.* Baltimore: Johns Hopkins University Press.

Hui, Po-Keung. 1995. "Overseas Chinese Business Networks: East Asian Economic Development in Historical Perspective." Ph.D. dissertation, SUNY-Binghamton.

Huskonen, Wallace. 2001. "China Adds Three New Steel Mills." *33 Metalproducing,* April:26–27.

Hymer, Stephen. 1979. *The Multinational Corporation: A Radical Approach.* Cambridge: Cambridge University Press.

Ikeda, Satoshi. 2004. "Japan and the Changing Regime of Accumulation: A World-System Study of Japan's Trajectory from Miracle to Debacle." *Journal of World-Systems Research* 10(2):363–94.

Inamura, Hajime. 1993. "Recent Port Development Strategies and Future Prospects in Japan." Pp. 1515–26 in World Conference on Transport Research, *Selected Proceedings of the Sixth World Conference on Transport Research*. Lyon: World Conference on Transport Research.

Innis, H. 1956. *Essays in Canadian Economic History*. Toronto: University of Toronto Press.

International Bulk Journal. 1999. "China's Surprise." October:23.

———. 2002. "China Has Its Irons in the Fire." May:28.

International Energy Agency (IEA). Various years. *Coal Information*. Paris: OECD.

Iron and Steel Statistics Bureau (ISSB). 2006. "ISSB News and Updates." www.issb.co.uk.

Irwan, Alex. 1995. "Japanese and Ethnic Chinese Business Networks in Indonesia and Malaysia." Ph.D. dissertation, SUNY-Binghamton.

Isard, Walter. 1948. "Some Locational Factors in the Iron and Steel Industry since the Early Nineteenth Century." *Journal of Political Economy* 63(3): 203–17.

Israel, Jonathan I. 1989. *Dutch Primacy in World Trade, 1585–1740*. Oxford: Clarendon Press.

———. 1995. *The Dutch Republic: Its Rise, Greatness, and Fall, 1477–1806*. Oxford: Oxford University Press.

Iwase, Nobuhisa. 2003. "Financial Record Shows a Good Start for JFE." *Steel Times International*, July–August:41.

Jalee, Pierre. 1968. *The Pillage of the Third World*. New York: Monthly Review Press.

Jansson, J., and D. Shneerson. 1982. "The Optimal Ship Size." *Journal of Transport Economics and Policy* 16(3):217–38.

Japan Iron and Steel Federation. 2006. "Statistical Data." www.jisf.or.jp.

Japan Port and Harbour Association. N.d. *Laws and Regulations on Ports and Harbours of Japan*. Tokyo: Japan Port and Harbour Association.

Japanese Industry. 1968. Tokyo: Foreign Capital Research Society.

JCN Newswire. 2004a. "Mistui OSK Lines Signs Deal to Transport Iron Ore for China's Maanshan Iron and Steel." March 17.

———. 2004b. "Nippon Steel and Rio Tinto Reach Basic Agreement on Comprehensive Alliance." April 9.

Jenkins, Rhys. 1987. *Transnational Corporations and Uneven Development: The Internationalization of Capital and the Third World*. London: Methuen.

Jisi, Wang. 2005. "China's Search for Stability with America." *Foreign Affairs* 84(5):39–46.

Johnson, C. 1982. *MITI and the Japanese Miracle: The Growth of Industrial Policy, 1925–1975*. Stanford: Stanford University Press.

Kahn, Joseph. 2003. "China Gambles on Big Projects for Its Stability." *New York Times*, January 13.

———. 2004. "China's 'Haves' Stir the 'Have Nots' to Violence." *New York Times*, December 31.

———. 2005a. "22 Million Chinese Seek to Block Japan's Bid to Join U.N. Council." *New York Times*, March 31.

———. 2005b. "Chinese General Threatens Use of A-Bombs If U.S. Intrudes." *New York Times*, July 15.

Karmon, Y. 1980. *Ports around the World*. New York: Crown Publishers.

Katz, Richard. 1998. *Japan: The System That Soured.* Armonk, N.Y.: M. E. Sharpe.

Kawahito, Kiyoshi. 1972. *The Japanese Steel Industry: With an Analysis of the U.S. Steel Import Problem.* New York: Praeger.

Kawata Publicity. 1971. *Japan's Iron and Steel Industry, 1971 Edition.* Tokyo: Kawata Publicity.

Keenan, Rebecca. 2006. "Portman Says China Likely to Accept Higher Iron Ore Price." *AAP Newsfeed,* May 24.

Kendall, P. 1972. "A Theory of Optimum Ship Size." *Journal of Transport Economics and Policy* 6(1):128–46.

Kenny, Henry. 2004. "China and the Competition for Oil and Gas in Asia." *Asia-Pacific Review* 11(2):36–47.

Keohane, R. 1984. *After Hegemony.* Princeton: Princeton University Press.

Kepp, Mike. 2002. "CVRD Looks to Copper." *Daily Deal,* May 7.

Kerr, Derek. 2002. "The 'Place' of Land in Japan's Postwar Development, and the Dynamic of the 1980s Real-Estate 'Bubble' and the 1990s Banking Crisis." *Environment and Planning D: Society and Space* 20:345–74.

Kiely, Ray. 1998. "Globalisation, Post-Fordism and the Contemporary Context of Development." *International Sociology* 13:95–115.

Kinch, Diana. 2003. "Will Iron Ore Restraints Hinder Slab Projects?" *Metal Bulletin Monthly* 394:27–33.

King, Neil, Jr., Gregg Hitt, and Jeffrey Ball. 2005. "Oil Battles Set Showdown over China." *Wall Street Journal,* June 24:A1, A10.

Kipping, Mathias. 1997. "How Unique Is East Asian Development? Comparing Steel Producers and Users in East Asia and Western Europe." *Asia Pacific Business Review* 4(1):1–23.

Kirk, William. 2003. "China's Emergence as the World's Leading Iron Ore—Consuming Country, Part 1." *Skillings Mining Review* 92(7):8–13.

———. 2004a. "BHP Billiton Iron Ore Supply Contracts and Expansions." *Skillings Mining Review* 93(11):5.

———. 2004b. "Domestic Firm May Supply Iron Ore to China." *Skillings Mining Review* 93(11):10.

———. 2005. "Iron Ore Down Under: A Rio Tinto Roundup." *Skillings Mining Review* 94(1): 4–5.

Kita, Hideyuki, and Hiroshi Moriwaki. 1989. "Financial Systems of Port Development under the Changing Needs to Port." *Reports of the Faculty of Engineering, Tottori University* 20:190–202.

Koenig, Philip, Hitoshi Narita, and Koichi Baba. 2002. "Lean Production in the Japanese Shipbuilding Industry?" *Journal of Ship Production* 18(3):167–74.

Koerner, R. 1993. "The Behaviour of Pacific Metallurgical Coal Markets: The Impact of Japan's Acquisition Strategy on Market Price." *Resources Policy,* March, 66–79.

Kojima, Kiyoshi, and Terutomo Ozawa. 1984. *Japan's General Trading Companies: Merchants of Economic Development.* Paris: OECD.

Kosai, Y., and Y. Ogino. 1984. *The Contemporary Japanese Economy.* Armonk, N.Y.: M. E. Sharpe.

Krasner, S. 1978. *Defending the National Interest: Raw Materials Investments and U.S. Foreign Policy.* Princeton: Princeton University Press.

Kudo, Kazuo. 1985. "Implementation of Port Development Policy in Japan: Problems and Countermeasures." Pp. 4–10 in United Nations Economic and Social Commission for Asia and the Pacific, *Port Development Policy*. Bangkok: United Nations Economic and Social Commission for Asia and the Pacific.

Kunio, Yoshihara. 1982. *Sogo Shosha: The Vanguard of the Japanese Economy*. Tokyo: Oxford University Press.

Kyodo News International. 2004. "Japan Traders Itochu, Mitsui to Invest in Iron-Ore Joint Venture in Australia." March 1.

Lague, David. 2003. "The Making of a Juggernaut." *Far Eastern Economic Review*, September 18:30–33.

Landes, David. 1969. *The Unbound Prometheus*. Cambridge: Cambridge University Press.

Lardy, Nicholas R. 1992. *Foreign Trade and Economic Reform in China, 1978–1990*. Cambridge: Cambridge University Press.

Lee, Armistead. 1952. "Australian Coking Coal for Japan." December 16. *Foreign Relations of the United States:* 843.2552/12/1652.

———. 1953a. "Further Progress in Australian-Japanese Coking Coal Trade." May 4. *Foreign Relations of the United States:* 843.2552/5–453.

———. 1953b. "Present Status of Blair Athol (Queensland) Coal Project." October 29. *Foreign Relations of the United States:* 843.2552/10–2953.

Lewis, C. 1983. *British Railways in Argentina, 1857–1914*. London: Athlone Press.

Lewis, Leo. 2003. "Japanese Industrialists Poised to Crack the Biggest Game in Town." *Times of London*, December 27:58.

Lieberson, Stanley. 1992. "Small N's and Big Conclusions,: An Examination of the Reasoning in Comparative Studies Based on Small Numbers of Cases." Pp. 105–18 in Charles C. Ragin and Howard S. Becker (eds.), *What Is a Case: Exploring the Foundations of Social Inquiry*. Cambridge: Cambridge University Press.

———. 1997. "The Big Broad Issues in Society and Social History: Application of a Probabilistic Approach." Pp. 35985 in Vaughn R. McKim and Stephen P. Turner (eds.), *Causality in Crisis?: Statistical Methods and the Search for Causal Knowledge in the Social Sciences*. Notre Dame, Ind.: University of Notre Dame Press.

Lincoln, Edward. 1984. *Japan's Industrial Policies*. Washington, D.C.: Japan Economic Institute of America.

Liu, Kezhang, and Xiaoyun Jin. 1994. "CC Gathers Speed in China." *Steel Times International*, January:40.

Lloyd's List. 2002. "Rio Tinto Takes Control of Its Charter Business." July 16:7.

———. 2005a. "CVRD Plans to Lift Annual Output to 300m Tonnes." September 29:4.

———. 2005b. "Global Sea Trade Rising 4% a Year." November 9.

———. 2006a. "No End in Sight for Rising Iron Ore Prices as China Stokes Demand." February 16.

———. 2006b. "China Backs Steel Mills' Price Battle." March 10:4.

Lloyd's of London. 1990. *Lloyd's Ports of the World, 1990*. Colchester: Lloyd's of London Press Ltd.

Lohr, Steve. 2005. "Unocal Bid Opens Up New Issues of Security." *New York Times*, July 13.

Luciw, Roma. 2005. "China Tries Oil Sands." *Globe and Mail*, April 12.

Lundmark, Robert, and Mats Nilsson. 2003. "What Do Economic Simulations Tell Us? Recent Mergers in the Iron Ore Industry." *Resources Policy* 29:111–18.

Lyday, Travis. 2001. "The Mineral Industry of Australia: 2000." Washington, D.C.: U.S. Geological Survey.

Mahbubani, Kishore. 2005. "Understanding China." *Foreign Affairs* 84(5):49–50, 51–56, 57–58, 59–60.

Maki, J. 1947. "The Role of the Bureaucracy in Japan." *Pacific Affairs* 20(4):391–400.

Mandel, E. 1975. *Late Capitalism.* London: Verso.

Manners, Gerald. 1971. *The Changing World Market for Iron Ore, 1950–1980: An Economic Geography.* Baltimore: Johns Hopkins University Press for Resources for the Future.

Marine Log. 2004. "Chinese Yards Extend Their Range." *Marine Log* 109(6):35–39.

Marshall, J. 1995. *To Have and Have Not: Southeast Asian Raw Materials and the Origins of the Pacific War.* Berkeley: University of California Press.

Marx, Karl. 1967. *Capital.* Vol. 3. New York: International Publishers.

Masuda, Hiromi. 1981. *Japan's Industrial Development Policy and the Construction of the Nobiru Port: The Case Study of a Failure.* Tokyo: United Nations University.

Mathias, P. 1969. *The First Industrial Nation: An Economic History of Britain, 1700–1914.* New York: Charles Scribner's Sons.

McCarthy, John. 2002. "BHP Set to Outlay $1 Billion on Iron Ore Expansion." *Courier Mail* (Queensland, Australia), April 4:25.

McCloskey, Gerard. 2006. "Hard Coking Coal Prices Cut by 8%." *Financial Times,* February 7:44.

McDougall, W. 1993. *Let the Sea Make a Noise: Four Hundred Years of Cataclysm, Conquest, War and Folly in the North Pacific.* New York: Avon Books.

McFarland, H. 1984. "Transport Costs and Processing." *Journal of Transport Economics and Policy* 18(3):311–15.

McGraw-Hill. 1992. *McGraw-Hill Dictionary of Science and Technology.* New York: McGraw-Hill.

McGregor, Richard. 2006. "China Excluded from Iron Ore Pricing." *Financial Times,* February 20:2.

McKern, Bruce. 1976. *Multinational Enterprise and Natural Resources.* New York: McGraw-Hill.

McMahon, L., and Stuart Harris. 1983. "Coal Development: Issues for Japan and Australia." Pp. 71–95 in Nobutoshi Akao (ed.), *Japan's Economic Security: Resources as a Factor in Foreign Policy.* Aldershot: Gower Publishing.

McMichael, P. 1984. *Settlers and the Agrarian Question: Foundations of Capitalism in Colonial Australia.* Cambridge: Cambridge University Press.

———. 1990. "Incorporating Comparison within a World-Historical Perspective: An Alternative Comparative Method." *American Sociological Review* 55:385–97.

———. 1992. "Rethinking Comparative Analysis in a Post-Developmentalist Context." *International Social Science Journal* 133:350–65.

McMillan, C. 1985. *The Japanese Industrial System.* 2nd ed. Berlin: Walter de Gruyter.

Meinig, D. W. 1986. *The Shaping of America: A Geographical Perspective on 500 Years of History.* Vol. 1, *Atlantic America, 1492–1800.* New Haven: Yale University Press.

———. 1993. *The Shaping of America: A Geographical Perspective on 500 Years of History.* Vol. 2, *Continental America, 1800–1867.* New Haven: Yale University Press.

———. 1998. *The Shaping of America: A Geographical Perspective on 500 Years of History.* Vol. 3, *Transcontinental America, 1850–1915.* New Haven: Yale University Press.

Minerals and Energy. 2004. "Corporate Control in Iron Ore Mining in 2002." *Minerals and Energy Raw Materials Report* 19(2):36–38.

Mining Journal. 2001. "Iron Ore in WA." November 2:336.

———. 2002a. "BHP Billiton Expands Iron Ore." April 5:241.

———. 2002b. "WA Iron Ore: China's Impact." November 29:377.

———. 2003. "Record Trade in Iron Ore." July 11:21.

Ministry of Energy, Mines and Petroleum Resources (MEMPR) of the Province of British Columbia. 1989. *1989 Review of the British Columbia Coal Industry.* Victoria: MEMPR.

———. 1992. *British Columbia Mineral Statistics.* Victoria: MEMPR.

Minter, Adam. 2004. "A Grinding Hunger for Scrap." *Far Eastern Economic Review,* March 25:26–29.

Mintz, Sidney. 1985. *Sweetness and Power.* New York: Viking.

Mitchell, Brian. 1980. *European Historical Statistics, 1750–1975.* New York: Facts on File.

———. 1994. *International Historical Statistics: Africa, Asia and Oceania, 1750–1993.* New York: Facts on File.

Miwa, Yoshiro, and J. Mark Ramseyer. 2002. "The Myth of the Main Bank." *Law and Social Inquiry* 27:1–20.

Miyaji, Yutaka. 1990. "Port Management: Japan's System and the United States' System." M.S. thesis, University of Washington.

Modelski, George, and William Thompson. 1996. *Leading Sectors and World Powers: The Co-evolution of Global Politics and Economics.* Columbia: University of South Carolina Press.

Moffett, Sebastian, and Phred Dvorak. 2004. "As Japan Recovers, an Unlikely Source Gets Credit: China." *Wall Street Journal,* May 4:A1, A12.

Moore, Jason. 2003. "Capitalism as World-Ecology." *Organization and Environment* 16(4):431–58.

Morita, A., with E. Reingold and M. Shimomura. 1986. *Made in Japan: Akio Morita and Sony.* New York: E. P. Dutton.

Morris, Jonathan, John Hassard, and Jackie Sheehan. 2002. "Privatization, Chinese-Style: Economic Reform and the State-Owned Enterprises." *Public Administration* 80(2):359–73.

Morrison, Kevin. 2004. "Voracious Demand Fuels Miners' Challenge." *Financial Times,* April 23:24.

Mosk, Carl. 2001. *Japanese Industrial History: Technology, Urbanization, and Economic Growth.* Armonk, N.Y.: M. E. Sharpe.

Murata, Kiyoji. 1980. "The Development of Manufacturing Industries." Pp. 15–22 in Kiyoji Murata and Isamu Ota, *An Industrial Geography of Japan.* New York: St. Martin's Press.

Murphy, R. Taggart. 1996. *The Weight of the Yen: How Denial Imperils America's Future and Ruins an Alliance.* New York: W. W. Norton.

Nafziger, E. 1995. *Learning from the Japanese: Japan's Pre-War Development and the Third World.* Armonk, N.Y.: M. E. Sharpe.

Nagatsuka, S. 1989. *Outlook for Demand-Supply of World Shipbuilding in the 1990s.* Tokyo: Japan Maritime Research Institute.

———. 1991. *Changes in the World's Shipbuilding Facilities for Large Size Vessels and Future Prospects Thereof.* Tokyo: Japan Maritime Research Institute.

Nakamura, Takafusa. 1981. *The Postwar Japanese Economy: Its Development and Structure.* Tokyo: University of Tokyo Press.

———. 1983. *Economic Growth in Prewar Japan.* New Haven: Yale University Press.

———. 1994. *Lectures on Modern Japanese Economic History, 1926–1994.* Tokyo: LTCB International Library Foundation.

———. 1998. *A History of Showa Japan, 1926–1989.* Tokyo: University of Tokyo Press.

Nakatani, I. 1984. "The Economic Role of Financial Corporate Grouping." Pp. 227–58 in M. Aoki (ed.), *The Economic Analysis of the Japanese Firm.* Amsterdam: North-Holland.

Nascimento Rodrigues, Jorge. 2005. "The China Factor and the Overstretch of the U.S. Hegemony." www.gurusonline.tv.

Nayar, Baldev Raj. 2004. "The Geopolitics of China's Economic Miracle." *China Report* 40(1):19–47.

New South Wales Government. 2003. *New South Wales Coal Industry Profile, 2002.* Canberra: New South Wales Government Department of Primary Industries.

Ng, Loretta. 2005. "Anglo American to Buy Shenhua Stake for $150 Million." *Bloomberg.com,* June 1.

Nikkei Weekly. 2003. "JFE Steel to Join Brazilian Firm in Iron-Ore Mining Venture." July 14.

Nishizawa, Tamotsu. 2002. "Ichiro Nakayama and the Stabilization of Industrial Relations in Postwar Japan." *Hitotsubashi Journal of Economics* 43:1–17.

Nolan, Peter, and Huaichuan Rui. 2004. "Industrial Policy and Global Big Business Revolution: The Case of the Chinese Coal Industry." *Journal of Chinese Economic and Business Studies* 2(2):97–113.

O'Brien, Patricia. 1992. "Industry Structure as a Competitive Advantage: The History of Japan's Post-War Steel Industry." *Business History* 34(1):128–59.

O'Connor, Gillian. 2000. "Japan Provokes Suspicious Mines: Anglo's Bid for North Has Led to Speculation about the Japanese Steel Groups' Intervention." *Financial Times,* July 26:36.

Odaka, Konosuke. 1999. "The Functions of Industrial Associations." Pp. 145–79 in Tetsuji Okazaki and Masahiro Okuno-Fujiwara (eds.), *The Japanese Economic System and Its Historical Origins.* Oxford: Oxford University Press.

OECD. 1985. *World Steel Trade Developments, 1960–83.* Paris: OECD.

———. 2003. *Statistics on Ship Production, Exports and Orders in 2002.* Paris: OECD.

———. 2005. "Bright Outlook for Steel Industry in 2005–2006 Forecast at OECD/IISI Conference." Paris: OECD.

OECD Working Party on Shipbuilding. 2004. *Statistics on Ship Production, Exports and Orders in 2003.* Paris: OECD.

Ohashi, Nobuo. 1992. "Modern Steelmaking." *American Scientist* 80(6):540–55.

Ohashi, Tetsuro. 2004. "Production and Technology of Iron and Steel in Japan during 2003." *ISIJ International* 44(6):941–56.

O'Hearn, Denis. 2001. *The Atlantic Economy: Britain, the US and Ireland.* Manchester: Manchester University Press.

Okazaki, Tetsuji. 1997. "The Government-Firm Relationship in Postwar Japanese Economic Recovery: Resolving the Coordination Failure by Coordination in Industrial Rationalization." Pp. 74–100 in Masahiro Aoki, Hyung-Ki Kim, and Masahiro Okuno-Fujiwara (eds.), *The Role of Government in East Asian Economic Development.* Oxford: Clarendon Press.

Okazaki, Tetsuji, and Masahiro Okuno-Fujiwara. 1999. "Japan's Present-Day Economic System and Its Historical Origins." Pp. 1–37 in Tetsuji Okazaki and Masahiro Okuno-Fujiwara (eds.), *The Japanese Economic System and Its Historical Origins*. Oxford: Oxford University Press.

Okimoto, Daniel. 1989. *Between MITI and the Market: Japanese Industrial Policy for High Technology*. Stanford: Stanford University Press.

Onishi, Norimitsu. 2005a. "The Japan-China Stew: Sweet and Sour." *New York Times*, January 19.

———. 2005b. "Japan's Fragile Foundation: Gold Eggs from Postal Goose." *New York Times*, September 16.

Osaka Port and Harbor Bureau. 1987. *Port of Osaka*. Osaka: Osaka Port and Harbor Bureau.

———. 1999. *Port of Osaka: 1999–2000*. Osaka: Osaka Port and Harbor Bureau.

Ouchi, W. 1981. *Theory Z: How American Business Can Meet the Japanese Challenge*. Reading, Mass.: Addison-Wesley Publishing.

Owens, Helen. 2002. "Rail Reform: Privatise, Corporatise, Franchise or Contracts; The Australian Experience." Canberra: Productivity Commission Australia.

Ozawa, T. 1979. *Multinationalism, Japanese Style*. Princeton: Princeton University Press.

———. 1986. "Japan's Largest Financier of Multinationalism: The EXIM Bank." *Journal of World Trade Law* 20(6):599–614.

Packenham, T. 1991. *The Scramble for Africa*. New York: Random House.

Paige, Jeffery M. 1999. "Conjuncture, Comparison, and Conditional Theory in Macrosocial Inquiry." *American Journal of Sociology* 105(5):781–800.

Panda, R. 1982. *Pacific Partnership: Japan-Australia Resource Diplomacy*. Rohtak, India: Manthan Publications.

Parker, William N. 1991. *America and the Wider World*. Cambridge: Cambridge University Press.

Pascale, R., and A. Athos. 1981. *The Art of Japanese Management: Applications for American Executives*. New York: Warner Books.

Pauley, E. 1945. "Letter to General Douglas MacArthur and President Truman." *Foreign Relations of the United States, 1945: The Far East*. Vol. 6. Washington, D.C.: United States Government Printing Office.

Paxton, Robin. 2003. "China Wants Key Role in Iron-Ore Price Talks." *Business Day*, November 14:5.

Pearson, Brendan. 2003. "Japan Lights Fire under Australian Miners." *Australian Financial Review*, September 19:26.

Peek, Joe, and Eric Rosengren. 2003. *Unnatural Selection: Perverse Incentives and the Misallocation of Credit in Japan*. Working Paper 9643. Cambridge, Mass.: National Bureau of Economic Research.

Pekkanen, Robert. 2004. "After the Developmental State: Civil Society in Japan." *Journal of East Asian Studies* 4(3):363–88.

Pekkanen, Saadia. 2000. "Chapter 4: Sword and Shield: The WTO Dispute Settlement System and Japan." *Japanese Economy* 28(5):3–26.

———. 2003. *Picking Winners? From Technology Catch-Up to the Space Race in Japan*. Palo Alto: Stanford University Press.

Pempel, T. J. 1998. *Regime Shift: Comparative Dynamics of the Japanese Political Economy.* Ithaca, N.Y.: Cornell University Press.

Penfold, A. 1984a. "Triangulation to Reduce Landed Costs?" *Bulk Systems International,* August:15–17.

———. 1984b. "Development Aid Funds Terminal Construction." *Bulk Systems International* August:26–29.

Peters, Anthony. 1988. "Iron and Steel." *Minerals Yearbook, 1988.* Washington, D.C.: United States Bureau of Mines.

Peterson, Avery F. 1955. "Counselor of Embassy, Canberra to State." January 17. Despatch No. 296, RG 59. *Foreign Relations of the United States:* 843.2552/1–1755.

Pine Valley Mining Corporation. 2005. "Corporate Information." www.pinevalleycoal.com.

Platts Coal Week International. 2003. "New Fording Partnership Shedding 15% of Workforce in Consolidation." 610:9.

Platts Coal Outlook. 2003. "Fording Affirms Luscar Closure; Will Delay Cheviot." 27(1)3:8.

Platts Energy. 2002. "Coal Mergers and Acquisitions, 2001." Platts Energy: www.platts.com.

Pollack, Andrew, and Keith Bradsher. 2004. "China's Need for Metal Keeps U.S. Scrap Dealers Scrounging." *New York Times,* March 13.

Porter, Michael, and Mariko Sakakibara. 2004. "Competition in Japan." *Journal of Economic Perspectives* 18(1):27–50.

Porter, Michael, Hirotaka Takeuchi, and Mariko Sakakibara. 2000. *Can Japan Compete?* Cambridge, Mass.: Perseus Publishing.

Pounds, Norman, and William Parker. 1957. *Coal and Steel in Western Europe: The Influence of Resources and Techniques on Production.* Bloomington: Indiana University Press.

PR Newswire Europe. 2006. "Performance of CVRD in 2005." March 7.

Prestowitz, C. 1988. *Trading Places: How We Allowed Japan to Take the Lead.* New York: Basic Books.

Priest, R. 1993. "Coal: Australia, 1946–1960." University of Wisconsin-Madison. Unpublished manuscript.

Queensland Department of Natural Resources and Mines. 2001. *Queensland Coal Industry Review, 2000–2001.* Brisbane: Government of Queensland.

Raggat, H. 1968. *Mountains of Ore.* Melbourne: Landsdowne Press.

Ragin, Charles. 1987. *The Comparative Method: Moving beyond Qualitative and Quantitative Strategies.* Berkeley: University of California Press.

Ramseyer, J. Mark. 2000. "Rethinking Administrative Guidance." Pp. 199–211 in Masahiro Aoki and Gary Saxonhouse (eds.), *Finance, Governance, and Competitiveness in Japan.* Oxford: Oxford University Press.

Raw, Silvia. 1985. "The Political Economy of Brazilian State-Owned Enterprises: 1964–1980." Ph.D. dissertation, University of Massachusetts, Amherst.

———. 1987. *The Making of a State-Owned Conglomerate: A Brazilian Case Study.* Kellogg Institute Working Paper #97. South Bend, Ind.: University of Notre Dame.

Reading, B. 1992. *Japan: The Coming Collapse.* New York: HarperBusiness.

Reuters. 2005a. "China Loans Russia $6 Billion for Yukos Deal." *Reuters,* February 1.

———. 2005b. "China Refuses Japan Request over Gas Project." *New York Times,* May 31.

———. 2005c. "Venezuela to Sell Fuel Oil to China." *New York Times*, June 18.

Ricardo, David. 1983. *On the Principles of Political Economy and Taxation.* London: J. Murray.

Rimmer, P. 1984. "Japanese Seaports: Economic Development and State Intervention." Pp. 99–133 in B. Hoyle and D. Hilling (eds.), *Seaport Systems and Spatial Change.* Chichester: John Wiley & Sons.

Robinson, R. 1978. "Size of Vessels and Turnaround Time." *Journal of Transport Economics and Policy* 7(2):161–78.

Robinson, William. 1996. *Promoting Polyarchy: Globalization, U.S. Intervention, and Hegemony.* Cambridge: Cambridge University Press.

———. 1998. "Beyond Nation-State Paradigms: Globalization, Sociology, and the Challenge of Transnational Studies." *Sociological Forum* 13(4):561–94.

———. 2004. *A Theory of Global Capitalism.* Baltimore: Johns Hopkins University Press.

Rodney, Walter. 1982. *How Europe Underdeveloped Africa.* Washington, D.C.: Howard University Press.

Rosenberg, N., and L. Birdzell. 1986. *How the West Grew Rich: The Economic Transformation of the Industrial World.* New York: Basic Books.

Rosenquist, Gail. 2006. "Alliance Promotes Geraldton Growth." *Skillings Mining Review* 95(4): 4–5, 25–26.

Rostow, Walter. 1960. *The Stages of Economic Growth: A Non-Communist Manifesto.* Cambridge: Cambridge University Press.

Rui, Huaichuan. 2005. "Development, Transition and Globalization in China's Coal Industry." *Development and Change* 36(4):691–710.

Ruiyu, Yin. 1999. "Steel Technology in China." *Steel Technology International* 2000:27–32.

Samuels, R. 1987. *The Business of the Japanese State: Energy Markets in Comparative and Historical Perspective.* Ithaca, N.Y.: Cornell University Press.

Sanchanta, Mariko. 2004. "Set for Take-Off after a 'Lost Decade' Japan." *Financial Times*, April 2:4.

Sasaki, H. 1976. *The Shipping Industry in Japan.* London: International Institute for Labour Studies.

Sassen, S. 1995. "The State and the Global City: Notes Towards a Conception of Place-Centered Governance." *Competition and Change* 1(1):31–50.

Sawabe, Norio. 2002. "The Role of Accounting in Bank Regulation on the Eve of Japan's Financial Crisis: A Failure of the New Capital Adequacy Regulations." *Critical Perspectives on Accounting* 13:397–430.

Schiff & Hafen. 2003. "China." 8:32.

Schmidt, Lisa. 2003. "Cuts Mean Miners Face Grim Prospects: Fording Closes Hinton Mine; Shelves Cheviot." *Calgary Herald*, April 3:B1.

Schneider, Karen, Wu Zhonghu, Dai Lin, and Vivek Tulpule. 2000. *Supplying Coal to South East China: Impacts of China's Market Liberalisation.* Canberra: ABARE.

Schumpeter, Joseph. 1934. *The Theory of Economic Development: An Inquiry into Profits, Capital, Credit, Interest, and the Business Cycle.* New York: Oxford University Press.

Scott, W. 1979. "Australian Coal Promises Rapid Industrial Growth". *Energy International*, August:13–15.

Sengupta, Somini, and Howard French. 2005. "India and China are Poised to Share Defining Moment." *New York Times,* April 10.

Serchuk, Alan. 2001. "Chinese Steel: Rousing the Phoenix." *Modern Metals* 57(1):32–43.

Shaw, M. 1997. "The State of Globalisation: Towards of Theory of State Transformation." *Review of International Political Economy* 4:497–513.

Sheard, P. 1994. "Interlocking Shareholdings and Corporate Governance in Japan." Pp. 310–49 in M. Aoki and R. Dore (eds.), *The Japanese Firm: Sources of Competitive Strength.* Oxford: Oxford University Press.

Simmons, Matthew. 2005. *Twilight in the Desert: The Coming Saudi Oil Shock and the World Economy.* Hoboken, N.J.: John Wiley & Sons.

Sinocast. 2004. "Four Chinese Steel Makers Acquired Overseas Iron Mine Equity." March 3.

———. 2006a. "New Shougang to Overtake Global Counterparts." January 20.

———. 2006b. "CVRD Said to Be Suspect of Violating Negotiation Rules." May 26.

Sinocast Transportation Watch. 2006a. "Samsung Heavy to Invest USD500MN in Weihai Shipbuilding." February 8.

———. 2006b. "China Shipbuilding Becomes Global No. 3." February 16.

Skillings Mining Review. 2004a. "CVRD/Baosteel in Long-Term Iron Ore Contracts." 93(1):17.

———. 2004b. "Rio Tinto Reaches Iron Ore Price Settlement with Nippon." 93(2):27.

———. 2005a. "CVRD's CEO Agnelli Comments on 2005 Iron Ore Prices." 94(1):11.

———. 2005b. "China Investing in Australian Iron Ore Mines." 94(10):5.

———. 2005c. "Rio Tinto Expanding Yandi Iron Ore, Dampier Port." 94(10):8.

———. 2005d. "Fortescue Sells Iron Ore to China." 94(10):8.

———. 2005e. "Cazaly Discusses Shovelanna Iron Ore." 94(12):9.

———. 2006a. "Alliance Promotes Geraldton Growth." 95:1:12.

———. 2006b. "Iron Mining to Resume on Koolan Island." 95(4):17.

———. 2006c. "Brazilian Iron Miners Ask Government to Confront China." April 21.

———. 2006d. "China Rejects CVRD Proposed 24% Price Hike." April 21.

———. 2006e. "Cape Lambert Iron Ore in MOU with Sinosteel." 95(5):10.

Sklair, Leslie. 1998. "Globalisation and the Corporations: The Case of the California Fortune Global 500." *International Journal of Urban and Regional Science* 22:195–215.

———. 2000. *The Transnational Capitalist Class.* Oxford: Blackwell Publishers.

Smart, Alan, and Jinn-Yuh Hsu. 2004. "The Chinese Diaspora, Foreign Investment and Economic Development in China." *Review of International Affairs* 3(4):544–66.

Smith, A. 1985. "Sanko: The Consequences Reach Out." *Bulk Systems International,* October:17–19.

Smith, Donald W. 1952. "American Consul General to Department of State." August 6. Despatch 60, RG 59. *Foreign Relations of the United States:* 843.2552/8–652.

So, Alvin. 2003. "The Communist Path of Developmental State: The Chinese Experience." Paper presented at the American Sociological Association annual meetings, Atlanta.

So, Alvin, and S. Chiu. 1995. *East Asia and the World Economy.* Thousand Oaks, Calif.: Sage.

Sorkin, Andrew Ross, and Jad Mouawad. 2005. "Bid by Chevron in Big Oil Deal Thwarts China." *New York Times,* July 20.

Stopford, M. 1988. *Maritime Economics.* London: Unwin Hyman.

Stover, J. 1961. *American Railroads.* Chicago: University of Chicago Press.

Sullivan, A. 1981. "Foreign Coal Ports Expand Capacity." *Coal Age,* May:110–15.

Supreme Commander for the Allied Powers (SCAP). 1946–67. *Japanese Economic Statistics.* Tokyo: Supreme Commander for the Allied Powers, Economic and Scientific Section, Programs and Statistics Division.

————. Natural Resources Section. 1949. *Japanese Natural Resources: A Comprehensive Survey.* Tokyo: Supreme Commander for the Allied Powers, Natural Resources Section.

Suzuki, Yoshio. 2000. "Strategies for Overcoming Japan's Economic Crisis." Pp. 9–16 in Masahiro Aoki and Gary Saxonhouse (eds.), *Finance, Governance, and Competitiveness in Japan.* Oxford: Oxford University Press.

Swan, Anthony, Sally Thorpe, and Lindsay Hogan. 1999. "Australia-Japan Coking Coal Trade: A Hedonic Analysis under Benchmark and Fair Treatment Pricing." *Resources Policy* 25(1):15–25.

Syddell, Mike. 2003. "Metals Outlook, 2004." *Australian Mining* 95(11):14–17.

Takamura, Osamu. 1990. "Construction of the Port of Osaka and Civil Engineers." *Bulletin of the Permanent International Association of Navigation Congresses* 68:148–52.

Takel, R. 1981. "The Spatial Demands of Ports and Related Industry and Their Relationships with the Community." Pp. 47–68 in B. Hoyle and D. Pinder (eds.), *Cityport Industrialization and Regional Development.* Oxford: Pergamon Press.

Tan, Hwee Ann. 2005. "Cleveland-Cliffs Agrees to Buy Portman for $465 Mln." *Bloomberg.com,* January 12.

Temin, Peter. 1964. *Iron and Steel in Nineteenth-Century America: An Economic Inquiry.* Cambridge, Mass.: MIT Press.

Teranishi, Juro. 1999. "The Main Bank System." Pp. 63–96 in Tetsuji Okazaki and Masahiro Okuno-Fujiwara (eds.), *The Japanese Economic System and Its Historical Origins.* Oxford: Oxford University Press.

————. 2000. "The Fall of the Taisho Economic System." Pp. 43–63 in Masahiro Aoki and Gary Saxonhouse (eds.), *Finance, Governance, and Competitiveness in Japan.* Oxford: Oxford University Press.

Tex Report. 1994a. *Coal Manual, 1994.* Tokyo: Tex Report Company.

————. 1994b. *Iron Ore Manual, 1993–94.* Tokyo: Tex Report Company.

33 Metalproducing. 1998. "Chinese Steelmaking to See More Restructuring." September:40–42.

Thurow, L. 1992. *Head to Head: The Coming Economic Battle among Japan, Europe, and America.* New York: William Morrow.

Tiffany, Paul. 1988. *The Decline of American Steel.* Oxford: Oxford University Press.

Tilton, Mark. 1996. *Restrained Trade: Cartels in Japan's Basic Materials Industries.* Ithaca, N.Y.: Cornell University Press.

Tilly, Charles. 1995a. "To Explain Political Processes." *American Journal of Sociology* 6:1594–1610.

————. 1995b. "Macrosociology, Past and Future." *Newsletter of the Comparative and Historical Sociology Section of the American Sociological Association* 8(1–2): 1, 3–4.

Todd, D. 1991. *Industrial Dislocation: The Case of Global Shipbuilding.* London: Routledge.

————. 1996. "Coal Shipment from Northern China and Its Implications for the Ports." *Dock and Harbour Authority* 76(868):49–58.

Tomich, Dale. 1994. "Small Islands and Huge Comparisons." *Social Science History* 18(3):439–58.

Tse, Pui-Kwan. 2000. *The Mineral Industry of China.* Washington, D.C.: U.S. Geological Survey.

Tsurumi, Yoshi. 1980. *Sogoshosha: Engines of Export-Based Growth*. Montreal: Institute for Research on Public Policy.

Ueda, Kazo. 1999. "The Financial System and Its Regulations." Pp. 38–62 in Tetsuji Okazaki and Masahiro Okuno-Fujiwara (eds.), *The Japanese Economic System and Its Historical Origins*. Oxford: Oxford University Press.

UNCTAD. Various years. *UNCTAD Commodity Yearbook*. New York: United Nations.

————. 1997. *Handbook of World Mineral Trade Statistics, 1990–1995*. New York: United Nations.

————. 2002. *Handbook of World Mineral Trade Statistics, 1995–2000*. New York: United Nations.

Unger, Richard. 1978. *Dutch Shipbuilding before 1800: Ships and Guilds*. Amsterdam: Van Gorcum.

United Nations Conference on Trade and Development (UNCTAD). Various years. *Review of Maritime Transport*. New York: United Nations.

United States Bureau of Mines. 1992. *Mineral Commodity Summaries, 1992*. Washington, D.C.: United States Bureau of Mines.

United States Bureau of Mines (USBM) / United States Geological Survey (USGS). Various years a. "The Minerals Industries of Japan." *Minerals Yearbook*. Washington, D.C.: United States Bureau of Mines / United States Geological Survey.

————. Various years b. *Minerals Yearbook*. Washington, D.C.: United States Bureau of Mines / United States Geological Survey.

United States Defense Mapping Agency. 1985. *Distances between Ports*. 5th ed. Washington, D.C.: Defense Mapping Agency.

United States Department of Commerce. 1989. *A Cost Comparison of Selected U.S. and Australian Coal Mines*. Washington, D.C.: U.S. Department of Commerce.

United States Department of Energy, Energy Information Agency. 2006. "Official Energy Statistics." www.eia.doe.gov.

United States Secretary of Defense. 2005. "Annual Report to Congress: The Military Power of the People's Republic of China, 2005." Washington, D.C.

United States State Department. 1949. "Basic Initial Post-Surrender Directive to Supreme Commander for the Allied Powers for the Occupation and Control of Japan." *Political Reorientation of Japan, September 1945 to September 1948*. Washington, D.C.: United States Government Printing Office.

Uriu, Robert. 1996. *Troubled Industries: Confronting Economic Change in Japan*. Ithaca, N.Y.: Cornell University Press.

Usui, C., and R. Colignon. 1995. "Government Elites and Amakudari in Japan, 1963–1992." Paper presented at the American Sociological Association annual meetings, Washington, D.C.

Van Ness, Peter. 2002. "Hegemony, Not Anarchy: Why China and Japan Are Not Balancing US Unipolar Power." *International Relations of the Asia-Pacific* 2(1):131–50.

Vance, James E., Jr. 1990. *Capturing the Horizon: The Historical Geography of Transport since the Transportation Revolution of the Sixteenth Century*. Baltimore: Johns Hopkins University Press.

Vernon, R. 1983. *Two Hungry Giants: The United States and Japan in the Quest for Oil and Ores*. Cambridge, Mass.: Harvard University Press.

Vigarie, A. 1981. "Maritime Industrial Development Areas: Structural Evolution and Implications for Regional Development." Pp. 23–36 in B. Hoyle and D. Pinder (eds.), *Cityport Industrialization and Regional Development.* Oxford: Pergamon Press.

Vogel, Steven. 2002. "Introduction: The San Francisco System at Fifty." Pp. 1–8 in Steven Vogel (ed.), *U.S.-Japan Relations in a Changing World.* Washington, D.C.: Brookings Institution Press.

Wailes, Graham. 2004. "Export Metallurgical Coal Mine Costs." *AusIMM Bulletin* 2:44–45.

Wald, Matthew. 2005. "U.S. Loans for Reactors in China Draw Objections." *New York Times,* February 28.

Wall Street Journal. 2004. "CVRD and Nippon Steel Reach an Agreement for the Supply of 70 Million Tons of Iron Ore." May 17.

Wallace, Stuart. 2002. "Xstrata to Buy Glencore Coal Units for $2.5 Billion." *Bloomberg News,* February 21.

Wallerstein, Immanuel. 1974. *The Modern World-System.* New York: Academic Press.

———. 1980. *The Modern World-System II: Mercantilism and the Consolidation of the European World-Economy, 1600–1750.* New York: Academic Press.

Wang, Gungwu. 1991. *China and the Chinese Overseas.* Singapore: Times Academic Press.

Wang, James, Adolf Koi-Yu Ng, and Daniel Olivier. 2004. "Port Governance in China: A Review of Policies in an Era of Internationalizing Port Management Practices." *Transport Policy* 11:237–50.

Waring, Peter, and Michael Barry. 2001. "The Changing Frontier of Control in Coal: Evidence from a Decade of Enterprise Bargaining in the Australian Black Coal Mining Industry." *Australian Bulleting of Labour* 27(3):216–37.

Warren, Kenneth. 2001. *Big Steel: The First Century of the United States Steel Corporation 1901–2001.* Pittsburgh: University of Pittsburgh Press.

Watson, Nick. 2005. "China Helps Rosneft Pay for Yukos." *Thedeal.com,* January 24.

Watts, Jonathan. 2005. "A Hunger Eating Up the World." *Guardian,* November 10.

Way, Nicholas. 2003. "Level-Pegging at the Pilbara." *Business Review Weekly,* March 27:22.

Wayne, Leslie, and David Barboza. 2005. "Unocal Deal: A Lot More Than Money Is at Issue." *New York Times,* June 24.

Wellman, Barry (ed.). 1999. *Networks in the Global Village.* Boulder, Colo.: Westview Press.

Welsh, Andrea. 2004. "CVRD Net Rose 14.4% in Quarter." *Wall Street Journal,* May 13.

Werner, Richard. 2004. "No Recovery without Reform? An Evaluation of the Evidence in Support of the Structural Reform Argument in Japan." *Asian Business and Management* 3(1):7–38.

Westar Mining. Various years. *Westar Annual Report.* Vancouver: Westar Mining.

Western Canadian Coal. 2005. *2005 Annual Report.* Vancouver: Western Canadian Coal.

Whitman, R. 1965. "Steel." Pp. 847–73 in United States Bureau of Mines, *Mineral Facts and Problems, 1965 Edition.* Bulletin 630. Washington, D.C.: United States Bureau of Mines.

Whittington, Floyd. 1953a. "Letter from Whittington to Benjamin Graham, Graham-Newman Corporation." February 26. *Foreign Relations of the United States:* 843.2552/2–2753.

———. 1953b. "Collinsville Coking Coal from the Bowen Basin, Australia, for Japan." July 24. *Foreign Relations of the United States:* 843.2552/1.2453.

Williamson, James. 1965. *A Short History of British Expansion: The Old Colonial Empire.* 3rd ed. London: Macmillan.

————. 1967. *A Short History of British Expansion: The Modern Empire and Commonwealth.* 6th ed. London: Macmillan.

Wilson, Alex. 2006a. "Rio Tinto Doubles Annual Profit to US$5.2 Billion." *AAP Newsfeed*, February 2.

————. 2006b. "Costello Calls for Market Prices in Wake of Iron Ore Reports." *AAP Newsfeed*, March 9.

Wolf, C. 2004. "Fault Lines in China's Economic Terrain." *Asia-Pacific Review* 11(1):58–72.

Wong, Craig. 2006. "Teck Cominco Reports Q4 Profit of $510M, Up from $285M a Year Ago." *Canadian Press Newswire*, February 1.

Woo, Jung-en. 1991. *Race to the Swift: State and Finance in Korean Industrialization.* New York: Columbia University Press.

World Coal Study (WOCOL). 1980. *Coal-Bridge to the Future.* Cambridge, Mass.: Ballinger.

Wu, John. 2001. "The Mineral Industry of Japan." *Minerals Yearbook, 2001.* Washington, D.C.: United States Geological Survey.

Wyatt, Stephen. 2000. "Jostling for Position to Lure Perfect Suitor: More Mergers Expected as Iron Ore Industry Enjoys Turnround." *Financial Times*, August 9:30.

Wyatt, Stephen, and Michiyo Nakamoto. 2000. "Joint Bid Launched for QCT Resources." *Financial Times*, August 29:24.

Xiaoguang, K. 2003. "Political Development and Political Stability in the Era of Reform." *Chinese Economy* 35(5):6–92.

Xinhua. 2004. "China's Shipbuilding Industry More Attractive to Global Market." January 16.

————. 2006. "China to Resist Iron Ore Price Increase at Global Negotiations." *Global News Wire*, February 17.

Yaghmaian, B. 1998. "Globalisation and the State: The Political Economy of Global Accumulation and Its Emerging Mode of Regulation." *Science and Society* 62:241–65.

Yakushiji, T. 1984. "The Government in a Spiral Dilemma: Dynamic Policy Interventions vis-à-vis Auto Firms, c. 1900–c.1960." Pp. 265–310 in M. Aoki (ed.), *The Economic Analysis of the Japanese Firm.* Amsterdam: North-Holland.

Yamamoto, S. 1980. "Shipbuilding." Pp. 163–75 in Kiyoji Murata (ed.), *An Industrial Geography of Japan.* New York: St. Martin's Press.

Yamamoto, S., and M. Murakami. 1980. "Iron and Steel." Pp. 139–51 in Kiyoji Murata and Isamu Ota, *An Industrial Geography of Japan.* New York: St. Martin's Press.

Yanaga, C. 1968. *Big Business in Japanese Politics.* New Haven: Yale University Press.

Yeung, Henry, and Kris Olds (eds.). 2000. *Globalization of Chinese Business Firms.* New York: St. Martin's Press.

Yonekura, S. 1994. *The Japanese Iron and Steel Industry, 1850–1990: Continuity and Discontinuity.* New York: St. Martin's Press.

————. 1999. "The Functions of Industrial Associations." Pp. 180–207 in Tetsuji Okazaki and Masahiro Okuno-Fujiwara (eds.), *The Japanese Economic System and Its Historical Origins.* Oxford: Oxford University Press.

York, Geoffrey. 2004. "China Frantic for Energy Supplies." *Globe and Mail*, November 29.

Yoshimatsu, Hidetaka. 2002. "Social Demand, State Capability and Globalization: Japan-China Trade Friction over Safeguards." *Pacific Review* 15(3):381–408.

Yoshino, M. Y., and Thomas Lifson. 1986. *The Invisible Link: Japan's Sogo Shosha and the Organization of Trade.* Cambridge, Mass.: MIT Press.

Young, Alexander. 1979. *The Sogo Shosha: Japan's Multinational Trading Companies.* Boulder, Colo.: Westview Press.

Yuzo, Kato (ed.). 1990. *Yokohama Past and Present.* Yokohama: Yokohama City University.

Zarocostas, John. 2005. "Global Sea Trade Rising 4% a Year." *Lloyd's List International,* November 9:5.

Zhu, Jieming. 2004. "Local Developmental State and Order in China's Urban Development during Transition." *International Journal of Urban and Regional Research* 28(2):424–47.

Zweig, David, and Bi Jianhai. 2005. "China's Global Hunt for Energy." *Foreign Affairs* 84(5):25–26, 27–30, 31–32, 33–36, 37–38.